College Admission Essays

2nd edition

by Jessica Brenner
and Geraldine Woods

for
dummies®
A Wiley Brand

College Admission Essays For Dummies®, 2nd edition

Published by: **John Wiley & Sons, Inc.,** 111 River Street, Hoboken, NJ 07030-5774, www.wiley.com

Copyright © 2022 by John Wiley & Sons, Inc., Hoboken, New Jersey

Published simultaneously in Canada

For general information on our other products and services, please contact our Customer Care Department within the U.S. at 877-762-2974, outside the U.S. at 317-572-3993, or fax 317-572-4002. For technical support, please visit https://hub.wiley.com/community/support/dummies.

Wiley publishes in a variety of print and electronic formats and by print-on-demand. Some material included with standard print versions of this book may not be included in e-books or in print-on-demand. If this book refers to media such as a CD or DVD that is not included in the version you purchased, you may download this material at http://booksupport.wiley.com. For more information about Wiley products, visit www.wiley.com.

Library of Congress Control Number: SKY10029987_092421

ISBN: 978-1-119-82833-4

ISBN: 978-1-119-82834-1 (ebk); ISBN: 978-1-119-82835-8 (ebk)

Contents at a Glance

Introduction 1

Part 1: Putting Yourself on Paper 5
CHAPTER 1: Becoming More Than a Statistic: What the Essay Does for You 7
CHAPTER 2: Exploring the Subject of the Essay — You 21
CHAPTER 3: Beginning to Self-Reflect 33

Part 2: Organizing Your Thoughts 47
CHAPTER 4: Writing as Process, Not Product 49
CHAPTER 5: Storming Your Brain: Idea-Gathering Techniques 59
CHAPTER 6: Steering Clear of Potential Landmines 81

Part 3: Writing the Rough Draft 95
CHAPTER 7: Writing for the Tired, the Poor (The Admissions Office) 97
CHAPTER 8: Building a Structure to Support Your Ideas 111
CHAPTER 9: Showing, Not Telling, Your Story 129
CHAPTER 10: Leading with Your Best Shot 149
CHAPTER 11: Constructing Good Paragraphs 159
CHAPTER 12: Going Out with a Bang: The Conclusion 171
CHAPTER 13: Overcoming Writer's Block 183

Part 4: I'd Like to Finish Before Retirement Age: The Final Draft 193
CHAPTER 14: Leaving a Good Impression 195
CHAPTER 15: Smoothing the Rough Edges: Polishing the Essay 207
CHAPTER 16: Navigating the Submission Process 219

Part 5: Analyzing Questions from Real Applications 229
CHAPTER 17: Composing Essays Starring You 231
CHAPTER 18: Describing Significant Strangers and Friends: Essays about Other People 253
CHAPTER 19: Focusing on More Essay Question Types 265
CHAPTER 20: Getting the Most out of Short Answers 277

Part 6: The Part of Tens 289
CHAPTER 21: Ten False Beliefs about College Essays 291
CHAPTER 22: Ten Great Essays to Inspire You 297

CHAPTER 23: Ten Absolute Musts for College Essays 303
CHAPTER 24: Ten Tips for Writing Supplemental Essays 307

Appendix A: Well-Written College Essays 313

Index 327

Table of Contents

INTRODUCTION 1

About This Book... 1

Foolish Assumptions... 2

Icons Used in This Book 3

Beyond This Book 3

Where to Go from Here 4

PART 1: PUTTING YOURSELF ON PAPER 5

CHAPTER 1: Becoming More Than a Statistic: What the Essay Does for You......................... 7

Understanding Why the Essay Is Your Key Opportunity 8

Factoring in Holistic Review and Test-Optional Schools 9

Forgetting about strategy................................. 10

Choosing authenticity.................................... 11

Familiarizing Yourself with the Common Application and the Prompts 12

Considering Alternatives to the Common Application........... 13

First Things First: Understanding Your Timeline............... 14

Considering Early Action and Early Decision deadlines...... 15

Working out how many essays you have to write 16

Factoring in supplementary writing 16

Writing Admission Essays While Having a Life 17

Taking advantage of spare time 17

Adapting one essay to several questions................... 18

Tempering Frustration: Greasing Your Wheels................. 19

Keeping Perspective 20

CHAPTER 2: Exploring the Subject of the Essay — You 21

Mining Your Life.. 22

Collecting the Stories of Your Life........................... 23

Dipping Your Toe in the Writing Pool: Freewriting 101 24

Identifying Themes in Your Autobiography...................... 25

Reviewing your life story 26

Revealing significant themes............................. 26

Writing about difficult experiences....................... 27

Delving Deeper with Your Personal Statement.................. 29

Sparking growth.. 29

Picking the topic of your choice.......................... 30

But Enough about Me: Overcoming the Taboo against Bragging 30

CHAPTER 3: **Beginning to Self-Reflect** 33

Looking Closer at Family Ties. 34
Contemplating your parents' influence .34
Focusing on your siblings. 35
Scrutinizing your grandparents and extended family 36
Answering general family questions. 36
Hitting the Halls: School Days 37
Considering your strengths 38
Tackling your challenges 38
Identifying teachers' influence on you 39
Seeing how different learning styles have affected you 39
Reflecting on group experiences. 40
Ruminating on Your Community. 40
Seeing how your local community plays a role in
who you are 40
Musing on the global village 41
Contemplating the Future 42
Predicting your professional future 42
Looking into a crystal ball at how the world may be 43
Pondering Your Identity 43
Pinpointing How Other People Help You Figure Out
Who You Are. 44
Including the No-Category Category 45

PART 2: **ORGANIZING YOUR THOUGHTS** .47

CHAPTER 4: **Writing as Process, Not Product** 49

Separating Your Inner Creator and Editor. 50
Pre-Writing: The First Steps 52
Idea gathering 52
Narrowing down to a specific moment .53
Detail gathering 54
Structuring and outlining versus discovery writing 55
Taking the Final Steps. 56
Revising. 56
Completing one essay makes the rest easier 56
Sighing with relief 57

CHAPTER 5: **Storming Your Brain: Idea-Gathering
Techniques**. 59

Making a Mess — You Can't Build a Castle Until You
Dump the Blocks 60
Matching Personality and Technique 61

Gathering Ideas: The Techniques 62
    Visual brainstorming. 62
        Listing 68
        Braindumping 72
Reacting to a Specific Question. 76
Throwing in a Wrench — Figuring Out a Challenge 77
Generating a Memorable (and Successful) Topic. 78
Accepting Your Permission Slip for a Messy First Draft. 80

CHAPTER 6: **Steering Clear of Potential Landmines** 81
Buying an Essay on the Internet and Other Things to Avoid 82
Finding the Right Sort of Help 83
    Avoiding too many cooks in the kitchen 83
    Trolling for topics. 84
    Dialing for details. 85
    Overseeing the outline 85
    Roughing it 86
    Checking and revising. 87
    Having too many editors 87
Identifying Your Parents' Role 88
    Understanding why your parents may try to micromanage
    the process. 88
    Managing your parents' concerns and expectations 89
Locating Help When You're On Your Own. 90
Writing College Essays in the Technical Age: What You
Need to Know. 92

PART 3: WRITING THE ROUGH DRAFT. 95
CHAPTER 7: **Writing for the Tired, the Poor
(The Admissions Office)** 97
Meeting Your Readers: The Admissions Committee 98
    Understanding the counselors' duties 98
    Factoring in your timeline 99
    Strategizing for success 100
Keeping Their Attention When Yours Is the 200th Essay
They've Read Today. 101
Avoiding Irksome Writing Traits 103
    My thesaurus and me: Unnatural vocabulary. 103
    Flowery language. 104
    Untruths and exaggerations 105
    I am a people person: Clichés 106
Developing Your Voice on Paper. 107

CHAPTER 8: **Building a Structure to Support Your Ideas**........111
    Meeting the Major Players in the Structure Game................112
        Chronological order 112
        Interrupted chronological order...........................113
        Survey 115
        Description and interpretation............................119
        Cause and effect 120
    Structuring Your Meaning 122
        Understanding how different structures can work
        for your essay..122
        Selecting the structure for your essay 124
    Embracing Uncertainty.......................................125
    Using Structure to Explain Your Interest in your Major..........126
        Pursuing your interests in college........................126
        Answering the question: Why this field?...................127

CHAPTER 9: **Showing, Not Telling, Your Story**....................129
    Getting Down to Specifics 130
    Using All Your Senses 137
        Using the four senses besides vision 137
        Discovering sensory details 138
    Choosing the Best Details and Ignoring the Rest 139
    Selecting Strong Verbs and Nouns 141
        Verbs..141
        Nouns 142
        Adjectives and adverbs..................................143
    A Little Metaphor Won't Kill You 144
    Calibrating Expectations: "But 650 Words Is So Short!"..........146

CHAPTER 10: **Leading with Your Best Shot**.......................149
    Taking the Right First Step: What the Lead Does for Your Essay 150
    Capturing the Reader's Attention 150
        Sharing an anecdote....................................152
        Intriguing the reader....................................152
        Previewing the coming attractions 153
    Setting the Right Tone.......................................154
    Taking a Closer Look: Five Strong Openings 155
    Avoiding Common Pitfalls 157
    Parting with the Traditional Thesis...........................158

CHAPTER 11: **Constructing Good Paragraphs** 159
    Punctuating Your Points with Paragraphs.....................160
        Including some logic 160
        Adding some drama 161

Creating a Strong Scope Sentence 162
Placing Scope Sentences and Details 164
Starting with a scope sentence 164
Finishing with the scope sentence 165
Putting the scope sentence in the middle 165
One more word about details 166
Setting Up a Transition 167
Using linked transitions 167
Adding transitions later 169

CHAPTER 12: **Going Out with a Bang: The Conclusion** 171
Repeating Yourself and Other Non-Answers
to the Conclusion Question 172
Not a reworded introduction 172
Not a miniature essay 173
Not an announcement 173
Not a new topic 173
Concluding the Essay Effectively 174
Tying up loose ends 174
Creating a wider context 176
Coming full circle: Completing the experience 177
Forging the last link in a chain of logic .178
Making a strong impression 179

CHAPTER 13: **Overcoming Writer's Block** 183
Understanding Your Block 184
Confronting Your Application Anxieties 184
Overcoming a fear of failure 185
Coping with perfectionism and paralysis 185
Reclaiming power 186
Embracing change 187
Overcoming self-doubt 188
Gaining perspective 189
Leaping Over Writing-Related Blocks 189
Rising from the fog of details 190
Editing while writing 190
Stopping and starting with ease 191

PART 4: I'D LIKE TO FINISH BEFORE
RETIREMENT AGE: THE FINAL DRAFT 193

CHAPTER 14: **Leaving a Good Impression** 195
Considering How Multiple Essays Work Together 196
Getting Your Point Across 197
Verifying That You've Answered the Question 200

Conveying Strength. 201
    Projecting confidence 201
    Winning without whining 203
    Keeping perspective 204
Checking the Essay One Last Time 205

CHAPTER 15: Smoothing the Rough Edges: Polishing the Essay 207
Trying the Red Pen Exercise. 207
Writing Anew 209
Avoiding the Perils of Overediting 209
Creating Stylish Sentences 211
    Monotony 211
Saying It Once and Only Once 213
Reenlisting Your Support System 216
    Having realistic expectations. 216
    Keeping it tasteful 217

CHAPTER 16: Navigating the Submission Process 219
Getting the Lowdown on the Submission Process. 219
    Eyeing the characteristics of the process. 220
    Understanding how the process works .220
    Working with word count requirements 221
    Working on short-answer questions 222
    Submitting your application: The when .223
Creating a Submission Plan 224
Finishing Your Submission. 226
    Pasting your essays into the application 226
    Submitting your essay: What you need .226
    Finishing the process: Signing, submitting, and celebrating. 227

PART 5: ANALYZING QUESTIONS FROM REAL APPLICATIONS 229

CHAPTER 17: Composing Essays Starring You 231
Understanding the Supplemental Essays 232
    Dealing with "Why us" questions. 232
    Complimenting without flattery 235
Relating a Personal Experience 236
    Choosing relevant material 237
    Ranging over a long period of time. 238
    Taking the story inward 239
    Interpreting the story for the reader 240

Explaining Academic Experiences and Your Intended
Major (or Lack Thereof) 242
    Writing an essay with an undecided major 243
    Responding to the question of who you will be on campus. 245
Answering Questions on Diversity and Inclusion 245
Approaching Fun and Creative Questions. .248
Daydreaming Your Way into College 250

**CHAPTER 18: Describing Significant Strangers and Friends:
Essays about Other People** 253
Defining Others' Influence: You Are Who You Know 254
Writing about Friends and Relatives. 256
    Choosing the "big figure" in your life .256
    Focusing on your ties to a group. 257
    Selecting the scene 258
    Interpreting the influence 261
Relating Strangers' Lives to Your Own 262
Entering the Fictional Universe 263

CHAPTER 19: Focusing on More Essay Question Types 265
Responding to "Is There Anything Else You Want to Tell Us?" 266
Answering Literature and Writing Questions 269
    Discussing books. 269
    Writing creatively. 271
Discussing Current or Historical Events. 272
    Writing an essay about a current event 272
    Delving into the past. 275

CHAPTER 20: Getting the Most out of Short Answers 277
Saying a Lot in Little Spaces. 278
Answering the Most Common Short-Answer Questions. 281
    Playing favorites. 282
    Moving on: The transfer question. 285

PART 6: THE PART OF TENS 289

CHAPTER 21: Ten False Beliefs about College Essays 291
Drafting at the Last Minute Is No Biggie 291
Limiting the Focus to Your Achievements Is Wise 292
Requesting Help from Lots of People Strengthens Your Writing. . . .292
Figuring Out Your Story Is No Big Deal. 293
Focusing on a Certain Topic Guarantees Admission 293
Writing without Restraint Always Works 293
Talking about Ordinary Lives Is a No-No 294
Using Scholarly Language Is Impressive 294

Writing One Essay Is Enough 294
Believing No One Reads Your Essays 295

CHAPTER 22: **Ten Great Essays to Inspire You** 297
"Us and Them" by David Sedaris 297
"I Am Not Pocahontas" by Elissa Washuta 298
"Total Eclipse" by Annie Dillard 298
"A Talk to Teachers" by James Baldwin 299
"Professions for Women" by Virginia Woolf 299
"On Keeping a Notebook" by Joan Didion 299
"The Search for Marvin Gardens" by John McPhee 300
"Mother Tongue" by Amy Tan 300
"On Lying in Bed" by G.K. Chesterton 300
"Generation Why?" by Zadie Smith 301

CHAPTER 23: **Ten Absolute Musts for College Essays** 303
Saying Something They Wouldn't Otherwise Know 303
Keeping It Real 304
Answering the Question 304
Being Specific 304
Showing, Not Telling 304
Getting Personal 305
Avoiding Clichés 305
Holding Their Interest 305
Meeting the Deadline 306
Revising Your Drafts 306

CHAPTER 24: **Ten Tips for Writing Supplemental Essays** 307
Saying Something Distinct from Your Personal Statement 307
Starting Early 308
Being Direct 308
Grounding Your Response in Past Experience 308
Answering the Right Questions 309
Paraphrasing the Prompt 309
Looking for Patterns 310
Meshing with the College or University 310
Researching Specific Programs (and Knowing What's Available) 310
Being an Explorer 311

APPENDIX A: WELL-WRITTEN COLLEGE ESSAYS 313

INDEX 327

Introduction

Getting into college can be extremely difficult. More students are applying to four-year universities than ever before, tuition is higher than ever, and the number of college campuses has stayed almost exactly the same. There are no guarantees when it comes to college applications.

And yet one aspect of college admissions has never been more important: college essays. The impression you make and the stories you share can tip the scales in your favor and distinguish you from the thousands of other applicants with the exact same GPA and test scores. Whether you've been an aspiring storyteller since you first picked up a pen or the thought of writing anything longer than a text message makes you want to hide under the covers, you *are* capable of crafting memorable college essays. This book can explain how to write creatively, authentically, and *well* — giving you the best possible chance at admissions. Just as important, a well-paced writing process can help you discover valuable insights about yourself (and it's ideal that you know yourself well before going off to college) and even be enjoyable — much more so than working yourself into a frenzy days before your deadlines.

This second edition of *College Admission Essays For Dummies* gives you a road map around what I call *essay sand traps* (those unsubstantiated claims, vagueness, and cliched topics, among other things) that can sabotage your application, as well as strategies used by the most successful applicants. This book helps you decide what to write and then guides you through the process of creating essays that present your best self to the admissions committee. Because many scholarships require personal statements, this book may also pay off in cold, hard cash. Moreover, you'll find this new edition useful even after you plunk down your last tuition payment. Chances are a few employment-related letters and essays are in your future, especially if you're applying for internships or jobs on the professional level.

About This Book

If you're applying for admission or hoping that your eloquent essays will translate into scholarship money, you probably already have your hands full: You're asking for letters of recommendation, tracking down your Social Security Number, and assembling that resume you've been tinkering with for months. You don't need another chore, but you do need help. Never fear. This book demystifies the process of writing an application essay — from topic search through final draft, without wasting your time. Of course, I like to imagine you glued to these pages, devouring every syllable, but I'm a realist.

You can find information on the following topics (and so much more):

» A questionnaire — a personal inventory — that helps you discover the best topics for your essays

» Proven techniques for jump-starting your creative process

» Techniques to gather ideas, focus on a topic, and choose the best structure for your essay and how you can seek help without violating any university, school, parental, or personal code of honesty

» Tactics to demystify the rough draft, including why you should "show" not "tell" your story and the lowdown on topic sentences, use of detail, and strong introductions and conclusions

» Tips on overcoming writer's block

» Ways to put the finishing touches on a final draft

» Methods to finalizing your essays and knowing when you're done writing (for some, the tinkering and tweaking stage can go on forever!)

» Pointers on grammar and spelling without all those horrible terms that English teachers love so much and help with choosing the best tone, creating transitions, and avoiding wordiness and repetition

» Examples of real admission essays from students who were very happy when the colleges of their choice mailed out decision letters

» Guidance on how to address the most familiar types of *supplemental essays* (which are essays used to supplement your personal statement) and some uncommon question types, too

Foolish Assumptions

Although you know what "they" say about assumptions, here are a few assumptions I make about you:

» You want to choose — and be chosen for — the best possible university, and you understand that essay writing is a major component in ensuring your success.

>> You may be just a little insecure about writing, maybe not with regards to the usual English-report sort of paper, but certainly the "let-me-tell-you-about-myself" type of essay. And who isn't insecure about such a task? After all, summing up a life experience, at the age of 17 or the age of 71, is daunting.

>> You're aware of the wealth of information available to you — with regards to deadlines, application guidance, and major do's and don'ts of essay writing — but that the information you read or hear is often conflicting and confusing. Sifting through it and creating your own manageable plan might feel just a *bit* out of reach.

Everything in *College Admission Essays For Dummies*, 2nd Edition, is intended to calm your anxieties, improve your writing skills, and help you complete your application essays on time and on target.

Icons Used in This Book

Throughout the book are little signs located in the margins to guide you toward important information. Here's what each sign means:

The material accompanying this icon is more valuable than a message from a jockey about the favorite's chances to win the sixth race. The Tip icon alerts you to shortcuts, ways to improve writing style, and other helpful hints for writing a successful college admission essay.

This icon contains helpful content — you know, stuff worth remembering! Think of this icon as a speedbump asking you to slow down for a moment and take note of guidance.

The Warning icon is like the sturdy fence at the edge of a cliff. This icon tells you how to sidestep the most common errors of admission essays and prevent some seriously nasty falls.

Beyond This Book

This book is chock-full of examples, tips and tricks, and other pieces of helpful advice so you can write a college admission essay that can wow the admissions team and help you get into your dream school. If you want some additional tidbits of wisdom, check out the book's Cheat Sheet at www.dummies.com. Just search for "College Admission Essay Cheat Sheet."

Where to Go from Here

Head to the Table of Contents and index to see what's where. Then turn to the chapters that deal with the part of the process currently tying your stomach into a knot. After you've grasped what you need to do, plop yourself in front of the computer and get to work. Keep a copy of the book nearby, so the next time you're stuck, you can turn to the respective chapter in this book for more assistance.

For instance, if you've already finalized your college list, you may want to start by making a list of essay questions and deadlines. You may also consider beginning where most students do: by exploring the prompts and various approaches to the Common Application personal statement (a more thorough explanation of why this comes first is in Chapter 1). As you begin to understand your strengths and weaknesses as a writer, dip into the different chapters that address the parts of the writing process most likely to be hard for you. And take heart: You *will* write your college essays and you *will* survive the application era of your life.

My personal goal for this book is that any student coming out of any high school will be able to read it and get the information needed and deserved — for the price of a paperback or ebook. I want to put maximum control and empowerment in your hands. I hope the information in the coming chapters serves as a guide, inspires your curiosity, generates ideas, and overall makes you feel prepared as you tackle this important process in the manner that is right for you.

1

Putting Yourself on Paper

Understand the role of college essays in your college application process.

Create a timeline and plan based on the number of essays required by the colleges to which you're applying and the deadlines you hope to meet.

Consider various approaches to the Common Application writing prompts (and other prompts you're likely to encounter).

Reflect on your experiences and relationships to begin brainstorming for your college essays.

Gain an understanding of the genre and process of college essay writing.

Master the central do's and don'ts you should be aware of before you begin writing.

IN THIS CHAPTER

» Taking a look at yourself as the subject

» Knowing your audience

» Creating a timetable for writing

» Discovering how to live your life while writing the essay

» Focusing on the process of essay writing

» Maintaining a sense of perspective during the application process

Chapter **1**

Becoming More Than a Statistic: What the Essay Does for You

When's the last time you answered the question "Who are you?" with this response:

I'm a B average and a 1230 SAT. Pleased to meet you!

Not recently, I bet. Yet for the most part your admissions or scholarship application answers the "Who are you?" question in just that way. But you're *not* a standardized test score or a list of grades. You're a person. The admission essay is your chance to become more than a number to those who judge your candidacy.

In this chapter I explain *why* essays are a part of the college application process and *what* your writing should accomplish. I also tackle *when* — an important issue for people who are frantically overworked (in other words, everybody).

Understanding Why the Essay Is Your Key Opportunity

Most of my students begin the college essay writing process knowing very little, if anything, about the genre of personal or narrative writing. In fact, many of them are eager to discuss their test scores, their resume, their GPA — anything to shift the focus away from college essays. After all, writing an admission essay (or more than likely a series of essays — more on that in Part 4) about *yourself* feels murky and even vulnerable. How do you succeed?

Consider this analogy: A pile of forms is a pile of forms. Nothing's deeply personal about the information on a typical application: your name, address, Social Security number, date and place of birth, courses and grades, extracurricular activities, and standardized test scores. All that information is important. But you have *one* real opportunity to stop your readers — the admissions counselors sitting on the admissions committee — in their tracks. You may have the opportunity to follow up with an interview, but your writing is often be the first and only chance to tell your story in a way that will make it impossible for them to refuse you as a candidate for admission.

The chapters in Parts 1 and 2 help you reflect on your upbringing, the challenges you've faced, and other influences in your life to figure out the story (or stories) your application would be incomplete without. Maybe that includes your struggle to overcome your fear of physics and the 22 consecutive lunch hours you gave up in order to construct the perfect magnetism experiment. Or the change in your worldview after you read Virginia Woolf's great novel, *To the Lighthouse*. Numbers and basic data can't possibly convey your burning desire for social justice or passion for visual arts. Yet those factors are as much a part of you as your A in English or C in physical education.

Granted, the letters of recommendation submitted with your application may address your personality and experiences. However, you have no control over the content of those letters, and frankly, not all recommendation writers actually know how to write well. Their letters may be vague and limited to the scope of what they've seen from you in class. The only way you can be sure that the application paints a true portrait of you is to write at length about yourself. Enter the essay.

Specifically, an admission essay can

>> Show how you react to challenging situations ("When Coach asked me what really happened, I . . .")

>> Reveal your values and priorities ("Nothing is more important to me than . . .")

>> Explain factors in your background that have influenced you ("Growing up on the summit of Mount Everest, I . . .")

>> Interpret your academic record ("I used to believe that I would never be an A student . . .")

>> Discuss how you will contribute to the life of the institution ("I would love to join your chapter of . . .")

>> Relate the reasons why you and the institution mesh well ("I am attracted to the American Studies major because . . .")

>> Display your logic and writing skills ("Ultimately, I've realized that . . .")

Factoring in Holistic Review and Test-Optional Schools

The writing was on the wall long before the COVID-19 pandemic. The University of Chicago and the University of California went *test optional* in 2018 and early 2020, respectively — meaning that, for the first time, prospective students could apply without submitting any standardized test scores. By the fall of 2020, more than 1,500 schools were on the test-optional list — and many counselors like me knew that there would be no going back. Sure enough, many of these schools extended test-optional policies into the 2021–2022 admissions cycle and beyond.

Truth be told, colleges and universities have been debating the merit of the SAT (and ACT) for a while, with the term "holistic review" simultaneously factoring into many schools' admissions process. *Holistic review* refers to the process of evaluating candidates in terms of what they can contribute to a college campus and their qualities as a whole, not simply the metric of their GPA and test scores. (Schools like the University of Oregon, the University of Washington, and Louisiana State University have embraced the concept of holistic review for several years now.) With mounting data showing that wealthier students with greater access to resources (private schools, extensive tutoring, and so on) have advantages concerning standardized tests, using test scores as a metric of student performance is misleading.

So what does all of this business about the SAT mean for you, future essay writer? It means that, unlike other factors used in college admissions, the opportunity to introduce and distinguish yourself as a candidate *in your own words* has never been more important. Isn't it a relief to know that colleges will see you as more than a number?

Given that what colleges most want to learn about is *you* — the you beyond the numbers and statistics — the next few sections cover what you can keep in mind (and what not to worry about) as you begin to brainstorm what experience and characteristics you want to share in your essays.

Forgetting about strategy

"What do they want to read? I'll say anything!" Sound familiar? If so, you're hanging out with the wrong crowd. Too many applicants expend far too much energy attempting to analyze the admissions office, creating myths such as these:

>> **Every college has a magic topic that guarantees admission.** "If you want to go to an Ivy League school, write about how worldly and well-traveled you are." "*Always* mention winter sports in your essay for the University of Colorado." Rumors like these spread quickly, but they're a waste of time. Anyone who claims to know tricks that guarantee admission is indulging in wishful thinking.

>> **One mistake can sink your application.** "She uses semicolons? Dump her." "This guy spent four years in the debating society. He's gonna argue with everyone. Out he goes." Gimme a break. If you write the truth about yourself, you don't have to worry about breaking a rule you only imagine exists. You'll either get in or you won't, but your semicolon habit will have nothing to do with the outcome.

>> **Some topics are automatic turn-offs.** Various authority figures tell you with great confidence never to write about the Big Game, the death of a relative, or some other particular topic they've labeled taboo. Nonsense. Although a few topics can be especially hard to pull off (an essay about your first romantic relationship comes to mind), no topic is off limits if you handle it well and keep it focused on you. (See Chapter 2 for how to handle it well.)

>> **If a particular topic worked for one student, it will work for all.** "Jenelle wrote about paperclips, and she got into her first choice, so I'm going with a description of my office supplies." Good idea? No. Okay, reading other people's work may give you valuable tips on style and format. That's why I scattered some real student essays throughout this book and in the Appendix. But content is a different story. Jenelle didn't get in because of the paperclips.

She got in because of a host of factors you know nothing about, and she pulled off an essay that was probably highly memorable, but not worth trying to duplicate. The moral of the story: Write your own essay and forget about everyone else's.

To correct other misconceptions about the admission essay, read Chapter 21.

Choosing authenticity

In this section I state what the admissions officers *do* want to see in potential applicants. Keep the following in mind:

REMEMBER

>> **Self-awareness:** Have you ever noticed that when someone is truly honest about themselves, you're more than willing to forgive them a flaw or two? Or even that a moderate dose of self-deprecating humor makes someone *much* more likeable than a moderate dose of arrogance? That's because *self-awareness,* or knowing yourself well, is a great way to ensure that you can navigate your future relationships and responsibilities — flaws and all.

Know yourself before you go to college, and that's why the Common Application prompts (see the next section for more about the specific prompts) focus on getting you to reflect on the person you actually are and how you came to be that way. Granted, you should still present your best self, meaning if you choose to share what you might see as a shortcoming or personal challenge, you also want to showcase your efforts to grow. But your best self is still *yourself,* not someone else.

>> **Authenticity:** College admission essays are far more than a recap of your resume or a recitation of your achievements. In fact, being authentic and, above all, *true to yourself* is exactly what colleges want to see from you. Do they care that you're a human and willing to admit imperfection? No, because a student who speaks openly about how they've overcome past challenges is far more likely to be *equipped to handle future challenges*. In other words, if you've never been called to overcome difficulty before, then how does your reader know that you're ready for whatever your higher education throws at you — academically, socially, personally, or professionally?

>> **Thoughtfulness:** I once proctored a philosophy exam with only one question: Design an ideal society. Some students sweated for three hours, explaining the ins and outs of community structure and grappling with the tension between individual rights and group responsibility. Others finished in ten minutes; their papers made statements like "In my ideal community everyone will be happy." Guess which level of complexity is more appealing to the admissions committee? Answer: Door #1 — the thoughtful version.

>> **Good writing skills:** Good writing is vivid; it leaps off the page and takes the reader out of the armchair and into the subject at hand. Good writing is clear; the reader doesn't have to sit around wondering whether you're describing a redwood forest or a brokerage office as the site of your best summer ever. Good writing holds the reader's attention, even if they have an almost overwhelming desire for sleep. Write well — all the more so if you're not applying as a Humanities or English major, because the ability to self-reflect and communicate effectively shows that you have what it takes to thrive as a college student and for the rest of your life.

Familiarizing Yourself with the Common Application and the Prompts

The Common Application, affectionately known as the Common App, is where you can fill out a generalized college application (including basic information about yourself, your extracurricular activities, your courses, and your grades). Nearly 950 colleges and universities in the United States have agreed to accept applications via the same platform, so applying to colleges and universities have never been easier.

You can make an account anytime at www.commonapp.org to view which schools on your own list of prospective colleges use this application, as opposed to another platform. (The next section identifies some other applications that colleges use.)

As you start working on your personal statement, take the time to create an account and begin adding colleges of interest to view individual supplemental essays for each college.

The following section focuses just on the Common App. When you complete the Common App, you share one personal statement to all the colleges and universities you're applying to on the Writing section of the Common App, though most of these schools also have their own additional essays, called *supplementary essays*. (Part 5 addresses the supplemental essays.) In other words, the Common App personal statement is the mother of all college essays you'll have to write. You may submit it alongside a few other responses, or you may have to tailor it to a slightly different word count for a college that isn't on the Common App, but this personal statement is the central snapshot of yourself you'll be submitting to as many colleges as you can.

Here are the standard essay prompts on the Common App. You can submit a response of up to 650 words on one of the following topics:

>> **Prompt #1:** Some students have a background, identity, interest, or talent that is so meaningful they believe their application would be incomplete without it. If this sounds like you, then please share your story.

>> **Prompt #2:** The lessons we take from obstacles we encounter can be fundamental to later success. Recount a time when you faced a challenge, setback, or failure. How did it affect you and what did you learn from the experience?

>> **Prompt #3:** Reflect on a time when you questioned or challenged a belief or idea. What prompted your thinking? What was the outcome?

>> **Prompt #4:** Reflect on something that someone has done for you that has made you happy or thankful in a surprising way. How has this gratitude affected or motivated you?

>> **Prompt #5:** Discuss an accomplishment, event, or realization that sparked a period of personal growth and a new understanding of yourself or others.

>> **Prompt #6:** Describe a topic, idea or concept you find so engaging it makes you lose all track of time. Why does it captivate you? What or who do you turn to when you want to learn more?

>> **Prompt #7:** Share an essay on any topic of your choice. It can be one you've already written, one that responds to a different prompt, or one of your own design.

Considering Alternatives to the Common Application

Although I focus on the Common Application in this book, nearly all my advice and suggestions apply to the other applications. If the college or university you're applying to doesn't accept the Common App, you don't need to worry. You still need to write essays that capture the admission counselors' attention enough so they accept you in the fall's freshmen class.

Here are some of the other college applications you may encounter besides the Common App:

>> **Coalition Application:** More than 150 colleges accept the Coalition Application (www.coalitionforcollegeaccess.org). Like the Common App, it requires a central personal statement (the prompts tend to overlap nicely with those on the Common App) and supplements for most of the participating schools.

>> **ApplyTexas:** The saying "Everything's bigger in Texas . . ." certainly applies to the state's system of higher education. In fact, the ApplyTexas application is accepted by nearly 60 schools. You can find the essay questions at www.applytexas.org and click on the "View the 2021–22 essay prompts." Note that, like the Common App and Coalition App, you may also encounter individual supplemental essays for different schools.

>> **University of California:** The University of California has nine campuses (University of California at San Francisco offers health-focused graduate programs) that require this application exclusively. The essay structure for the UC Application is very different than other applications. Instead of one central essays, the UC App requires that you complete four 350-word Personal Insight Questions. You can find the prompts (you can choose from eight) at apply.UniversityofCalifornia.edu and search for the personal insight questions.

>> **Individual applications:** Although I list many of the big players on the application landscape, some schools (Georgetown comes to mind) continue to use their own application platforms and don't accept Common App or any of the other portals. This can certainly change anytime, but if you're having a hard time finding a certain school on the application you hoped to use, search online to find out whether you're searching in the right place.

First Things First: Understanding Your Timeline

Your second year of nursery school and you still haven't decided on an essay topic? Uh oh. You'd better catch up!

Calm down. I'm only kidding. You should start early, but not too early. If you're a current junior, the fall of your senior year is likely to be extremely hectic. You've probably chosen a demanding class schedule and arrived at the point of maximum responsibility in your extracurricular activities. You may also be facing a battery of standardized tests so knocking off all you can — especially the essays, which are typically the most time-consuming part of your applications — during the summer preceding senior year makes sense. When school begins, you're ahead of the game.

You can get the bulk of your essay writing (with the exception of a supplemental essay or two that may change on August 1, when the Common App relaunches each year) done as far in advance as you want, but you do need to know which colleges you're applying to so you know exactly how much writing you need to do what prompts to answer.

By getting an early start on your admission essays, you will be equipped for early deadlines and any unexpected developments that may come your way during the fall of your senior year. In the following sections I review these possibilities.

Considering Early Action and Early Decision deadlines

Having the option to apply early is one of the many ways that getting your writing done over the summer can benefit you. Depending on the school, you may have two options if you've completed the bulk of your work and are on track to submit applications with early deadlines:

>> **Early Decision (ED):** If you're applying ED, you're telling just one college that it's *the* university of your dreams. You promise to attend if admitted (in other words, this is a *binding* admissions plan), and in return this college gives you a fairly quick decision. Most ED applications are due November 1 or 15 of the academic year before enrollment, though some colleges have introduced "Early Decision II," a secondary round due at a later date. The results of November applications are released in December or January.

>> **Early Action (EA):** EA applications aren't binding (in most cases, however Stanford has something called Restrictive Early Action, meaning you can't apply EA anywhere else). Typically, EA means you send in your application by an earlier deadline (usually also in November) and the college answers within a few weeks or months.

Both ED and EA can dramatically increase your chance of being accepted to the college of your choice, mainly because the admissions committee reads your application among a much smaller pool of applicants and because you're showing initiative and readiness earlier than the general pool. Chapter 7 provides more details.

Working out how many essays you have to write

The number of essays you have to write depends on your college list. For all intents and purposes, when English teachers and other authority figures refer to "your college essay," what they're talking about is the Common Application's (or similar application) personal statement (you can find the prompts for that essay in the section, "Familiarizing Yourself with the Common Application," earlier in this chapter). In addition to this essay, the Common App also offers an optional essay (Chapter 19 gives you more info on how to write that essay), so that's two main essays that nearly every school you apply to will read.

In addition, many schools on the Common App also have their own supplemental essays (some schools have none, where others have up to five or six). And if you're applying to schools that don't use the Common App, like the University of California, they have their own requirements (refer to the section, "Considering Alternatives to the Common Application," earlier in this chapter).

TIP

Aim to figure out your working college list as quickly as you can — ideally relatively early in the summer after your junior year. You can make changes later, but if you work out the broad framework of how much writing you're working with, your future self will be grateful. You may also figure out your "Tier 1" schools, to which you may or may not opt to apply EA or ED; that way, you can always write an extra supplement or two for your January deadlines or if you decide to add a college later, but you'll still have the majority of your work done.

Chapter 7 provides a detailed timeline to help you strategize for success when applying to the schools of your choice.

Factoring in supplementary writing

Most schools on the Common App or elsewhere also have their own short essays called supplemental essays in addition to your personal statement. Supplemental essay prompts are already available to you (you just have to create a Common App account or search online for last year's application), but sometimes a college decides to change a supplement or two, releasing their new prompts on August 1 when the Common App goes live for each new batch of seniors. (Chapter 24 gives you ten tips to answering supplemental essays.)

TIP

You can start ahead of time on the supplemental essays, but I suggest focusing first on your main essays. Prioritizing your personal statement and getting a head-start on additional essays ensures that you're in prime shape by early fall — and more than on track for your deadlines.

Writing Admission Essays While Having a Life

When I was writing my own admission essays (not quite during the rock-and-chisel stage of human communication, but nearly), I was blessedly ignorant enough to apply to only one school as an ED candidate (which I don't recommend). Now, most of my students apply to 10 or 12 universities or even more. They also take more difficult courses and cram more activities into their days than my generation did. So the task has become harder and the time to complete it more limited. Efficiency is definitely the name of the game. If you want to come up with a great admission essay and still fit in sleep, schoolwork, and trips to the mall/nightclub/nature preserve (pick one), this section's for you.

Taking advantage of spare time

Some words to live by as you apply to college or grad school: Every minute counts. I mean this statement literally. If you take advantage of five minutes here and ten minutes there, you'll find that a great deal of the work of writing an admission essay evaporates. Of course, you need a block of uninterrupted time at some point, but not as much as you would if you hadn't grabbed every second. Here are a few ways to squeeze essay-writing into your day:

>> **Family gatherings:** Sit next to the relative who knows you the best and talks the most. (If those qualities are in two separate people, sit between them or divide your time.) Explain that you're writing about key aspects of your personality and experience. Ask for suggestions. You may emerge with unexpected insights about yourself, your role in your family, or how people saw you as a child that can serve as fodder for essays.

>> **Trips:** On the bus to a soccer meet? Put your cellphone on Airplane Mode for a brief stretch so that you can stare out the window and daydream. Spend a few minutes imagining that you're signed up to give a TED Talk about one moment in your life. Which moment should it be? Before you leave the bus, jot down your thoughts. Later, those thoughts may form the basis of an essay.

During the topic-search period, jot down ideas whenever they occur to you. As you write the rough draft, use spare minutes to record great details or phrases. When you have one complete draft, keep a printout in your backpack. Glance at it whenever you can, fixing grammar errors, correcting spelling, and so on. Chapter 5 gives you more suggestions for generating ideas.

Adapting one essay to several questions

The University of Oregon asks in its supplemental essay prompt how you'll share your "experience, values, and interests with [its] community." The University of Colorado at Boulder asks you to "Pick one of your unique identities and describe its significance." These questions are different, but the answers may not be. An essay you write for one may do the trick for both, with some minor tweaks.

For example, suppose you write an essay for Boulder about your summer as a mascot for a minor-league baseball team. Your essay talks about the freedom you discovered the minute you covered your head with a giant plastic baseball. The anonymity, you explained, allowed you to discover your inner child and made you realize that mascots are "almost spiritual in that they draw people out of everyday reality." Okay, I'm being slightly ridiculous, but you get the idea. You've got an essay that reflects on an unusual July and August. Assuming it's a good essay, why not send it to several other colleges as well?

TIP

When I encourage students to recycle an essay that may work for a few different supplemental responses, I mean they use the same general topic or even the opening paragraph of the same essay, but they make some minor changes in the later paragraphs in order to truly reflect each distinct prompt. You may also have different word count requirements for one essay than another. In other words, you can recycle a topic or experience you want to write about more often than you can recycle and entire piece, word-for-word.

WARNING

If you do recycle your supplemental essays, make sure you change any reference to the school in question. You're not impressing anyone when you're applying to the University of Colorado but the essay refers to Indiana University.

WARNING

One particular question you should *never* adapt for more than one application: the "Why us?" essay, as in "Why do you want to attend our university?" If you answer the question honestly (as you should), you'll include details about your interest in this particular school that aren't relevant to another institution. And if your essay is so general that it applies to several schools, it isn't good enough for any of them. That doesn't mean, however, that you can't share details about yourself and what you have to offer on a college campus to more than one school. Refer to Chapter 17 for more help in tackling the "Why us?" question.

Tempering Frustration: Greasing Your Wheels

Some students put their fingers to the keyboard and stunning prose comes out. (And by "some students," I mean less than five students over the course of 12 years as a counselor.) The vast majority of the time, you need to write a certain number of pretty unfortunate drafts before you get to the good stuff. Don't fight that process. You're just greasing your wheels.

That metaphor has especially helped my students who actually love writing, and therefore put a ton of pressure on themselves to do a great job on this process.

Think of your favorite writer in the world. Chances are, they weren't published any younger than the age of 35. Do you think your writer picked up a pen for the first time at 34, or even at 30? Um. No. Your writer probably started writing at a young age, and most of their early work was probably garbage. Poorly constructed sentences, revised four or five times. And all of it was absolutely essential. That's what I mean by greasing your wheels.

I'm not suggesting you need several decades to write your personal statement (though several months is pretty typical!), but I do mean you have to extend yourself grace and forgiveness when it comes to the imperfect stuff that's going to burst forth from your pen or fingers when you first begin to write.

Here's yet another way of looking at an infuriating first draft — writer Anne Patchett calls it the amethyst butterfly effect. Say you're lucky enough to actually have a perfect vision of what your essay is going to focus on and sound like in your head. In the excitement of brainstorming (see Chapter 5), you just *know* your essay is going to be brilliant. Yet, as soon as you actually start to crystallize your ideas and write, your ideas come out all clunky and weird and fall dramatically short of your vision. In other words, you're having a hard time grabbing that elusive butterfly with both hands.

So how do you write and cope with the disappointment? Some writers give up when their words don't meet their expectations — without realizing that this part of writing is normal and inevitable. If you can tolerate your dull, flat beginnings and keep chasing your vision, you'll probably arrive at something far closer to perfection than you imagine in your most frustrated moments. That's all part of the process.

Keeping Perspective

Need I state the obvious? It's "just" an essay. Yes, what you write will have an impact on your chances for admission, and certainly you want to do the best job you can — after all, that's why you're devoting a significant chunk of time to letting your ideas marinate. But how good a job can you do if you see the admission essay as the only possible path to everything you ever wanted out of life? "My entire future depends upon this sentence" is *not* an attitude likely to bring out your best performance. (And just in case you do find yourself too flustered to operate at some point in your writing process, I devote all of Chapter 13 to overcoming writer's block and getting yourself back on track.)

REMEMBER

Writing a college admission essay isn't as hard as most of the other things you've already done, such as learning to tie your shoelaces and telling your mom about the time you borrowed and lost her favorite necklace. Yes, it may be the most challenging piece of writing you've ever written. And yet, your only job is to tell "the truth, the whole truth, and nothing but the truth" about a subject you know very well — your own life. No one is more qualified for the job.

Chapter **2**

Exploring the Subject of the Essay — You

I sometimes get a particular look from students the first time we discuss college essays. Most commonly, it's the wide-eyed gaze of someone about to take a test they didn't study for. Those students occasionally shoot an accusatory expression toward a parent, if one happens to be present or nearby. And the look is usually followed by a statement like: "I really don't know how I'm going to do this. Nothing interesting has ever happened to me." Sometimes, the feedback is even more direct: "I'm pretty boring!"

You're on the wrong path if you think that only a dramatic, life-altering experience provides fodder for an admission essay. In fact, everyone's life is packed with potential essay material, just waiting to be unearthed. In this chapter I show you how to dig into the subject of your essay — yourself. I also explain why you're the subject of *all* college admission essays, even if you think you're writing about something completely different.

Mining Your Life

Miners move tons of earth looking for a few precious bits of ore. Their task is dirty, dangerous, and tiring. Fortunately for you, "mining your life" for college admission essay topics carries none of the risks of chopping real minerals out of the earth, though you may tire (mentally, at least) after a long trek down memory lane. Plus, mining your life is actually pretty interesting; you get to poke around inside your own head, dredging up all the best moments from your past. You may find yourself reflecting on the challenges that have shaped you, too — and I encourage you to meet those memories with an open mind, if you can. I share more about that in the section, "Writing about difficult experiences," later in this chapter.

REMEMBER

College admission essays are often regarded as a true rite of passage, and some of the essay prompts quite literally focus on the transition from childhood to adulthood. That's because you're at a crossroads. You can gain valuable self-knowledge from this process that you can take with you into your future. By taking this essay writing seriously, you're paying close attention to not only this moment in your life, but also what you value from your past and what you want for your future.

When you mine your life for material, you're in search of stories. You're *not* seeking a bunch of general statements like "I'm a very strong person. When I face a challenge, I don't give up." General statements are boring — they *tell*, when you need to *show* (and Chapter 9 is devoted to this very topic). Broad claims also offer very little information. But tell a story — everyone loves stories — and you'll capture your readers, making them experience your reality for a few moments.

Of course, when you write an admission essay, you present more than the story. You must convey why the story matters, or consider the theme of the story and what you're trying to reveal about yourself. In the next section of this chapter, I explain how to uncover the stories you need. In a later section of this chapter, "Identifying Themes in Your Autobiography," I show you how to define the themes of your stories.

TIP

Many supplemental essays, especially if you're applying to a specialized program, like film, business, kinesiology, or nursing, ask you why you're interested in that particular major. (Supplemental essays are essays written for just one school or program, and you can find out more about them in Chapter 17.) Mining your life to answer this question involves thinking about people in the profession you've met or experiences (an illness or a court case, perhaps) that made you appreciate these jobs. See Chapter 3 for additional questions that prod your memory and help you define why you chose your career path.

Collecting the Stories of Your Life

The big moments — the winning touchdown, the award, the opening night of the play — can be a good place to start your search for stories. They're also fairly easy to remember. Here's how to collect memories of important events:

>> Flip through your family's photo albums (or through your camera roll or your social media accounts) or mentally review the milestones you've passed — birthdays, graduations, "firsts," and so on.

>> Talk with your parents or other relatives, urging them to tell you stories about your childhood. Look for patterns — or surprises! — in the ways they remember you.

>> Chat with your best and oldest friends and take note of the stories they seem to remember best.

TIP

Use a notebook or open a new note on your phone's Note app or a new document on your laptop. Name the file or note something like "Mining" or "Memories." Fill it with a list of all the memories you've gathered. Put a star next to turning points — the times when something changed.

Then turn your attention to the small stuff. Life's little events are important too. The quiet walks with your grandfather around the pond in his backyard. The hobbies you enjoyed as a kid (or now!). The first time you helped a family member prepare a traditional holiday dinner. As you review your past, collect a long list of stories — memories, really — of those times.

I recommend you gather moments in terms of intervals: listing at least one memory from two years ago, five years ago, ten years ago, and so on until you run out of time. The moments you choose to remember from a typical day at each of those ages may provide fine essay material. (Chapter 3 contains a series of questions that can help you remember the small stuff of life.)

After you have a slew of stories, think about them carefully. Is there a story you'd share with people you've just met to help them get to know you better? Is there a story family and friends love to tell about you? Which ones reveal something important about your character? Which ones do you want the admissions committee to hear? Do any of your memories relate to the questions on the application? Does any story have a theme that you want to communicate to your reader? (For more information on theme, refer to the section, "Identifying Themes in Your Autobiography," later in this chapter.)

REMEMBER

Mining your life is *not* writing the essay. At this stage you're just collecting material, not trying to punch it into shape for that large blank spot on your application. Don't worry about the rest of the process yet; just dredge up as many memories as you can and list them in a computer file or in a notebook.

Dipping Your Toe in the Writing Pool: Freewriting 101

Now you're ready for a quick dip — about ten minutes or so — into the writing pool. Not to worry, this first endeavor is fairly low risk and painless. In these beginning stages, your goal is to turn off your filter (no, not your Instagram filter) and allow yourself full freedom of expression. If you've ever kept a journal before, you're at an advantage, because *freewriting* — this initial writing stage — is just that: letting your stream of consciousness pour onto the page. Unlike brainstorming, outlining, or braindumping ideas, freewriting is about loosening up and writing without a prescribed plan. Your goal should be to simply say everything you can possibly think of with regards to a given memory or idea.

However eager you may be to jump into writing a structured draft, you aren't ready yet because you have no idea where you're headed. If you simply follow your train of thought, though, you'll see that what emerges is more raw, honest, and genuine than if you tried to plan everything you will cover in your essay. In other words, you may not know what you're trying to say until you see it on the page.

Freewriting helps you create a road map for your essay. To do this freewriting exercise, try these simple steps:

1. **Find a quiet room with no distractions.**

   Turn off Netflix, your phone, and any music. You need to focus all your attention on this exercise.

2. **Use a notebook or open a file in the word-processing program of your choice.**

   You may feel more comfortable writing or typing, but whichever you choose isn't important.

3. **Select a topic that interests you — either a memory or aspect of your personality that came up as you began to mine your life.**

   Refer to the section, "Collecting the Stories of Your Life," earlier in this chapter for suggestions on how to gather material and the section, "Revealing significant themes," later in this chapter for some ideas.

4. **Write (or type) for a finite time — shoot for 15 minutes — about this topic unless you're inclined to go longer.**

Don't hold back. Because this freewriting exercise is just for you, you have no responsibility to think about punctuation or grammar.

5. **Reread your freewrite.**

Mark anything that strikes you as an interesting detail, an important insight, or otherwise worthy of consideration. You might also add notes to yourself on how to develop your ideas ("Expand on this?").

6. **If you're inspired by the idea of freewriting but aren't convinced you have any useable material, try another 15-minute freewrite on a different topic or memory.**

Remember that if all that you've accomplished while freewriting is breaking the ice to get a bit more comfortable with writing about yourself and your life, it was worthwhile. You can now experiment with different approaches, always keeping your earliest freewrites as raw material you might revisit later.

REMEMBER

If you find yourself wandering off and writing about a new topic, that's okay. Most students start their writing process thinking they're going to write about one thing and find that their final draft is actually a synthesis of several initial ideas that they had. Maybe you're planning to write about soccer, for example, but your freewriting turns to a conversation you had with your grandmother whose Italian identity impacted your family's dynamic.

College essays often start with a vivid moment or opening anecdote of some kind. So even as you freewrite you may consider adding as much sensory information or details related to the five senses as you can. With your filter off, can find details that you had no idea were within you.

Identifying Themes in Your Autobiography

The stories of your life are an important ingredient of the admissions essay, but they're not the only ingredient. You also need to identify the themes that run through the information you present about yourself. A *theme* is a general category or big idea that seems to apply to the most important memories of your past. Creative works have themes too; in English or art class you've probably had to identify the themes of novels or other artworks (poems, plays, musical compositions, paintings, and so on). How do you find the themes that are relevant to your essay? Read on.

Reviewing your life story

Your life has an objective reality: hours worked, food eaten, friends greeted, tasks accomplished, and so forth. But apart from that dry list of details, everyone also makes an internal movie, *The Story of Me*. In *The Story of Me* you are the star, the scriptwriter, and the director. You create the characters (the way you see yourself and others) and select events to film (decide which events are important to you). From time to time you project *The Story of Me* onto the screen of your mind, watching the events (that is, remembering them) and, in the process, weaving a set of random happenings into a plot that makes sense. To identify themes, turn yourself into a movie critic, interpreting and analyzing *The Story of Me*.

For example, your own personal film may revolve around compassion. When you peer into the past, you remember how you helped that little boy in kindergarten who dropped his glob of clay and how you sat for hours with an elderly neighbor as she regaled you with stories of her childhood in Hungary and her career as a cigar roller. Your inner review of *The Story of Me* proclaims, "This film is a moving account of a girl who never met anyone she wasn't interested in helping. The main character is driven and motivated by her concern for others." (Do you cringe at boasting? Check out the section, "Overcoming the Taboo against Bragging," later in this chapter.)

Revealing significant themes

Identifying themes is crucial because you can't write about your life coherently unless you understand why particular events are significant *to you*. Moreover, if you identify a theme and express it clearly, the reader (that is, the admissions office) will understand how to put the information you're providing about your background, your qualities, and your life experiences into context. And the more deeply your reader understands your character, the better off you are.

Here's a selection of themes that may apply to your life:

>> **Identity:** How do you define yourself? Think about gender, race, ethnicity, economic level, age, and all the other factors that contribute to your identity. Then think about times when you were particularly aware of those factors. Can you match any memories to these issues? If so, you may have an essay topic.

>> **Challenges:** What barriers have you overcome? What difficulties have you gone through? When have you almost lost courage? Think of challenges relating to family, school (both academic and social), and community. What incidents can you relate that illustrate how you have handled tough situations?

>> **Curiosity:** What would you like to know about the world? Whom would you like to meet? Where would you like to visit? Have any situations sparked a hunger inside you — not the "I'll faint if I don't get a lunch break" sort of hunger, but the kind that moves you to explore? Check your memory bank (and Chapter 3). What situations have provoked your curiosity?

>> **Future:** When reporters attend your 100th birthday party, what will they hear the speakers say about you? What will you have accomplished in that long life? If your imagination stalls before the century mark, concentrate on something simpler — your life 5, 10, or 15 years from now. What memories would you like to create as you move through your future?

>> **Time:** How do you spend your days? When does time fly for you, and when does it drag? Are you a planner, a seize-the-moment type, a nostalgia buff? How does this approach impact how you relate to the world?

>> **Passion:** No, I'm not talking about physical passion. (This is a family-friendly book!) I'm talking about what moves you intellectually, artistically, emotionally, politically, or spiritually. When you feel with intensity, what are you doing? Or, what do you want to be doing? The issues or situations that get you going are worth writing about.

>> **Learning:** How do you learn best? What types of activities or teaching styles match your learning style? Which assignments do you remember? Why those? Can you illustrate your identity as a student with one particular experience?

>> **Failure:** I'm not suggesting that you paint yourself as a total loser, because of course you're *not* a loser at all. But if you're human, your reach has occasionally exceeded your grasp, as the poet says, and you've failed. What did you discover from that failure about yourself? How did you change your methods or goals as a result? A memory of failure may become a great essay topic.

>> **Context:** Where do you fit in? *How* do you fit in — in your family, school, neighborhood, country, world, universe? Or, how *don't* you fit in? See yourself as a small tile in a large mosaic. What is your role?

>> **Personality:** What qualities or traits are part of your personality? How do you deal with day-to-day life? Collect some descriptive terms, but don't stop there. Look for memories that illustrate those qualities in action — so that you can show and not tell. For example, if courage is one of your most important qualities, hunt for moments in which you had to be brave.

Writing about difficult experiences

When you read sample essays or even the Common Application personal statement prompts, you may notice a surprising emphasis on writing about memories you may not recount with love and affection.

Until 2017, Prompt 2 on the Common App focused explicitly on failure. In fact, it read, "Recount an incident or time when you experienced failure." The prompt has been softened to "Recount a time when you faced a challenge, setback, *or* failure," (emphasis added) because many students responded to the word "failure" just as you would expect — with horror!

You may be wondering why you would tell colleges about a time when you failed rather than about your achievements, and how doing so would still allow you to present yourself in the best possible light. I have two reasons why you should:

>> **If you've failed, you're a risk-taker.** You have to be willing to do hard things in order to fail. You can't fail while drinking lemonade in a hot tub. If you've known the feeling of falling flat on your face, you must know the value of a challenge, and more than likely you know how to set goals.

>> **Failure means you're in good company.** Many people assume their heroes were born into greatness, when what most beloved public figures actually have in common is an understanding that setbacks are inevitable, and a refusal to be deterred by them. Here are a few examples of familiar people who attribute their eventual success to failing early and often:

- Steven Spielberg (rejected twice from USC's film school)

- Thomas Edison (teachers labeled him as "too stupid to learn anything")

- Beyoncé (lost on *Star Search* and endured nearly a decade of financial hardship before any commercial success)

- JK Rowling (before she wrote *Harry Potter,* she was a broke, divorced new mom struggling with depression)

(UNIVERSITY OF) CHICAGO FIRE

The University of Chicago is notorious for having fun with its supplemental essays. Every year, admitted students and alumni are encouraged to submit creative prompts — from the zany to the brain-busting — for hopeful students to respond to. Past examples have included "So where is Waldo, really?" and "Find X." (Honestly, those are both real.)

You're probably wondering why I am sharing this with you now. Well, because you're at the cusp of generating *a lot* of ideas. After you narrow the focus of your main essay — your personal statement — you may think you're not going to be able to share those other stories anywhere. However, you might. The University of Chicago's paradoxically ambiguous and specific prompts are one example of when you might pull out a story or anecdote you really liked but weren't sure where to include . . . so long as you can tie your material to the theme of the prompt.

That's why the most successful application essays are about challenging oneself *and* handling inevitable setbacks. The reason why you should be honest about the difficult experiences and setbacks you've gone through isn't because those "challenges, setbacks, or failures" define you. Rather those experiences are often the beginning of you. They reveal the stuff you're made of.

Delving Deeper with Your Personal Statement

The personal statement, or the main essay you hope to submit to every college you apply to (see the complete list of prompts in Chapter 1), should provide your reader with a snapshot of who you are and how you came to be that person. Obviously, though, *many* experiences, characteristics, and influences encompass who you are. In these sections, I offer a deeper look at several key ideas you should keep in mind when you review the prompts and begin to narrow your topic.

Sparking growth

You may still be searching for the right realm for your topic. Prompt 5 on the Common App asks you to describe an "accomplishment, event, or realization" that sparked personal growth. Prompt 1 invites you to convey a "background, identity, interest, or talent" that your application would be incomplete without.

Great! You may be thinking. I can write about an aspect of my life where I shine. Maybe that's Irish dancing, or your first internship, or being a natural at STEM subjects. Those experiences may indeed make for great essay material. However, the application has an entire section devoted to extracurricular activities where you can discuss tangible things you've achieved, as well as supplemental essays.

REMEMBER

The key to writing about a significant experience in your life is how it helped you to grow and what you learned about yourself. You risk boring your reader to tears if you insist on writing your personal statement as a lengthy recitation of your resume.

Colleges want to know more about you. That's not to say that you *can't* write about a work experience, a talent or passion, or an experience of leadership — that often is exactly where you should start! But if you're going to do so, you're expected to *dig deeper*.

Don't simply write about how you love science so you decided to pursue an internship at a lab where you learned a lot from valuable mentors. The Activity section on the application provides that information. Rather, write about your deepest feelings (how you always felt that as a girl, you could never be successful in the sciences), challenges (the first day of your internship you wanted to run home), and other insights (how it was your grandmother's immigration story that actually prepared you to enter this field). You'll need that level of depth to write well about an activity you've participated in.

Picking the topic of your choice

The last personal statement prompt on the Common App is the mysterious "Topic of your choice." Other college applications also tend to offer a prompt which is equally vague, such as "Tell a story from your life . . ."

REMEMBER

The fact that this prompt exists is meant to free you, not to add to your stress. You have the freedom to write a personal statement about an aspect of your life that isn't tailor-made to any of the other prompts. You don't need to feel bogged down by adjusting your narrative to fit a particular question. Just focus on your raw material — your life and your stories — as you work through this brainstorm stage. Keep in mind that this is *The Story of You*, or if you prefer a different analogy, your TED Talk. You may have to figure out your themes and characteristics a bit more before you can decide the right lens, or prompt, for your essay.

But Enough about Me: Overcoming the Taboo against Bragging

There is an old joke about a bore at a cocktail party who remarks, "But enough about me. Let's talk about you now. What do *you* think about me?" The joke relies on the fact that nearly everyone has met someone so self-absorbed that they may as well paste mirrors on the inside of their sunglasses. And nobody wants to be the cocktail party bore who's star-struck with his own magnificence.

However, you *can* talk about yourself without unnecessary bragging. And to submit the best possible application on your own behalf, you need to be comfortable conveying your strengths, whether in the form of your essays or in the Activities or Honors section of your application. But if you're like most people, you learned early on to play down your accomplishments:

> YOU: Oh, that little medal? It's the (*mumble mumble*) prize.
>
> FRIEND: The what prize?
>
> YOU: The Nobel Prize. So, do you think it's going to rain?

But applying for admission (or for a scholarship) is *not* a time for humility. It's a time to reveal all the good stuff you usually smile about only when you brush your teeth. However, revealing isn't the same as boasting. When you reveal your good points, you speak honestly and specifically, as in the following:

> In my senior science class I was appointed lab technician, responsible for setting out the chemicals or other supplies needed for each day's experiment. Last week, for example, I had to place 5 grams of radioactive xylophonium on each table. After the experiment, I was in charge of phoning the National Safety Board so that they could come to school to interview the survivors.

Just kidding about the radioactive stuff. Now read this paragraph, in which the writer qualifies for the "I Love Me" Award:

> In my senior science class the teacher, stunned by my natural talent, gave me the most responsible and important job in the class. No one else could be trusted with the task of putting out the radioactive xylophonium and calling the National Safety Board.

Do you see the difference? In the first example, the writer states exactly what she has done and lets the reader decide to affix labels such as "trustworthy," "mature," "reliable," and so on. In the second example, the writer draws conclusions for the reader — always an annoying habit, but particularly offensive when those conclusions are praise for the writer.

Bottom line: Be clear and specific about your accomplishments and character and leave the admiration to your reader.

Chapter **3**

Beginning to Self-Reflect

S ome students have a difficult time working through the process of reviewing their life on their own. If you can identify with that difficulty, you're not alone. To make self-reflection easier for writing your college admission essay, being interviewed or asked questions can help the process. As any podcast fan knows, a skilled interviewer can elicit the best material — including insights or memories that the subject hadn't planned or thought to share.

With the right questions, you, too, can unearth insights and memories that may never have occurred to you otherwise. (Refer to Chapter 2 for more help in looking at your life as if it were a movie, with the broad goals of figuring out themes and collecting interesting stories.)

Don't be discouraged by the number of questions in this chapter. You don't have to answer them all, and you don't have to answer any of them in detail. Work your way through the categories that seem most appealing, jotting down a phrase or two — just enough to remind you of the answer. If you're inspired by any particular question, grab a sheet of scrap paper or open a file on your computer and write everything that occurs to you.

TIP

Even if you don't use all your brainstorming material, getting to know yourself at a deeper level can only better equip you to write college essays. Some of these questions dig fairly deeply into your personal life, but you're certainly not obliged to share the most private parts of your life with your admissions readers. So if secrets surface as you answer these questions, remember that you're still in charge of what to do with them, and what you write in a *freewrite* (an unfiltered, stream-of-consciousness way of pouring your thoughts onto the page) or in your early notes doesn't always have to remain as raw or revealing in a later draft.

Looking Closer at Family Ties

Applications frequently ask you to describe an important person, someone who has influenced you. Or you may be faced with a question about your identity — how you define yourself. Family stories may be useful for these essays.

The following questions prompt you to think about your family background and interactions. I even include a couple of questions about your most distant ancestors, people who lived long before you were born, because sometimes thinking about your family's heritage helps you understand its current reality. (Still another great essay topic!) Don't worry if your family falls firmly into the nontraditional category. Plug your own definition of family into these questions and answer away. If you want, answer the same questions about your stepparents or other parental figures in your life.

Contemplating your parents' influence

Whether you hope to model yourself after their example or simply learn from it, your parents or parental figures were your very first teachers — and are often the most natural place to start when brainstorming admission essay ideas. When it comes to the parental figures in your life, here are some questions to ask yourself:

» What are your parents' backgrounds? Think about their upbringing (economic, social, cultural, and so on) and yours. How have those factors influenced you?

» Have your parents told you any stories about their lives that struck you as important in some way? If so, what was the best story?

» Does your upbringing differ from your parents'? Do you feel fortunate because of those differences? Do you feel deprived because of those differences?

» What is the best lesson your parent(s) taught you? What were you doing when you learned this lesson — or when have you head a chance to put their wisdom into practice?

» What's your favorite memory of your parent(s)? Why is this memory important?

» Have you and your parents struggled over any issues? Which ones? Why? What was the outcome of the struggle? How did you grow from that struggle?

In addition to these questions, sometimes I ask students to try writing a typical scene around the dinner table with their parents and other family members. Doing so can provide a more organic route of defining some of the "characters" in your life — and seeing how you relate to them.

Focusing on your siblings

Some of the best personal statements I have read have been about siblings — about witnessing or helping a sibling who was struggling, receiving support from siblings, and even, on occasion, about the absence of siblings.

As you think about your family makeup, these questions can help you in your self-reflection:

>> Has the size of your family or your birth order (oldest, middle, youngest, or one of more than three) impacted you? How do you see your role in the family?

>> Describe a situation where you see the influence of your siblings — perhaps where you leaned on them, or they leaned on you. Is this situation how you typically relate to one another, or was it the exception to the rule?

>> What is your favorite memory of your sibling(s)? Least favorite memory? Why?

>> What have you learned from your siblings? Describe the situation you were in when you learned this lesson. What were you all doing? What did they say? How did you react?

>> What have your siblings learned from you? Describe the situation in which they learned this lesson. What were you all doing? What did you say? How did they react?

TIP

If you include an important relationship in one of your essays, remember that you don't have to title it "Why my older sister is my idol, hero, and basically a modern-day Mother Theresa, in 650 words or less!" Maybe your relationship with your sister has really taken time to evolve, or you've gone through some hardships and often butted heads — but she has absolutely had a defining role in your life. In other words, when you think about influential relationships in your life, just as with your important memories, they may include shades of gray, and the tough moments can be just as meaningful as the blissful ones. (And if you're worried about what your sister or other family members may feel when they read that essay of yours, turn to Chapter 6.)

Scrutinizing your grandparents and extended family

Maybe you're one of the fortunate ones — fortunate enough to know your grandparents pretty well. Grandparents can play an important role in understanding the bigger picture of your family. Sometimes the loss or absence of grandparents also plays a role in how you have experienced your family dynamic, in which case you might consider what you do know — by reflecting on these questions independently or discussing with a parent or sibling. These questions can help you discover more about who you are, through a family lens:

>> Do your grandparents see you often? Have your grandparents passed down any special traditions to you? What are those traditions? What do those traditions mean to you now, in the 21st century?

>> Have your grandparents had very different lives, in comparison with your own life? How? Have they made any decisions or sacrifices that shaped your life?

>> Do you have any family heirlooms? What are they? Describe the objects. Why are the objects important? What traditions do these heirlooms represent? What will you pass along to your heirs someday?

>> What family legends have you heard (about any family member, including ancestors)? What do those stories mean to you?

>> Are any special places associated with your family? Think about homelands, vacation spots, the site of historic events, the family house, and so forth.

Answering general family questions

You may have come up with your own reflective questions about how you relate to the important people in your life, based on the unique structure of your own family. Use these questions to jump-start your self-reflection:

>> When was your family most proud of you? Why? How did they show their pride? How did you react?

>> When was your family disappointed in you? What did you learn from that event?

>> What qualities do you appreciate most about your family? Why? How does your family show those qualities?

>> What would you change about your family, if you could? Why?

>> Have you ever helped your family? When? What did you do? How did they react?

>> Have you ever wanted to help your family but were unable to do so? How did you feel? Why couldn't you help? What did you do instead?

>> Describe a typical holiday celebration of your family. What do your customs reveal about your family and your place in it?

>> Describe a typical Saturday morning, Friday night, weekday evening, and/or weekday morning in your house. What does your routine reveal about your family and your place in it?

>> How are you different from your family? What does that difference reveal about your own identity?

Hitting the Halls: School Days

Though you may not write your personal statement about your academic life (because most of the essay prompts invite you to share something more personal), more than likely you'll write about your school experience for the various *supplemental essays* (those specific essays or short answer questions required by only one institution).

Reviewing your life at school may even help you with "why us?" questions — for example, why are you applying here, and what do you hope to achieve on our campus? Having a full understanding of what you value and what may have been missing from your high school experience can help you define what you seek in your college experience.

The questions in this section are designed to draw forth your thoughts on your school days — what you learned in and out of your classes and about yourself. You may also find material here for questions about your successes and failures, your role models, or your most memorable intellectual experiences.

REMEMBER

Sometimes teachers writing your letters of recommendation may want you to provide them with a short reflection on your work in their class so that they're best equipped to advocate for you, so don't be surprised if they send you a survey with questions similar to these questions.

Considering your strengths

As you reflect on who you are as a student, you want to be able to articulate your strengths and preferences in a more sophisticated way than "I like English because it's easiest for me." These questions can help you dig into the areas where you naturally excel:

>> What is your favorite subject? Why do you like it? Describe a typical day in this class. What sort of activity in this class do you most enjoy? Describe yourself taking part in that activity.

>> What skills or talents do you have that you must apply in your favorite class or classes? In what activities (lab reports, term or research papers, tests, discussions, projects, and so on) do you excel?

>> Describe a project you're proud of. How long did you work on it? How did you go about your work? Why was this project special?

Tackling your challenges

Even if you never want to think about your hardest class ever again, remember that growth doesn't happen when things are easy-breezy. Your most important lesson about learning might have happened when you were knee-deep in frustration. These questions might also help you with the "Anything Else You Want to Tell Us?" question (I explain this essay in detail in Chapter 19), where you have the option to explain how you overcame adversity in your learning experience:

>> What subject is hard for you? How did you meet that challenge? Were you successful? What did you take away from your success or failure?

>> Describe a project or assignment that you wish you could do over. Why were you dissatisfied with the initial result? What would you do differently now? What did this project teach you about your own strengths and weaknesses as a student?

>> Who has helped you through tough times in school? What did they do? How did you react? What changed because of their help?

>> Have you had any semesters or time periods where you struggled as a student? What do you attribute that difficulty to and how did you overcome the difficulty?

Identifying teachers' influence on you

Though you may have much to say about your recent teachers (especially if you've been considering who may be willing to write a letter of recommendation on your behalf), by no means do you need to limit yourself to high school when you consider these questions. Maybe there was an early classroom experience that was extremely formative for you, nurturing an enthusiasm for a given subject (or possibly the opposite). These questions can help you to consider the figures who have influenced you throughout your learning process:

>> Who is your favorite or most influential teacher? Why? Describe a typical experience with that teacher. Describe a special, out-of-the-ordinary experience with that teacher.

>> What did you learn about yourself from this teacher? What message would you like to give this teacher?

>> Have you had a teacher who was tough on you? How did you react to the challenge? What did you learn about yourself from this teacher?

Seeing how different learning styles have affected you

Before you enroll in college, have a good sense of who you are as a learner — meaning, understand what techniques and approaches help you to be successful academically. These questions can help you to reflect on the strategies that work for you (and which ones don't).

You may use this information in an essay about an academic experience or how you overcame a challenge as well as to better equip yourself to enter a whole new learning environment:

>> Think about silent study, discussion, notes, creative projects, writing, and other academic tasks. Which ones are hard and which ones are easy? Why?

>> How do you budget your time? Can you describe a long-term project and how you scheduled the work?

>> Would you define yourself as a visual, auditory, or hands-on learner? How has that impacted your approached to studying? Are there adjustments or strategies you use when a class isn't taught in your preferred learning style?

>> How do you handle pressure? Describe one time when you felt nervous or stressed out about an assignment. What did you do? What did you learn from that situation?

>> Are you the same student you were ten years ago? Five years ago? Two years ago? What have you learned about yourself as a student?

Reflecting on group experiences

I was never a big fan of group projects in high school. But the belief that "learning is social" is a huge part of many academic programs, and so think about how you feel and operate in groups, especially if you're applying to a program or school that puts a strong emphasis on collaborative work. These questions can also help you realize what kind of professional environment would be best suited to you:

>> Describe a group project that went well. Why was the group successful? Did everyone participate? Did anyone goof off? How did the group handle the goof-off? Were you a leader? What did you do? What would you do differently?

>> Describe a group project that did not go well. Why did it fail? What would you do differently if you were assigned that project again? What did you learn from that project?

>> Do you have a preferred role in group projects? Is your role consistent or does it change depending on the subject or project?

Ruminating on Your Community

"No man is an island," wrote poet John Donne. (No woman is either, I might add.) You live in a community, and increasingly, in a global village. The questions in these sections are designed to clarify your thoughts about your role in these contexts. Answers here might apply to essays asking about (surprise, surprise) your community, culture, or background, but they're also relevant to questions about your values.

Seeing how your local community plays a role in who you are

Sometimes when I ask students what they're looking for in a college community, their answer is "Somewhere nothing like my hometown." Other times, they explain that they're seeking somewhere with similar values to those they've grown up around. But what are the values and characteristics that define your current community?

No matter what you seek in the next chapter of your life, you can benefit from understanding the world you come from, and these questions can help:

» Describe your local community. What makes it unique? When you think about the community, how do you fit in? How does the community see you?

» Have you contributed to your community? In what way? How did that experience affect you?

» If you could change one thing about your community, what would it be? Why? Realistically, can you change your community?

» Which values of your community do you share? What makes you different from others in your community?

» What issues face your community? Think about the environment, social interactions, government, the economy, and so forth. Which issue is most important to you? Why?

» Do you still live in the community of your birth? If not, why did you move? What was the experience of moving like for you and for your family? What does your community of origin mean to you, now that you no longer live there?

» What are you seeking in a college community — socially, academically, and culturally?

Musing on the global village

These questions are a bit broader in scope and invite you to consider your awareness of global events. You don't need to start skimming news articles. Instead, you can use these questions to gauge what global issues already stand out to you and what kind of exposure (or lack thereof) you have had to other cultures and communities:

» How connected do you feel to events happening in other countries? Which events concern you the most? Why?

» Have you had the opportunity to experience a culture different from your own? What did you admire about it? What would you like to learn more about?

>> When you think about your future, are your drawn to the idea of working globally? What could that look like?

>> Think about the environment, diplomacy, the economy, health, nutrition, war, terrorism, and so on. Which global issue is most important to you? Why? What can you do about the issue?

Contemplating the Future

The application era of your life is future-oriented. You're thinking about the four years, at least, and each college or university you apply to is considering the next few years with you. But you're also pondering your long-range plans: career or personal goals. Similarly, colleges want to know what contributions you hope to make, in the classroom, on campus, and afterward. These matters are sometimes addressed directly by questions such as "What are your career plans?" and "How would you be involved in campus life?" Material from this section may also be useful for a general "Write about yourself and your goals" question or the "issue important to you" question.

Predicting your professional future

Although many students don't truly find their career path until they're enrolled in college or afterward, you may encounter questions like the following on your college applications. Jot down a few notes and see if you can get comfortable with considering the possibilities.

These questions can help familiarize you with the ways you might be asked about your career goals:

>> What are your career plans? Why are you hopeful about this particular career path?

>> What type of environment would you like to work in? Why?

>> How do you hope to contribute to your intended field? How will you go about making that contribution?

>> What branch of the field most attracts you? Why?

>> What current trends in your field will shape the future of the profession? Which trends will fade away? Explain your reasons.

>> Borrowing from an infamous UCLA scholarship application prompt: You've just written a 200-page autobiography. What does it say on page 165?

TIP

Not having an idea what your career plans are or even what your major will be is okay. After all, the average college student changes their major several times. If you're met with a question like USC's "Describe how you plan to pursue your academic interests and why you want to explore them at USC specifically" and have no idea how to respond, I recommend leaning into a few different subjects that intrigue you and be honest and excited about the prospect of exploring them at college. In other words, you're entitled to be a well-rounded student who sees many possibilities for the future — and it makes sense why you need a little more time (in other words, your freshman year of college) to explore possible paths before committing to one.

Looking into a crystal ball at how the world may be

These questions may make you feel a bit like you're running for office, but they can also help you to begin to consider what matters most — not just for you, but for the society you live in. These insights can even inform some of your thoughts about what you want to major in or what career(s) you hope to explore. If you encounter a question similar to one of these among your supplemental essay prompts, you can read more about possible approaches in Chapter 19.

>> What will your generation contribute to the world? How will your generation be different from those that preceded it?

>> What is the greatest danger to the future of the world? What is the world's greatest hope?

>> Think about any element of modern society (computers, books, the media, cars, and so on). How will that element change in the future? Why? How will society be different because of that change?

Pondering Your Identity

Your identity is made up of a set of descriptions that you apply to yourself or that others apply to you. Some factors that create your identity are your race, ethnic background, nationality, religion, gender, sexual orientation and gender identity, and age.

Here are a few examples:

>> Think about your race, ethnic background, religion, gender, and other aspects of your identity. How do these factors affect how you see the world or how others see you? Describe a situation in which one or more of those factors mattered.

>> Have you experienced being a minority compared to those around you in terms of your race, identity, gender, ability, or beliefs? How did you feel? What did you learn from that experience?

>> What adjectives (descriptive words) apply to you? Why? Think of situations in which you displayed those qualities.

>> What's the first thing about yourself that you would tell a new friend? Why?

>> What does your best friend know about you that no one else knows?

>> What has been most important in shaping your personality? Name one person. Describe one event.

Pinpointing How Other People Help You Figure Out Who You Are

"People who need people are the luckiest people in the world," sang Barbra Streisand. So everybody's lucky, except perhaps for a hermit or two in a far-off desert. *You* certainly need people, and not just the admissions counselors who will read your essays. Yet sometimes students shy away from writing about important relationships or influences, wondering, "Isn't this essay supposed to be about *me*? I'm finally getting used to that idea, and now you want me to brainstorm about *other people*?"

REMEMBER

The truth is anything you write about a figure who is important to you is a reflection of your specific perspective — the way you see others and what you value about them. For example, when you write that your football coach taught you what it means to be accountable to those around you (and that he imparted this lesson through shouting, sweat, and even a few tears), if you write the essay vividly enough, the admissions counselors are learning about you, not your coach. The essay will convey *your* response to a strong authority figure and *your* development of discipline (through specific examples, of course). Your reader doesn't need a biography of your coach. The focus is your own impressions and direct interactions and the impact he had on you.

Without further ado, these questions help you pinpoint figures that have been important in shaping your life.

>> Scan the section, "Looking Closer at Family Ties," earlier in this chapter, and pick out people who have been important to you. Describe their influence on you. Think of situations in which that influence was obvious.

>> Think about world figures, both present day and historical. Whom do you admire? Why? What contributions do you attribute to those people? Would you like to contribute in the same way or in a different way? If you could sit down to chat with any of those people, what would you say?

>> Review the books you read for school or for pleasure. Which characters made a strong impression on you? Why? If you could chat with one of those characters, what would you say? How do you imagine the character would answer you? Why?

Including the No-Category Category

I call this section "no category" because "general" is too boring. Here are the questions that don't fit anywhere else

>> What books have you read recently? Which was best? Why?

>> What media do you consult regularly (television, Internet, radio, newspapers, magazines, books, anime, video games, and so forth)? What are the advantages and disadvantages of those media? How would you change the medium if you could?

>> What is the most creative element of modern life? (Think film, computers, art, whatever.) Why? How do you create?

>> Where have you traveled? What made a strong impression on you? Why?

>> What was the best summer of your life? Why?

>> Have you participated in any volunteer programs? What did you learn? What did others learn from you?

>> What does art mean to you? How about beauty? Wisdom? The price of tomatoes? (Sorry. Big philosophical terms make me yearn for the concrete details of life.)

>> Describe your ideal roommate. Why have you chosen these characteristics? (Or you can take a stab at one of Stanford's prompts: "Write a letter to your future roommate.")

2

Organizing Your Thoughts

Understand the writing technique most appropriate to your strengths and personality.

Gather the details and stories you'll use in your college application essays.

Move through several brainstorming exercises to help get you actively moving on your essays.

Figure out your personal statement topic based on the details and ideas you have gathered.

Establish the helper(s) who will oversee your writing process (while setting boundaries with parents and other well-meaning advice-givers!).

IN THIS CHAPTER

» Focusing on the process

» Keeping your inner creator and editor separate

» Gathering ideas: Pre-writing

» Putting your words on paper — the drafting stage

» Finalizing your essay

Chapter **4**

Writing as Process, Not Product

You sit down, type as rapidly as you can, and then stand up. Does this sound like your writing process? If so, you're focused on the product — the finished paper or essay. Bad idea. Naturally, you can't ignore the product completely when you write. After all, that's why you're writing! You want to end up holding a piece of paper with words on it, preferably words that actually make sense and, as a bonus, sound good. But if your mentality is to simply to get your college essay writing done as quickly as possible, focusing only on the product, you're setting yourself up for frustration. In other words, you can plan and then write, or write without a plan and then sift through your raw material (I explain these approaches in the section, "Structuring and outlining versus discovery writing," later in this chapter). What you *can't* do, however, is bypass the writing process altogether and expect to produce a submittable draft on your first attempt. You aren't pulling a rabbit out of a hat!

I see this emphasis on product whenever I assign a timed, in-class essay. Before the essay begins, I explain the ideal schedule to the students, given a total writing period of 40 minutes: 5 minutes of idea gathering and outlining, 30 minutes of writing, and 5 minutes of revision. Yet when I hand out the question (which hasn't been announced in advance), half of the students open their bluebooks and immediately start stringing words together. They're still at it 40 minutes later when I rip the booklets off their desks, mid-word. These students are sure that writing furiously (both in speed and in mood) for the entire time gives them a better result than writing for 30 minutes, with before and after steps.

Unfortunately, they're wrong. Here's what happens when you see the essay as a 100-meter dash: You start out with the first idea that pops into your head. If you get a better idea later, too bad. You're committed to one direction and can't change course mid-essay. As you work, you omit some terrific points because you're too busy writing to think much about the content. You're concentrating on mechanics (the English teachers' term for grammar and spelling, not automobile specialists), so you can't spare any brain cells for creative flourishes. Nor can you expend any energy creating a logical structure for the essay. Result: a weak, disorganized, spotty product, probably filled with mechanical errors you would have caught had you gone back for a second reading.

Granted, you have more than 40 minutes to write a college essay, and you will (please, please) recheck your work. But if you write your essay in a product-oriented way, you're cheating yourself. You're leaving your best writing buried inside.

As you tackle the personal statement essay, you may think that every light you glimpse at the end of the tunnel is the headlight of a train, rushing to mow you down. Take heart! This chapter provides a set of powerful fluorescent lights, illuminating an efficient and painless route through the writing *process* — the way in which you should prepare to write, draft, and finally revise your work. The best part about process-oriented writing is that it's incredibly easy. No matter who taught you to write — an old-time, memorize-every-rule-in-the-book English teacher or a groove-with-the-universe and throw-structure-to-the-wind type — you can improve your technique by taking the task of writing your admission essay one step at a time.

Separating Your Inner Creator and Editor

The writing process divides into three parts:

>> **Pre-writing:** The stage during which you gather your thoughts, consider focus and theme, choose a structure, and outline the essay. Chapters 2 and 3 provide some exercises to help you start.

>> **Drafting:** The first couple of rounds of slinging words onto the page until you have one complete version of the essay.

>> **Revising:** The stage during which you function as a stern critic, reading over the essay, clarifying and polishing until it's perfect.

About half of the process — from pre-writing through the first rough draft, minus the structuring and outlining stage — depends upon free-flowing creativity. The other half — from the second draft through the final product — depends more upon a critical eye. (Structuring and outlining also fall into the critic's corner.) To come up with the best possible essay, you've got to keep both halves of the writing process completely separate.

Here's what I mean: Two little workers inhabit your brain, a left-brain editor and a right-brain creator. No kidding, sort of. Scientists who have studied brain function have determined that most of the creative impulses come from the right side of the brain. The left brain is in charge of critical, logical, and analytical thinking. So the right brain gives you great ideas, and the left brain puts those ideas in order and inserts commas and capital letters. Both your inner editor and creator are useful — even essential — to your essay.

The problem is that they fight. Like co-workers who can't share an office without shooting paper clips at each other, the editor and the creator battle for dominance. Your goal is to make sure that neither side wins. What you do is employ them in shifts. Send the editor out for coffee while the creator produces ideas (the pre-writing stage of gathering thoughts and mulling over focus and theme). After you have a lot of ideas, invite the editor back to weigh in about structure. While the editor is busy, give the creator a rest. After a quick coffee break, blindfold the editor and let the creator crank out a draft. Then sit on the creator while the editor revises the essay.

WARNING

I hope I didn't lose you in this analogy. In plain English, what I most commonly see is a student's self-editing take over the writing process, stunting or slowing the results. Why? Because the student wants the essay to come out *perfectly* in a first draft. If you're prone to this issue, you may write a sentence or two, and then want to go back and immediately tinker with what you've written until it reflects your best possible sentence construction. Or you may get repeatedly stuck on words and want to mess around with your best friend, Thesaurus.

If you've just facepalmed yourself and are muttering, "That's definitely me," you have to find a way to send that inner editor out for lunch (or stop them in their tracks). Though telling yourself that you're going to write without an active filter may feel a bit strange at first, by doing so, you'll find that you can say what you want to say and not censor your most interesting thoughts. Your creator needs freedom; your editor will have plenty of opportunities in later stages. (If you tend toward perfectionism and can identify with this example, check out Chapter 5 for more important information on freewriting. Chapter 8 offers you tips on how to choose an essay structure as you progress from a freewrite into a more formal draft.)

Still wondering which half of your head is stronger — the creative right side or the logical left side? Try this completely unscientific but fun test:

1. I read the last page of a mystery novel first so I can find out the name of the murderer.

2. I *loved* proving theorems in geometry class.

3. I *hated* art class when the teacher told us to play around with the paint and just "let it happen."

4. I always link one idea to another with words such as "consequently," "after," "therefore," and "on the other hand."

5. I hate it when people hop around in conversation with no understandable order.

Do you have more "yes" answers? You like order and logic, so your left brain is probably the one that tends to take over. More "no" answers? Your creator probably calls the shots. Regardless of the results of this test, remember that you need *both* sides of your brain to write a good essay — not that you can't rely on a trusted outside voice for editor help, especially if you're an impressionist creator for whom revision and structure really don't come naturally (more on that in Chapter 6). Just be aware that one part of the process will probably be easier for you than the other. Don't give in when you hit the difficult bit!

Pre-Writing: The First Steps

Before you put a single finger on a single key (or a single word on the page) of the actual college admission essay, you should be exercising your brain cells. The following sections cover the pre-writing steps.

Idea gathering

While you're idea gathering, you write down any and every possible essay topic without worrying about what your final focus will be. Helpful methods for idea gathering include

>> Journal-keeping (jotting down ideas and observations)

>> Chatting with friends and relatives about possible topics

>> Exploring your memories (Chapters 2 and 3 explain how to do so)

>> Visual brainstorming, listing, and freewriting — three idea-gathering techniques I explain in Chapter 5

After you have a good number of ideas — at least five or six possible topics — you're ready to move to the next stage.

Narrowing down to a specific moment

You're on the hunt for *the* topic (or overlapping topics) for your personal statement, your premiere college essay that you'll want read by every school you apply to. You thumb through your idea list, separating topics into "possibles" and "What *was* I thinking?" Soon one topic emerges as having the most potential or appeal to you. If that topic is a theme or a broad idea more so than a specific memory, at this time you may want to try to come up with a singular moment that you can use as a jumping off point to talk about your topic. As I discuss in Chapter 10, a common way of approaching the personal statement is to begin with an opening anecdote or a moment you can illustrate in great detail. Then you can shed light on that moment in broader context.

Table 4-1 lists some examples of real students' broad topics and the *specific* moments they came up with to use as a launching point for their essays.

TABLE 4-1   **Broad Topics and Specific Moments**

Broad Topic	Specific Moment Used in Essay (As a Gateway to Reflect on the Topic)
Art as an outlet and creative passion	Working with a blowpipe in the glassblowing studio
Working to overcome social anxiety	Accepting the Tri-Athlete Award in front of student body
Dance as a means for developing self-awareness and self-discipline	Taking in the moment of silence before dancing first-ever solo
Values developed from immigrant parents	Organizing a food pantry during the first week of COVID-19 lockdown
A lifelong curiosity about math and science	Completing a Rubik's cube for the first time at age seven

The next few sections help you (as I tell my students) to write the heck out of the moment you choose. After you have the makings of an interesting story, you can begin to anticipate the next steps of your essay: what that story says about you, your character, and your growth. Is that moment symbolic of a trait you're trying to show? Does it represent a challenge you've overcome? Is it a defining moment that shaped your perspective or beliefs? If you can answer "yes" to any of these questions, you know you're on the right track.

Detail gathering

As in the first gathering stage ("Idea gathering," described earlier in this chapter), in the detail-gathering stage you list everything you can think of that relates to your chosen topic. Once again, don't worry about whether or not you'll use the details in your final product. Just write them down. If you're writing about a memory, take care to include *sensory details* — the sights, sounds, smells, tastes (if appropriate), and tactile or touch sensations associated with the memory. Depending upon your topic, you may not use all or any of these sensory details in the finished essay, but recalling them helps to make the memory more vivid.

Here are some strong examples of lines from college essays including sensory details (your detail-gathering notes don't have to be this precise):

> The shuffle of leather shoes echoes throughout the stage. (Sound)
>
> I watched, indifferent, as six inches of glossy hair fell to the tile floor. (Sight)
>
> The lemonade dripped down my chin and into a sticky, sugary mess. (Touch)
>
> I scavenge the coveted catalog from the pile of junk mail and immediately inhale its inky scent. (Smell)
>
> I lance, squeeze, and watch as blood oozes from the end of my dirty, calloused finger. (Sight — and no need to worry about the blood! This memory was from a diabetic student testing his blood sugar levels.)
>
> Walking through the door of the apartment, I'm greeted by the rattling of our ancient gas oven and the sizzling of Dad's Hungarian meatballs. (Sound)

In addition to practicing sensory details, you may also consider what will constitute the reflective part of your essay: what you believe this story will show about who you are as a person or how you've grown or changed.

Structuring and outlining versus discovery writing

Some students may need to create a structure and outline with a list of bullet points before they're comfortable trying to articulate a complete sentence. If you're one of those people, outline away. Map out your moment or your key details and insights about your topic and come up with a handful of bullet points about what you want to say with your essay.

REMEMBER

I confess, though, that I'm not much of a believer that you need to outline your personal statement before you begin to write. That's because you may not know what you're trying to say until you see it on the page and begin to understand and (finally) organize what you've written into something logical and compelling. In other words, you may need to do a bunch of freewriting and then go back and outline after you figure out what it is you're trying to say about yourself.

REMEMBER

If listing, planning, and outlining don't feel like vital steps to you before you draft, you may prefer to think of yourself as a Discovery Writer. Discovery Writers like to plunge in. They know they have the seed of a good story, but they don't have any idea where they'll end up. That's more than okay — there's room for discovery. If you identify with being a Discovery Writer, freewriting may be your greatest ally. I discuss freewriting in greater detail in Chapter 5.

Whether you're a Planner or a Discovery Writer, what you're looking for is a way to gather the must-haves for a strong essay: details (sensory details and other specifics) and development (how the experiences and relationships in your essay have impacted you as a person).

REMEMBER

Don't completely erase any drafts. You never know when you might need them. You might delete a sentence from the first draft that seems perfect for a later version of the essay. But if you've shredded the earlier draft, set fire to it, or poured leftover spaghetti sauce all over it, you're out of luck. That perfect sentence is gone forever.

After you have a complete rough draft, you may want to show it to a college counselor, a helpful teacher, or a friend. They can tell you whether you're on the right track or not. (Chapter 6 explains in detail what sort of help is appropriate and what is out of bounds.) Bring the rough drafts with you. Your helpers may see value in something you discarded.

Taking the Final Steps

When you've got a good rough draft, the hardest stage of the battle is over. In my experience, editing your essay and working to make it better can be the fun part — and certainly doesn't compare to wrestling with the blank page. Keep the following sections in mind as you begin to narrow down the framework for your personal statement essay.

Revising

"To revise" is literally to "re-see" your work. Revision is actually a tough skill to master. If you're like most people, you tend to fall in love with your own words fairly quickly. It's hard to dump a really great phrase or idea just because it doesn't mesh with the final version of your essay (author William Faulkner called this "killing your darlings"). Or, you might get to a place where you've read your essay so often that you truly can't see it anymore. Your eye skips over missing letters or awkward phrases because you're on automatic pilot. So before you revise, take a break. Eat a snack, walk around the block, or study for the next chemistry test. Later, return to the essay with fresh eyes. Bring everything you know about voice and style to the front of your mind. As you ruthlessly read your essay again, sandpaper the rough, clarify the vague, and correct the missteps.

Chapter 14 offers plenty of strategies for making sure that *every* sentence of your essay is both well-constructed and serves a clear purpose.

Completing one essay makes the rest easier

If you're applying to colleges that require supplemental essays (refer to Part 5 for more about them) in addition to your personal statement, you may feel concerned that you're spending so much time on one essay — after all, you have 10 to 15 ignored prompts left to go. Do you have to expend the same amount of creative energy on each one?

REMEMBER

Don't worry. The first essay — your personal statement — is the hardest to write, both because most students lack experience in writing about themselves and because it is *the* essay you're submitting to every school that requires a personal essay. (Remember that some public universities, such as the California State University system, don't require any writing in order to apply.)

You may wonder why your first essay is the hardest. Pretty often, something kind of magical often happens after you have that personal statement essay about yourself of which you're proud. You may look at your supplemental essay prompts and think, "These questions are *so* much easier than trying to articulate the most important aspects of myself in 650 words" or even, "Gosh, I didn't get a chance to talk much about XYZ anywhere in my application . . ." and find that some of your supplemental essay prompts sound like a cakewalk. In fact, trying a different topic or figuring out what else it is you want colleges to understand about you may seem sort of fun. In other words, don't expect your supplements to drain or challenge you in the same way that your personal statement may have (though of course you'll want to give each one its due time). That's not just because they're usually shorter. It's because you're a seasoned veteran!

Sighing with relief

Just kidding. (Sort of.) After you're satisfied with your personal statement, set it aside while you work on the other components of your application, including your supplemental essays. Check out the chapters in Part 3 for some techniques you can use to ensure the emergence of your best possible writing.

Chapter **5**

Storming Your Brain: Idea-Gathering Techniques

You've collected a mountain of memories (No? Chapters 2 and 3 can help), but you can't seem to turn any of them into an essay. Every time you sit down to write, your thoughts logjam. Sound familiar? A lot of writers find themselves facing this dilemma, especially when they're in a high-stakes situation such as college admissions.

In this chapter I provide three great techniques to unclog the jam. I explain how to select the technique that fits your personality and guide you as you narrow your focus, moving from random memories to topic and theme and then to details that make your essay come alive.

Making a Mess — You Can't Build a Castle Until You Dump the Blocks

Say you're five years old, sitting next to a container of blocks that is almost as tall as you are. You decide to make a castle. You reach into the container and take out the first block. Perfect! Just what you need to start. Then you reach in and grab the ideal second block. The third block you touch is the one you intended all along to place on top of the other two. In fact, every block you take out is *exactly the one you need*. Each fits into the right spot in the castle, and you never have to move a block after it's already in place.

Are things ever that easy? No way! Even when you were five, you knew you couldn't build a castle or anything else that way. You made a mess, or you dealt with the frustration of multiple fruitless attempts — most likely not only while you were building castles, but also when you were painting in your art class, when you were practicing a defensive move for a game (if you were on a sports team), and when you were brave enough to attempt that 1,000 piece jigsaw puzzle. You had to dump every single multicolored piece before you even made your first move.

So what makes you think you can *write* without making a little bit of a mess first?

Here's how you really built a castle when you were five years old: first, you made a big mess. But pretty soon, you grabbed a snazzy red block, that little purple guy over in the corner, and maybe the green one that skittered under the couch. You moved them around a bit, experimenting, and pretty soon you had a little tower. Only then did you say, "Hey! This is a castle!" and knew you were on your way. Every once in a while you swept the whole thing away and started again. Eventually you ended up with a castle Lancelot would be proud of. (And then the dog or your brother knocked it over, but that's another story.)

You have to write your essay the same way you build a castle. Here are the simplified steps you can take:

1. **Dump the blocks; in other words, throw all the possibilities for your essay onto the paper.**

   Instead of saying, "My essay is about my camping trip and my first sentence is . . . followed by my second sentence . . . and so on through the 34th and last sentence," write down every idea on the paper (or type everything on the screen).

2. Sift through your blocks — the ideas.

You find a red block (memory of the time your mom took you to see the whale at the aquarium) and a green one (the 10th grade kick-off party for a beach clean-up project) and maybe a yellow one (getting your license as a swim instructor).

3. Sort through details, move a few things around, and occasionally sweep the whole thing away.

Finally you end up with a concept you can use. The idea sprouts details, themes, and images. You're on your way. Chapter 8 tells you more about possible essay structures, and in Chapter 10 you can read more about how to determine your essay's opening moment.

Matching Personality and Technique

Three strategies — visual brainstorming, listing, and braindumping — help you gather ideas for your college admissions essay. Each technique works best with a particular personality type, so before you try one, take a moment to consider which category you lean toward most:

>> **The artist:** Do you love visual arts — films, paintings, drawings? Do you understand everything better when you draw a little diagram, with lots of arrows connecting ideas? Are your school notebooks filled with doodles? When you think, do pictures fill your head? Do you see things that your friends miss?

>> **The logician:** Do you love order, method, reason? Are your favorite classes the ones where you can find concrete answers? Are you the last person you know to carry a traditional planner just so you can have multiple copies of your to-do lists?

>> **The free spirit:** Do you love to daydream, to float around in a fantasy world? When you chat with your friends, do you hop from topic to topic seemingly at random? When you studied poetry, did you love digging into levels of meaning, decoding similes and metaphors? Does your school notebook contain stories or bits of writing that have nothing to do with the subject?

If you're an artist, visual thinking is one of your strong points. Try the technique I call "Visual brainstorming." Logical types usually have success with "Listing." Free spirits typically embrace the open-ended nature of "braindumping": get all of your thoughts down now; organize them later! The following section shows you how to utilize each technique — though you're welcome to try all of them.

TIP

Human beings are complicated creatures, so some of the categories overlap. No problem. Try a couple of techniques until you discover which one is right for you.

Gathering Ideas: The Techniques

In this section I take you through the big three — proven techniques for "dumping the blocks" and gathering the ideas that are rattling around in your head. (See the previous section for more information.) Each technique meshes best with a particular personality type. But don't feel that you have to limit yourself to one technique only. If you're in the mood, try all three!

Visual brainstorming

Variations of visual brainstorming have been around for years, each with a different name. Visual brainstorming never goes out of style because it's such an effective way to tap into your creative brain cells. In visual brainstorming, you create a picture of your thought process. You also trick the critical portion of your mind (also known as the *inner editor* — refer to Chapter 4 for more details) into taking a coffee break so that your creativity can take center stage. Finally, visual brainstorming forces you to step away from your usual habits of writing so that truly new ideas may emerge. These sections examine in plain English how to brainstorm.

Brainstorming as easy as 1, 2, 3, 4

You can use visual brainstorming to select a topic for your essay or to amass detail after you've settled on a topic. It's also a great way to discover the theme of your essay (see Chapter 2 for more information on theme) and to uncover the metaphors (creative comparisons) that light up your writing.

For this technique you need old-fashioned pen and paper. (Don't worry; I'm sure you can find these somewhere in your house.) Give your computer a rest, get ready to have some fun, and do the following:

1. **Take a clean sheet of paper, preferably one without lines.**

   If the paper does have lines, ignore them. Don't hold the paper the usual way. Turn it on a diagonal or upside down — something to make it look different. You want to break down the habitual categories in your brain.

If you usually write with a pen, use a pencil. If pencil is your medium of choice, try a pen. Again, the point is to do something to change your pattern.

2. Write a word or phrase in the middle of the paper.

Which word? Any will do, but a promising idea from the "Personal Inventory" in the Appendix or from the self-discovery exercises in Chapter 2 is a good choice. If you can't find any good candidates, write your name or an abstract word like "loyalty," "friendship," or "challenge."

Don't obsess over which word to write in the middle of the page. I'm not a psychologist, but I do believe that a part of your mind is active while you're not consciously aware. Whatever you write down has some significance, even if you can't figure out exactly why you chose that particular word.

3. For about ten minutes, look at the word or phrase in the middle of the page and write down everything that comes to mind.

Don't try to control the direction of your thoughts. Just jot down the ideas. Some ideas will flow as a group. Write them near each other on the paper.

Sometimes you'll sense that you're starting a new set of ideas. Put these thoughts in a new area of the paper. A picture may emerge as you write. Fine. Don't spend forever drawing in the details, but go ahead and sketch whatever you like.

4. When the flow dries up, stop.

Look at what you've written. Circle the ideas that go together or connect them with lines.

Check out the visual brainstorm example in Figure 5-1. The key word is "change." "High school to college" led to "leaving home," which led to "going to camp." Then the idea of camp shifted to "afraid of water," "swimming lessons," "first race," and "medal." Now a new idea surfaced: "living away from home," then "year in Madrid," which drifted to "new language" and "dinner at 10 p.m." Somewhere during this process "snake" slithered in, with "shed skin" and "open to injury" and "danger" following.

Don't edit while you're brainstorming. Whatever you're thinking, don't allow yourself to say, "That's ridiculous. I'll never use it." Just write it. You're not committing to a 30-year mortgage. You're just jotting down ideas! (See Chapter 4 for a complete explanation of why editing and brainstorming don't mix.)

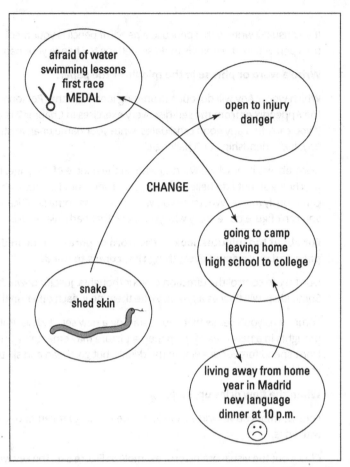

FIGURE 5-1:
An example
of visual
brain-storming.

Doing a second round of brainstorming

After you complete one round of visual brainstorming, take out a second sheet of paper and do the following:

1. Change writing implements if you like.

A different color for each stage of brainstorming can help you see the progression of your ideas.

2. Examine your first visual brainstorm.

TIP

Are you at all intrigued? Do you see any possible topics? If not, put a different word in the center of the new sheet of paper and try again. Repeat as often as necessary until something appeals to you.

3. **When one part of a brainstorm has possibilities, explore it further.**

   Put a word or phrase from the possible topic in the center of a new sheet of paper. For ten more minutes, jot down the ideas that come to you as you think of the centered word or phrase. Again, place thoughts that seem to belong together in a bunch. Whenever your mind skips to a new track, put those thoughts in a different section of the paper.

4. **When you're done, draw lines between ideas that connect to each other and/or circle related thoughts.**

In Figure 5-1, the visual brainstorm centered on the word "change." Two possible topics emerge. One has to do with "How I Overcame My Fear of Water and Became an Olympic Medalist" (or something like that) and the second concerns "My Adjustment to Madrid." For the second round of visual brainstorming, you can choose either one of these topics and place either "swimming" or "Spain" in the middle of the page.

Figure 5-2 displays a visual brainstorm centered on "swimming." Notice that the details all relate to competitive swimming. The brainstorm includes some of the hardships ("frizzies," "permanent head cold," "5 a.m. practices," and "green hair"). Some of the advantages came to mind also ("independence," "team spirit," and "body image"). With this visual brainstorm, the writer is in good shape to write about the joys and sorrows of going for an Olympic medal in the backstroke.

TIP

When I mention the writer has *two* possible topics, that doesn't mean she can't mention both swimming and Spain in the same essay, especially because they share an overlapping theme: change. However, one of these stories will probably become the *focal point,* or topic that the student is focusing on. She may mention the other topic more in passing as evidence of the same theme. Maybe she never would have had the guts to sign up for the exchange program in Madrid if she hadn't first challenged herself as a swimmer, which was her first major leap into discomfort, but that leap was transformative enough to lead to others.

Trying another brainstorm for more ideas

If the writer needs more material, it's time for another visual brainstorm. In Figure 5-3, for example, she brainstormed around "team spirit." She wanted to include a paragraph in her essay about the joy of working with 20 other permanently wet people, but she couldn't figure out how to say so. After brainstorming, she uncovered several relevant memories, including "homework on bus with teammates," "help Marjorie when injured," and "set coach's shoe on fire" — a cooperative and extremely unwise activity the team indulged in after the last meet of the season. Now she has enough ideas for a fine essay showing what she learned about cooperation and team spirit from her experience on the swim team.

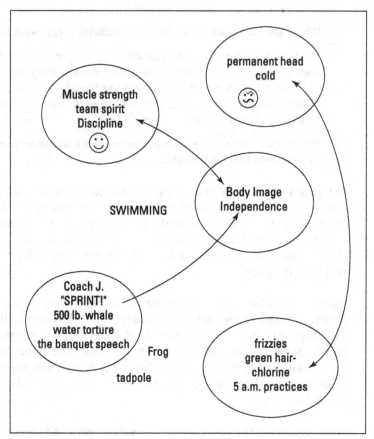

FIGURE 5-2:
An example of
second-round
visual
brainstorming.

TIP

Sometimes a really strange idea will keep popping into your mind while you're in the midst of visual brainstorming. You may be brainstorming about your first day of band practice, noting things like "clarinet," "out of tune," and "saliva." But the word butterfly floats again and again into your consciousness. *Write it down.* Later, look at all the weird items in your brainstorm. Ask yourself if any of them are metaphors (poetic comparisons) for the meaning of your experience. Maybe your first band practice, when no two notes in a row were correct, was your musical self as a caterpillar. About 5,000 band practices later, when you and your fellow musicians sounded great (okay, at least tolerable), your musical self was a butterfly. Now you've got a working metaphor for your essay.

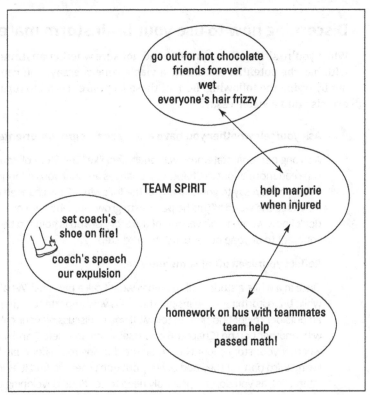

go out for hot chocolate
friends forever
wet
everyone's hair frizzy

TEAM SPIRIT

help marjorie
when injured

set coach's
shoe on fire!

coach's speech
our expulsion

homework on bus with teammates
team help
passed math!

© John Wiley & Sons, Inc.

FIGURE 5-3:
An example of
third-round visual
brainstorming.

In the brainstorming stage, you still haven't determined whether or not the metaphor will be spoken or unspoken in your essay. For example, a line like, "Like a caterpillar transforming into a butterfly, I have come into my own as a violinist" can be a bit much on the cheesiness scale or verge into cliché territory, depending on how you build up to it and your writing style, but at the very least the metaphor can be something you keep in mind as you write. It can give you a sense of what you want your reader to infer.

In Figure 5-1 earlier in this chapter, the "snake shedding its skin" may have slithered in as a metaphor for the feeling of change. You've got a shiny new self, even though the process of getting it hurt as much as peeling off your epidermis.

After a couple of rounds of visual brainstorming, you should have a pretty good idea what you want to write about (the topic). You should have some details you want to include. You may also have an idea for a theme (see Chapter 2 for more on themes) and perhaps a metaphor or two. You're ready to write.

If you need more details or an idea for a theme or if you have your heart set on finding the perfect metaphor, simply center a word and brainstorm again. Keep centering and brainstorming until you have everything you need.

Discerning how to use your brainstorm material

When you're sifting through ideas and not sure whether anything you've come up with has the potential to become a viable college essay, you can usually figure it out by trying the following. Both of these steps are crucial to turning a brainstorm exercise into a viable essay.

1. **Ask yourself whether you have a story that is growth-oriented.**

A strong personal statement will ideally feel like "The Story of You" (which you can read more about in Chapter 2). Chances are that you've found the Story of You if you can say to yourself any of the following: "This changed me." "This is how I see the world." "This helped me to grow into who I am now." But if you don't know whether *this* version of the Story of You is going to be interesting or coherent to anyone but you, try the next step.

2. **Reflect your idea off of someone else.**

Once in a while a student of mine has what I call a personal "A-ha!" moment while brainstorming — an insight that feels very important to them but one that an outsider might find hard to follow. If you're discussing your college writing with another person (Chapter 6 discusses in greater detail) and aren't sure whether your story should be left on the drawing room floor, pitch it to your loving third party. If they nod politely but don't seem to find it as important or interesting as you do, you probably need to continue developing your ideas.

In Chapters 8 and 9, I discuss more about how you can turn your raw material — your brainstorms — into a formal draft and how to ensure that you relay the details of your stories and ideas by showing, not telling.

Listing

I love lists. I makes tons of to-do lists, just so I can have the joy of crossing off (scratching into oblivion, actually) the chores I've completed. I also make lists when I'm getting ready to write. The order and logic of a list appeals to me. (But I don't get carried away; I haven't alphabetized the contents of my freezer for years.) The following sections give you the lowdown on how to use listing.

Making a list with no censoring

You can list alone, but listing is even more fun with a friend. Here's the method:

1. **Pick a word at random, perhaps something from self-reflective questions in Chapter 3 or a memory that you uncovered after reading Chapter 2.**

    If you can't decide on a word, try "family," "project," or "challenge." (I've had a lot of luck with those.)

2. **Take a sheet of paper or open a new file on the computer.**

3. **List titles for ten stories you could tell about yourself in relation to the word at the top of your list.**

    For example, if you chose "family" as the keyword, you should have ten titles for stories you can tell about you and your family (or even the concept of family).

    In Figure 5-4, the writer lists ten possible titles flowing from the keyword "challenge," including "physics labs," "waiting last Wednesday for phone call," "learning to parasail," "writing with a broken arm," and so forth.

CHALLENGE

Physics labs
Waiting past Wednesday for lover to call
Learning to parasail
Writing with a broken arm
Washing hair in desert
Avoiding dessert when on a diet
Getting the little tab into the slot when assembling furniture
Writing an essay
Speaking out about the new grading policy
Throwing out old shoes

© John Wiley & Sons, Inc.

FIGURE 5-4: An example of listing technique.

4. **If you absolutely positively can't come up with ten titles, stop.**

    Don't let yourself off the hook if you have fewer than five. Try again with a different keyword. Chances are one of the stories will grab hold of your imagination. Bingo! You're ready for the second set of lists.

5. **Write the title of the chosen story at the top of a new sheet of paper or type the title on a blank computer screen (a new file, or just scroll down until you've got a clean slate).**

6. **List details about the story.**

   Write everything you remember, one item after another, until you can't think of anything else. Concentrate on sense memories: what you saw, what you heard, what you smelled, what you felt (sensations from your sense of touch, as well as emotions), and, if appropriate, what you tasted. Check out Figure 5-5. The writer decided to list details about "physics labs" from the first list.

7. **If you remember any conversation, write the words.**

PHYSICS LABS

Working every lunch hour for the entire winter
Sneaking out of study hall when the lab was closed
Picking the lock on the equipment cabinet
Rival group working in the corner of the room
Band practice outside
Very noisy
Broken tuba – sounded terrible
Band leader: "And a one and a two and a three…" all day long
Dusty smell of old chalk
Dirty floor – ruined two pairs of pants
Mr. O'Conner really proud of our results
Lab report was 20 pages long for some experiments
The balance we made to weigh a feather
The momentum experiment
At least 10 kids didn't finish, but we did
Demonstrating the momentum experiment to the other class
Submitting our experiments to the science fair
Lots of blocks, like kindergarten, and some motors
None of the motors worked
Shocks from the batteries
The water trough

FIGURE 5-5: Creating list of details.

© John Wiley & Sons, Inc.

REMEMBER

Don't censor yourself. As you write the list, don't stop to worry about whether a detail is worth including or not. Just list it. Later you can always decide to leave the detail out of the essay.

How long should your detail list be? The longer the better. If you have 20 to 30 details, you're more than fine.

Working with a partner or alone

If you're working with a partner, retell your chosen stories to each other, using as many details as possible. After hearing each story, ask questions: "What did your mother say when you signed up for the bowling team?" "What color was the horse you fell off?" "Did you hear any noise when the president pinned the medal on your shirt?" The more you ask, the more detail you get, and the more you have to work with.

TIP

If you're working alone, consider enlisting a relative or friend to play the role of detective, quizzing you about your story until you truly can't remember anything else.

If any part of the story is still unclear, write the new keyword at the top of a new page or insert a page break in your computer file and make another list. In Figure 5-5, the writer listed details about the chosen story, "physics labs." But when he tried to write about the physics labs, he got stuck on "momentum experiment." He couldn't figure out what to say.

Check out Figure 5-6, which is the list he made about the momentum experiment. After that list was done, he had a lot more to work with!

MOMENTUM EXPERIMENT

A little car, like a child's toy
Green car
No motor, headed down an incline
Need to stop car at the bottom
Glued a plastic ruler in place – my little red ruler that I had used in geometry
Timing crucial to speed
Used my watch – digital
Then we bought stop watch
Sent the car down the incline
Timer went off
A huge crash when the ruler broke
Nothing stopping the car
Right through the window
Glass everywhere
We got into such trouble
The glass cost $40 and we had to replace it
The other lab group used a pillow to stop their car
Why didn't we think of that

FIGURE 5-6:
Creating a new list of details.

By the time you finish listing, you should have a topic, all the details your little heart desires, and perhaps even a metaphor or two to guide you as you write.

Braindumping

Braindumping is the pen-and-paper or computer screen version of downloading your thoughts. For a set period of time, you write everything that pops into your mind, hoping that something in the stream of ideas will turn out to be an idea you can use or raw material that you can organize later. I discuss how you can "dump" the contents of your brain in the following sections.

Reaching deep into your mind

Braindumping, like visual brainstorming (refer to the section, "Visual brainstorming," earlier in this chapter), reaches deep into your mind by tricking the conscious, critical portion of your brain into nodding off for a few minutes. Trying a braindump exercise also relies on strong finger muscles; guaranteed, especially if you're using the pen-and-paper strategy, your knuckles will cramp halfway through. Follow these steps in detail:

1. **Remove yourself to a quiet place where you can trust you won't be interrupted.**

   In other words, put your phone in a drawer with the volume off and tell your family not to interrupt you for 30 minutes. If you wish, put some music on — not music you usually listen to, but something different. Or, work in silence.

2. **Open a new file, or take a pen or pencil and turn to a clean notebook page.**

   Be sure that you're comfortable physically.

3. **Concentrate for a few seconds on a memory or idea that you've been considering as a possible essay topic.**

   If you've got no ideas at all, turn to Chapters 2 and 3. If nothing surfaces, no problem. Just sit quietly for a few moments thinking about nothing in particular.

4. **Begin to type or write every thought that comes into your mind.**

   Don't stop until you have documented every detail, insight or observation that occurs to you with regards to your memory or idea.

   TIP

   Two nanoseconds after starting to "dump" your thoughts onto the page, you'll realize that your mind hurtles along at supersonic speed while your fingers resemble a car in a traffic jam. You simply can't write as quickly as you can think. Don't worry! Just write everything you can.

As you braindump, don't attempt to make complete sentences, spell words correctly, or punctuate your work. If those things happen naturally, fine. If not, just keep writing.

During this process of downloading your thoughts, the mind hops from topic to topic with no clear links. That's good! Go with the flow, however illogical it appears at the time. The randomness is what makes this technique work. You'll sift through your material later.

5. **When you're confident that you've poured every possible thought about your idea onto the page, rub your fingers, take a short break, and then reread what you wrote.**

   Do you see why I told you to send everyone away? If you've done this exercise correctly, some of the thoughts you've written down or typed will be extremely private. (You can shred it later, at some point when you've extracted everything interesting — sometime between now and when you're packing up your room for college.)

   As you reread, underline anything that looks interesting. You're consciously looking for essay material, of course, but if you like something on the paper, underline it, even if you can't quite figure out how you might use it. Sometimes this magical thing will happen where you'll point your finger at a line halfway down the page and say, "What an opening line that would be!" Other times, you'll see something you think you might like to expand on but it'll need lots of fine-tuning in order to be useable.

Check out Figure 5-7, the result of one student's braindump exercise that starts with a vague idea about a library job. Notice that some of the material relates to the library job, but some doesn't, like the remark about the fire engine spurred by the sirens the writer heard. That remark, by the way, led the writer to a memory about a child in the library who wanted books about fire engines. Also notice that some words are spelled wrong and the grammar is far from perfect. After rereading this passage, the writer underlined some items, including how hard it was to work on Thursday nights with a chem test every Friday, learning how to do research, story hour, and Ferdinand the Bull. Any one of those could grow into an essay topic.

Braindumping, Round 2

After you underline a couple of items, it's time for round two in your braindumping exercise. Just follow these steps:

1. **Set yourself up as before, with a blank screen or page, and think about one of the items you underlined for a moment or two.**

2. **Write the underlined idea at the top of a new sheet of paper (or at the top of a new, blank screen) and begin writing again.**

started on my 16th birthday couldn't wait to have a real job worked after school for three hours and six on Thursday with a full day on Saturday. <u>Alway had a chem test on fri so the Thursday night gig was hard</u>, but still the money was nice - spending money for stuff I couldn't get before, but still saving for college what is that noise outside? a fire engine? and then the little kids in the children's room were so cute I liked that little red-headed kid who always wanted a book about fire engivnes I bet he thought I was so grown up. He should have seen me playing leapfrog in the aisle with Mary when the boss was on a break. And then there was the <u>advantage of learning how to do research</u> which I still use today and which I would not have known otherwise. I think I could have been flipping burgers for more money but I liked th library the people were mostly nice there was one guy who always took out the "dirty" books and then complained when he returned them that the library shouldn't have books like that but he always took out some more I guess he thought that he could have his cake and eat it too. I can't figure out what to write now I can't figure...okay now I'm thiking about story hour <u>when I read picture books "under the pink umbrella"</u> under the tree in the bakyard to all those little guys that was fun I also discovered all these great authors that I wouldn't know about otherwise and stories I loved like <u>Ferdinand the Bull what a great charcter</u> he is I think that Curious George is a good role model too, though I'm not sure about the man with the yellow hat what's that about?

FIGURE 5-7:
An example of a braindump.

© John Wiley & Sons Inc.

Every once in a while pull your mind toward the underlined idea you chose. Don't stop writing while you do so; in fact, don't stop for anything. All the same rules apply to this round: ignore punctuation, don't censor yourself, and exhaust every thought and idea with regards to your topic.

3. **As you reread the second round, again underline the sections that appeal to you.**

Do you have an essay topic yet? Repeat for as many rounds as necessary until you have settled upon the main idea of your essay.

Take a look at Figure 5-8, the second round of braindumping about the library job. This time the writer concentrated on working Thursday evenings with chemistry tests on Friday mornings. Notice the underlined material. Do you see an essay topic emerging? The job led the writer to become a more responsible student.

The technique of braindumping can be used over and over again until you're satisfied with the topic and the number of details gathered. Each round starts with a moment of concentration on the main idea.

Alway had a chem test on fri so the Thursday night gig was hard

why did we have a chem test every week? I guess he wanted a lot of grades, but boy did those tests take up a lot of time and boy were they boring. All I remember about chem is those tests and the occasional cloud of purple checmicals that my lab partner unleashed he was always adding a little more stuff to the experiment, tryiung to see what happened when he did so and usually we had to evacuate the chem lab when he was done. but working on Thursday nights was good - a good long time, not too busy, and a little overtime too it <u>made me organize the week very carefully</u> I had to start studying for chem on Monday nights and do a little at a time each day once I had the job I definitely got more organized and more focused . I didn't want my grades to go down, so I had to be careful to study when I had the time, not when I used to, at the last minute before the test. <u>So when I got the job I actually became a better student</u>. Imagine that. I guess I never realized that before. Mr. Bernstein, the chem teacher, we called him Bunsen Bernie, he told me that I was always well prepared I remember he quoted poetry all the time in class, and he always tripped over one spot on the floor near the door we could never figure out what he tripped over because the floor looked even to us there goes a garbage truck outside now there always seems to be a truck on the street when I'm freewriting the lab smelled bad - lots of things like rotten eggs. Do chemists become chemists because they like making a mess? Is there an appeal to stinkiness?

FIGURE 5-8:
A second round
of braindumping.

Here's one more example of braindumping about the library job. Read Figure 5-9, a portion of a braindump exercise done after the writer decided upon the main idea: becoming a more responsible person after taking the job. With each round of writing, more details emerge. As always with braindumping your thoughts, lots of the material is clearly useful, and some will probably be left out.

TIP

If you find yourself wandering into a totally new topic during any round, you have two choices: You can switch topics, or you can refocus. How do you refocus? Not by saying, "I am going to think about everything but elephants now (assuming that "elephant" is the topic you've been drifting into). If you tell yourself not to think about elephants, those big gray animals will sit in your mind and blot out everything else. You won't be able to think about anything but elephants! Instead, every time you realize that you are drifting away from the main idea, say to yourself, "I am thinking about the time I swam across the Atlantic" or whatever your preferred topic is. Pull yourself back into focus with a positive, not with a negative.

FIGURE 5-9: A third round of braindumping.

© John Wiley & Sons, Inc.

Reacting to a Specific Question

The techniques I discuss in the previous sections are also helpful if you're reacting to a more specific question. Don't give up on visual brainstorming, listing, or braindumping. You simply need to adapt the method of your choice to the question at hand. (See the section, "Matching Personality and Technique," earlier in this chapter for instructions on selecting a method.) Here's what to do:

>> **Visual brainstorming:** Extract the core word or phrase from the question and place the word or phrase at the center of the paper. As you brainstorm again and again, keep the question in mind. Be sure that the centered idea relates to the question you're attempting to answer.

>> **Listing:** Take the most important word or phrase from the question and place it at the top of your first list. Every time you start a new list, be sure that the word at the top of the list relates to the question.

>> **Braindumping:** Before each round of braindumping, take a moment to concentrate your mind on the question. Write a key word from the question at the top of the page or screen. As you record all of your thoughts, gently pull yourself back to the question whenever you realize that you're wandering.

Here's an example of how to adapt the three techniques to a specific question. Suppose you're asked to choose a photo and explain its significance. You unearth a photo of grandfather standing in the backyard of his house. At the center of the first visual brainstorm or at the top of your first list, write "Grandpa's yard." If you're braindumping, look at the photo for a minute before you begin to write. You may also place the photo on the desk or write "Grandpa's yard" at the top of the braindumping page.

Throwing in a Wrench — Figuring Out a Challenge

Often (and especially after a few of the idea-generating exercises that I discuss in this chapter) students come to me with a pretty clear idea of their dominant strength, character trait, or an important influence, and tell me that that's exactly what they want to write about. Here are some examples of that pitch:

"I want to write about theater! It's everything to me."

"I want to write about how I fell in love with photography."

"I want to write about my love for connecting with others. That trait drives me as a person."

"I want to write about how leadership comes naturally to me, like my role as team captain."

That's great! I say. There's definitely a lot there. Knowing what you love or what has shaped you makes for a wonderful start to an essay, but it's not enough.

REMEMBER

In English class, your teacher may have introduced you to the idea of the "So what?" factor. By the end of every essay, you need to make your argument poignant, take it deeper, and make it more universal. Whenever you write a claim, ask yourself, "So what?" to make sure that you have a point about why it all matters.

For example, Macbeth is plagued by doubt and guilt. So what? So, his behavior is an indication of how power can corrupt a person's character. Gatsby's whole life has been about his obsession with Daisy. So what? So, he is a representation of how nostalgia and idealization can be surprisingly powerful motivators. Holden Caulfield is defined by a mad case of Peter Pan syndrome. So what? So *Catcher in the Rye* is a novel about the pain of growing up, taken to the extreme.

You may be asking, "So what? I'm not writing an English essay." However, if an essay about a novel requires you to dig for layers of meaning, just think how much more a personal statement essay requires it.

TIP

If you fall into the category of wanting to write about a love, talent, or passion, embrace the strategy of trying to throw in a wrench — my way of instructing you to dig a little deeper — which often means adding some conflict. An essay about something you're naturally good at, with no conflict or problems, has the potential to be . . . well, *boring*. So say you're mad with love for photography, or soccer, or architecture, so much so that this interest has to be your essay topic. Don't forget to consider questions like the following:

>> What was your biggest challenge in this pursuit?

>> What stressors can you leave behind when you're engaged with your passion?

>> Who has been most supportive, and have you ever felt misunderstood in your pursuit?

Just keep digging, and know that figuring out a difficulty that you've had to wrestle with is a great way to add depth to your essay, so that its main premise goes beyond "Something I'm really good at."

Generating a Memorable (and Successful) Topic

You don't have to obsess about coming up with the world's most unique topic or angle for your college essay. After all, you've been searching through material from your own life, not anyone else's. The more you try to twist your real and honest stories into something you think is going to make you stand out more, the more your essay may begin to reek of inauthenticity. (Just ask someone close to you to read your draft, if you're concerned; if they don't immediately recognize the person in your essay, that should give you some food for thought as you revise or go back to the drawing board. Chapter 6 gives you pointers on how to identify someone to give you feedback.)

However, before you wallow too much, I'm here to make your decision of what to write about a tad easier. You have a vast, nearly limitless potential of essay topics. If you're still stumped after trying the exercises in the section, "Gathering Ideas: The Techniques," earlier in this chapter, you may want to consider some of my favorite essay topics that my students have come up with, according to theme:

>> **On adversity:**

- The cheating culture at a student's high school — and her decision to opt out (admitted to Stanford)

- Signing up to teach peers about sex — and failing (admitted to Brown)

- On semiannual flights between Beijing and San Francisco (admitted to the University of Michigan)

- Lying to a parent who used to be your best friend (University of Miami)

- Learning about mental health from a pathologically anxious dog (admitted to Kenyon)

>> **Personal quirks:**

- Sweaty palms as a running motif in a student's life (admitted to the University of Miami)

- Socks as a form of self-expression (admitted to Santa Clara University)

- Navigating life with severe food allergies (admitted to USC)

- Stickers and Pinterest — and how they can stave off depression (admitted to St. Andrews)

>> **More traditional topics and interests:**

- A fishing trip to Alaska with Dad (admitted to the University of Michigan)

- On how a student knew she wanted to be a nurse (admitted to UC San Diego)

- Cultivating sensitivity by growing up with a sibling with special needs (admitted to Loyola Marymount University)

- Overcoming debilitating shyness to become senior year class president (admitted to Clemson)

The trick is to start early so you can infuse your pieces with the dialogue, description, and detail to make them riveting. Part 3 can help you flesh out these important elements.

Because you can easily get caught up in the do's and don'ts, remember that every rule has an exception to that rule. For example, a student of mine was recently accepted to NYU's Stern School of Business by writing about his father's bout with cancer and how that experience helped him get over his anger at his father for divorcing his mother — a combination of two of the biggest no-no's! (Those no-no's are death and divorce. While I'm at it, breakups are also typically a no. I discuss other essay traits to avoid in greater detail in Chapter 7.) So write your truth, and the right school for you will hear your voice — if you use your time wisely and follow the guidance in this book.

Accepting Your Permission Slip for a Messy First Draft

If you imagine that writers are people who sit at their desks with a hot cup of tea and then do some triumphant typing, with perfect clarity as to what they want to say, you're dreaming. So what does writing look like? Even for the very best of writers (you can picture your favorite, most seasoned author or screenwriter), it includes puttering around the house, maddening moments in front of a computer screen, scrapping pages, and pulling out plenty of hairs. I hope you understand that you'll need to put in the time to write the type of admission essay you want to get you into the college of your choice. In other words, the type of essay you want to wow admissions counselors isn't something you jam out in a single day. Or a week.

Your essay needs time to marinate, in a manner different from any other writing you have done. You're going to have to revise it and revise it again — you'll scrap lines you loved when you first crafted them and lines you never liked. In the writing world, this process is called *killing your darlings.* Part 4 examines revising your essay and preparing it for submission.

When you start your college application writing, you have to give yourself permission to write imperfect drafts. College admission essays require a willingness to write messily, at least at first, about things that might be uncomfortable or that you've never put into words. That first draft will probably bear no resemblance to the finished product or feel like anything you could submit to an actual, bonafide college. But you must start somewhere!

REMEMBER

Here's your permission slip from me: You have my full consent to show this to anyone who tells you otherwise or questions your methods of accepting the inevitable experience of the inevitable experience of first-draft imperfection.

IN THIS CHAPTER

» Avoiding illegal pitfalls

» Getting constructive help with your essays

» Dealing with parental over-involvement

» Setting boundaries for your application process

» Finding help when you don't have any

Chapter **6**

Steering Clear of Potential Landmines

They may be everywhere — pacing the room as you gather ideas and leaning over the computer screen to follow every keystroke. Bugging you for "just a glimpse, we promise" of the first draft. Patiently explaining, for the 15th evening in a row, the topic chosen by "that nice boy down the block, the one who got into all the Ivies." They may be your parents, your teachers, your friends, or any of the people who are trying to help with your college admission essays. They mean well, and they can in fact be worth their weight in acceptance letters. But not all potential helpers know the rules for how to appropriately help you.

Or they may be nowhere. You may be sitting alone in your room facing a blank screen, reading contradictory or overwhelming advice and ready to scream, "HELP! Will somebody please talk to me about this essay!"

Whatever your situation, this chapter has information for you. It explains how to ask for and manage legitimate assistance with your college admission essays. In this chapter I also provide some strategies for dealing with over-eager helpers. And if you're one of the applicants with few-to-no helpers at all, I tell you where to look for assistance.

Buying an Essay on the Internet and Other Things to Avoid

By this stage in your life, you know your way around the Internet. So you know that essays on just about any topic abound, and some of them are for sale. But you've already rejected that option. After all, you bought this book, and you're reading it at this very moment. Good for you! The Internet-purchase route is a bad idea for several thousand reasons. The essays procured this way are canned, generic pieces of writing — not about you at all! (How could they be, when you didn't write them?) Also, every college admissions office employs at least one person who knows how and where to find essays-for-hire. You may get caught if you try to cheat, and frankly, you should. Dishonesty isn't an attractive quality, as some well-known actresses discovered after news broke that they paid exorbitant bribes for their children's college acceptances.

So congratulations on choosing the route of authenticity. But that route doesn't come with the world's clearest road signs. College admissions committees know that at some point in the process, someone is likely to help you a bit, and they made peace with that fact a long time ago. But the fact that the institution you hope to attend understands that you'll have *some* help doesn't mean that soliciting help on your college essays is a free-for-all. And even if in some alternate universe (the one in which ice cream is a health food) the university didn't mind parents or teachers more or less writing the essay for you, such involvement would still be a bad idea. Why? Because *you* are going to college or grad school, not your essay-helpers. For the sake of your self-esteem and to ensure a good fit between you and the institution, you should do your own work.

The general principle of legitimate help has two simple rules:

> **Rule #1**: They can help.
>
> **Rule #2:** They can't write the essay for you.

REMEMBER

If at any point in the process you're not sure what assistance is acceptable, check with the college counselor at your school or even an English teacher who may be familiar with your writing style. (If your school has no separate college counselor, the guidance office is a good bet.) College counselors in particular are used to dealing with the issue of help from parents and teachers. They've thought fairly deeply about the line between honesty and dishonesty, and they generally have a strong interest in maintaining the integrity of the application process.

Some applications come right out and ask you whether you received any help writing the essay, and if so, what kind. The Common Application, which is accepted by nearly 950 schools, asks you to sign and agree before submitting any application that the work you're submitting is your own. Once again, honesty rules. You *must* answer such questions truthfully. If you have qualms about accepting any sort of help, talk with your college or guidance counselor *before* you work on the essay.

Finding the Right Sort of Help

Others can help you, but not overhelp you, in writing an admission essay. That's a good rule, but it's not specific enough to keep you out of trouble. In the next few sections, I take you through each part of the process and explain what help is ethical and what's unethical for the college admission essay.

Avoiding too many cooks in the kitchen

You want to make a definitive decision about whose help you're going to enlist. Often, students mistakenly involve several people in the essay writing process, especially early on. You don't want multiple viewpoints on an early draft because of the phenomenon that I call "too many cooks in the kitchen." That happens when each person has their vision of where your essay is going or should go, which does nothing but confuse and distract you.

So how many people should help? My general rule is only *one* person should see your early writing. Yes, you read that correctly. One person should be your confidante and your cheerleader. Early-round help is simple: You can ask that one person questions, and they can point out where they see potential or where they feel confused as they read what you're generating. During the early stages they should keep their hands *off* the keyboard or page. In the later stages, they may offer feedback or suggestions, but you should still remain in the driver's seat and only make changes you understand and approve of.

If you're working with a professional, like an independent counselor, they should already know what early-round help looks like. Additionally they can help you break the news to your parents or others that they'll need to wait to read your writing until you have something more polished to share. (If your helper, whether paid to be helping you or not, doesn't seem interested in giving you the time and space to craft your own essays, consider it a red flag. You probably need to enlist someone else you trust for help in assessing whether this person is the best fit to support you.)

Make sure that your chosen confidante is someone who you truly trust, because you'll more than likely engage in several rounds of writing that only they're privy to see. See the section, "Locating Help When You're On Your Own" later in this chapter if you're not sure who to turn to for help in the essay writing process.

If you have more than one mentor or friend who wants to help, be firm with them. Tell them you've made your decision to have one person assist you. They'll ideally back off willingly if they know you're in good hands. "Thank you so much for wanting to help, but I'm really in a groove discussing my essay with so-and-so" is a great way of setting boundaries while you're in the thick of writing.

At some point, after you feel confident in a polished essay, such as your personal statement, you may ask for an extra pair of eyes or two to review it. Again, you get to be the one to decide what kind of help you want — often, that comes down to simply asking your secondary reader(s) what they take away from reading your essay, which should ideally reflect what your intention was when writing the essay.

If they start making notes or suggestions all over your essay that you're not sure what to do with (which can feel overwhelming when you think you're done with a piece, but it does happen), thank your secondary reader for their input and review their suggestions with your initial confidante, who can help you decide what, if anything, you should implement from this new round of feedback.

Trolling for topics

One of the most difficult aspects of writing an admission essay is deciding on a topic. (Chapters 2 and 3 give you pointers.) People who know you well — your immediate family, teachers who've spent a lot of time with you, your college counselor — can provoke a ton of good ideas just by asking the right questions. And as you generate two or three possible topics, the Helper Units in your life (parental or otherwise) may legitimately give you their opinion about the topic most likely to succeed.

No one can define a topic that is *guaranteed* to succeed. However, other people are good at suggesting topics because they have an outsider's perspective on your life that you can't achieve. And because the admissions committee will read your essay from exactly that viewpoint — the outsider's — it's worthwhile to hear about that viewpoint before, not after, you mail your application.

Although helpers can comment on the topics you're considering and even suggest some to you, they can't make the final decision, as in "Write about your relationship with Grandma — she'll love that!" You must remain in control of the choice. Your parents may also have the expectation that your topic will be something achievement-oriented, and if you're writing about a challenge you've faced, they might express skepticism or concern. (Feel free to direct them to Chapter 2 to understand more about why you might go this route.) For this reason, especially, waiting until you have a pretty polished essay before you allow family members to read it can be key. If you've done your job right, the story you've told in your essay will be all too clear, and your loved ones will be able to see that it's an essential one in getting to know who you are and the factors that have shaped you.

Dialing for details

After you decide on a topic, you may certainly ask those who were involved with the events to help you remember the details that will make your story come to life (and if you're especially sly, you may not even need to let them know early on that you're gathering details for college essay purposes).

For example, suppose you'd like your essay to touch on the inspiration you've received from your ancestors, focusing on your grandmother's immigration to the United States. Your mom may remember why Grandma left, how she traveled, where she lived, and so on. Interview your mom or phone Grandma and take notes. Or perhaps you're writing about the science fair that you and your best friend entered. Call your best friend for the lowdown on stuff that has completely slipped out of your mind, such as the comments the judge made as she examined your entry or the way that gooey stuff looked on her face just after the project exploded.

WARNING

In the search for details, one tall temptation stands before you: fiction, also known as lies. If you can't remember a detail, skip it. Don't make it up. As someone who reads countless drafts every year, I'm almost always stopped in my tracks when a detail reeks of exaggeration. Usually when I prod, the essay writer will look down and say sheepishly, "I thought it sounded better that way — how did you know?" (I *know*, and your admissions readers will probably know, too. Tall tales, and even tall details, are far more obvious than you think.) You can, however, speculate or imagine, as long as you make the reader understand where you've wandered off the reality path into novel territory, as in "I always imagine that she wore a red dress, a green apron, and a Yankee cap on the day she arrived in America."

The detail-gathering stage is totally open to your helpers, as long as none of them turn those details into sentences to be included in your essay.

Overseeing the outline

When you begin to structure your ideas, putting the details in order, you may want some feedback. No problem, as long as you keep control of the work. Helping you write the essay or create the outline is fine if what your helper is doing is mostly sitting beside you and asking questions. Doing the writing or arranging of content for you, however, is out of bounds.

Here are a couple examples of imaginary comments made after you've shown an outline to a helper. In each pair, one comment is okay and one is too intrusive:

Okay comment: I don't understand why you're explaining the party and then suddenly jumping to your relationship with Uncle Willie.

Why it's okay: The comment makes you think (emphasis on the "you") about why you want to discuss Uncle Willie after the party. If you have a reason, you'll probably keep the order as it is. If you don't, you may change the order. Either way, the control remains in your hands.

Butting-in comment: Here's a marked-up copy where I dumped Uncle Willie and moved up that story about the fishing trip. Then I showed how you can tie the party back in at the end.

Why it's butting in: The helper isn't truly helping; they're creating the outline for you.

Okay comment: Are you sure you've mentioned enough about your extracurricular experiences? Right now there's only one: your role with GSA.

Why it's okay: Granted, the comment is a thinly disguised criticism of the number of extracurricular experiences you describe in the essay (and remember the application has a separate part of the application where you can transcribe your resume, which takes the pressure off doing so in your personal statement). Nevertheless, the comment merely prods you to reconsider your ideas.

Butting-in comment: Let's add something right here about the times you helped out at Aunt Margaret's office.

Why it's butting in: The helper has made a decision for you about content (adding the office work) and one about structure (where to place the additions). Helpful reminders are okay, but this helper is trying to take the reins.

Roughing it

If you sit down to write and your helpers intrude, you're in trouble. You need, to paraphrase Virginia Woolf's famous statement, "a room of your own," preferably one with a lock on the door. Maybe you worked out a topic or outline with your chosen helper, but as you start stringing the sentences together into a real draft, you need some time to go it alone. Any help at this stage is pretty much guaranteed to be a no-no.

Your family can cook you a special dinner, or be on standby with your favorite show for after you're finished with your writing session. They can summarize a grammar rule you're stumped on, or remind you of a detail you wanted to include but don't see in your notes. But as you spill the whole essay onto the page or screen, by and large you'd better be working by yourself. After the rough draft is complete, the helpers can read it and make suggestions. (See the next section for details.)

Checking and revising

After you've given your best shot at a first draft (and if you're feeling a sense of letdown reading it back, see Chapter 5 for some encouragement) it's time to invite your dedicated helper to read your progress, and give you some pointers for revisions. But — and this is an emphatic *but* — make it clear that you're asking for feedback, not rewrites. Your helper may tell you which sections of the essay are unclear and ask you questions about the puzzling parts.

Also okay are comments like these:

> You started to lose me right around paragraph 3. Then I got bored. (I didn't say these comments were good for your ego, just for your integrity and the ultimate quality of your essay.)

> You move from one idea to another very quickly. How about some transitions?

> I like the story, but I'm not sure what point you're trying to make. Maybe you should clarify the last paragraph.

> I don't think you actually answered the question.

> Clearly ready for publication in *The New Yorker*.

One more time: Your helper can point you in the right direction, but not pilot the boat. *You* have to do the rewrites.

Having too many editors

If you show your essay to too many people, you're asking for trouble, even if each reader gives you only within-bounds help. The most likely scenario is that all the readers will identify the same problem(s) in the essay, but more than likely each will choose a different way to correct it.

One reader may say something like, "I think the section on your first root canal is too long" whereas another may say they'd like to read more about the root canal and less about your visit to the dental school.

Both are reacting to a lack of focus in the piece. But faced with contradictory advice, you won't know whom to follow. Choose one primary helper and stay with that individual. If others insist on reading the essay, take their advice with a grain of salt.

Identifying Your Parents' Role

They love you. They worry about your future. They also pay the bills. Is it any wonder that your parents want to help you concoct the perfect college application? But . . . it's your application, your future, and your essay. So is it any wonder that dealing with excess parental "help" is a real pain in the neck?

REMEMBER

I say "they/their" and "parents" in this section not because I assume every student reading this has a two-parent household, a white fence, and a Golden Retriever, but because regardless of your family structure you may still have to cope with interference (sorry, *assistance*) from those who love you. If too much help is a problem, simply plug in the pronouns that suit your particular situation. Also replace the word "parents" and substitute whatever term applies to your living arrangement. Then read on!

In this section, I outline strategies for identifying the parts of the application process that should be yours and yours alone, or where parental help is likely to be anxiety-driven and not especially helpful. (See the section, "Finding the Right Sort of Help," earlier in this chapter, for specific guidelines.) But before I explain how to dissolve the superglue currently attaching them to your back, you should give some thought to *why* the adult figures in your life are so hyper about your college applications.

Understanding why your parents may try to micromanage the process

Most parents (and I say this as a parent myself) begin to mourn a loss of control around your senior year. Assuming you won't be commuting from home to college, your parents won't know your friends, your social routine, your study habits, or little details like what time you come home after a party. Faced with the reality that you're about to leave both the family home and the family power sphere, your parents may have a harder time handling the change than you will. After all, it's not called empty-nest syndrome for nothing.

They may attempt to micromanage the application process, I believe, because they want to set you up for success — and because they cherish still having the ability to weigh in on your decisions. Also, some parents hold onto the illusion that controlling (er . . . helping you decide) where you go to college will allow them to have some control over what you do when you get there. (Unlikely.)

Having worked with nearly every kind of family dynamic, I haven't quite decided whether it's preferable for parents to know absolutely nothing about the college process or to know perhaps a little *too* much. In either case, avoiding a little tension at home isn't easy. That should come as no surprise — after all, your parents have probably been a part of every important decision in your life thus far and had a fair amount of control over what you were doing and *where* you were going for your entire life. (And if they haven't, they might use this moment as an opportunity to make up for lost time.)

This moment is a wonderful opportunity for you to practice the independence that will be required of you to be a successful college student. A bit of worrying on your parents' part or tension between your own wishes and theirs is just part of inevitable growing pains.

Managing your parents' concerns and expectations

If your parents have inserted themselves into the essay you're writing, your best bet is to show them that you're mature enough to handle the application process on your own. Here are some tips you can use to navigate this process as gracefully as you can — that is, with minimal arguing:

>> **Time management:** Show them that you're in control of the timing by starting early and working at a manageable pace. Consider sharing your application schedule, which includes your benchmarks and a checklist of everything you'll do before submitting applications. Let them know you have plans to enlist trusted input from somewhere and will probably want to share your final draft with them in several weeks (or whatever window of time you feel you still need). Frantic all-nighters don't breed parental confidence, but a thought-out to-do list will. (See Chapter 1 for tips on time management.)

>> **Requests for appropriate help:** Be specific in what you ask. Don't say, "I can't figure out what to write." Instead say, "Tell me what you think are the most significant moments in my childhood" or "I'm thinking of writing about Grandpa Bob's work at the nature center. Do you think that would explain why I want to be a marine biologist?"

>> **Politeness:** "Back off, MOM!" isn't exactly the most courteous response to parental pressure. Try "Thanks for offering to help, but I think I should tackle this essay on my own. I'll let you know how it's coming along in the next

couple of days." After they recover from their fainting spell, they should leave you alone. I always tell my students' parents that writing and reading your personal statement draft can feel a bit like writing and reading your diary, which is why discussing essays with a professional or stranger is often easier.

>> **Alternatives:** Give them some other way to help. Most parents are especially interested in helping you through the process of creating a list of which colleges to apply to — a task that is far more concrete than a personal essay and one that also requires their buy-in (literally and figuratively).

Some helpful responses to topics on your parents' minds might include

- "I know you're worried about debt and student loans. Here's what I'm doing to make sure I remain cost-aware as I finalize my college list."

- "Right now, I'm working on my personal statement. When I get to the extracurricular page in the application, we should sit down again. I'd love if you could help me with that by making sure I didn't forget anything." (I like this template because it allows you to share just enough to empower your parents and lets them know when they can expect to be able to offer more active input.)

>> **Authority figures:** If you're dealing with hardcore interferers, you may have to bring in some hired guns. Make an appointment with the guidance counselor or college advisor and explain your problem. Then you can confidently (and courteously) state, "Mom, I appreciate your wanting to help me with the essay, but Mr. Getin told me that I should do this part by myself." When you show the finished product to your parents, try this statement: "Here's the essay, Mom. Mr. Getin read it, and he thinks it's ready to go."

If none of these tips seem to quite do the trick, leave this book where they'll see it conveniently open to this section in this chapter. If they won't listen to you, perhaps they'll listen to me.

Locating Help When You're On Your Own

In writing this chapter, I assume your problem is too much help, but you may have the opposite problem — no help at all. You may be the first in your family to apply to college or the only one with a command of the English language. You may attend a large, scandalously understaffed high school where the guidance counselor's first open appointment is six months after the application is due. Not to worry! A few avenues of assistance are still available to you.

You've already gotten some help by reading this edition of *College Admission Essays For Dummies.* Good for you! Here are some other possibilities for assistance:

>> **A sympathetic teacher:** Most teachers are willing to spare you a few minutes, even if they have to chomp down a sandwich while reading a rough draft. Your English teacher is the logical choice, but teachers of other disciplines can help as well. Check out the section, "Finding the Right Sort of Help," earlier in this chapter for tips on appropriate and inappropriate help.

>> **Relatives:** Assuming they can remain at a respectful distance from the keyboard while you're writing, relatives have a lot to offer. Experience in higher education isn't necessary because your relatives know the most important subject — you. They can discuss your upbringing with you, tell you family stories, and help you remember or define important aspects of your life and character. They can also tell you if the person who comes through in your writing feels authentic to the person they know and love — the real you.

>> **Your friends and other mentors:** Your friends can help you in the same tasks and for the same reasons as your relatives. Apply the strategy explained in the preceding bullet to your peers. Sometimes, another sort of mentor, like a tutor, job supervisor, or other figure in your life, is also ideally suited to weigh in and give you their general observations on your essay, but like I discuss in the section, "Avoiding too many cooks in the kitchen," earlier in this chapter), remember to limit the amount of voices you invite to contribute so that you aren't overwhelmed or confused.

>> **Your older peers:** Chances are that you have a cousin, friend, or even a sibling who is a few years older than you and remembers all too well what it was like to be applying to college and writing admission essays. They may be willing to show you their own writing as a reference and offer the advice that was most helpful for them to hear when they were in your shoes.

>> **The Internet:** Though the Internet is the last on this list for a reason (see the next section), you can still find many helpful answers to questions you might have, such as how you may interpret a given essay prompt, online. You can also watch videos about other aspects of the application process and take virtual tours of various campuses as you work on building your list. Remember that during the COVID-19 pandemic, colleges had to do *all* their information sessions and outreach online, because many campuses were devoid of students and faculty — and much of that content remains available to you now.

Writing College Essays in the Technical Age: What You Need to Know

You can easily blur boundaries with shared documents and other features during the essay writing process. You can't just go into a cave with a feather quill and blank scroll — though I sometimes wish that applicants could. When you're soliciting feedback, keep the following points in mind:

» **Don't let anyone touch a single word of your essay without your permission.** When you're ready for edits, from either your early-round helper or secondary readers, make sure your readers use Track Changes. (You can also go with an even safer option: printing a hard copy of your essay and asking your reader to write out their suggestions.) However reassuring their feedback is or how tempted you are to click "Accept All" to their digital edits, review every single edit before accepting (or rejecting) it. Your college writing is yours, and not even a comma should find its way into an essay without your careful review and approval.

» **Don't compare your messy freewrite to someone else's finished draft.** It doesn't matter if it's an essay that another student shared with you or one you found online. In fact, while you're deep in the writing process, take a break from reading sample essays because you can easily get discouraged when you compare someone else's finished product with your work-in-progress. Chapter 5 discusses the freewriting process in greater detail.

WARNING

» **As you write, work in a word-processing program and not directly in an online application.** Feel free to use whatever program of your choice — Microsoft Word, Google Drive, or Pages. Just make sure you never write an essay, not even a short-response essay, directly in the application for a few main reasons:

- Inevitably your work won't save properly and you'll have to redo it.

- Most applications also don't check for grammar or spelling mistakes, so you'll want that extra layer of protection offered by a writing program with these features.

- Your readers can't leave you any comments or edits in the application like they can in programs like Word and Google Drive.

After you're 100 percent confident, you can copy and paste your work into the application before you submit. Chapter 16 discusses these and many other reasons why this practice is smart.

KEEPING BRANDING AT BAY

Unless you're talking about a major retailer, I usually cringe when I hear the word "brand." Still, in the age of social media influencers, it's somewhat inevitable that the tendency to think of yourself as a marketable product would spill into the world of college admissions. (Read Chapter 1 for more on why authenticity is the best approach.)

I probably shouldn't have been surprised when Natalie's mother announced, "We think Natalie should brand herself as a STEM buff with an entrepreneurial spirit." In the course of several sessions, Natalie, too, seemed pretty attached to her pitch, always pivoting to "But if I want them to see me as a STEM buff with an entrepreneurial spirit . . ."

Because her very well-intentioned parents had so ingrained this idea (Natalie *was* a STEM buff, but that wasn't nearly as interesting as everything else about her), it took some time to coax her into trying a different approach for her personal statement. I also had to reassure her parents that while reading her unfinished draft would be like tasting uncooked pizza dough (in other words, unnerving), Natalie knew where her essay was headed: a great finished product, which would be worth the wait if they would allow her the time to "cook" (ahem, write and revise).

They waited, and both parents were moved when they eventually read Natalie's personal statement, which focused primarily on her close relationship with her cousin, who had a variety of cognitive disabilities, and how that relationship impacted her sense of self and family. Natalie's parents were especially pleased when they were able to look over her full application before submission, which included her extensive resume (naturally revealing her emphasis on entrepreneurship) and a few supplemental essays on her interest in pursuing an engineering degree program in college and her experience with STEM. Without the focus on self-marketing and with some breathing room to work out how she wanted to express herself, Natalie got into her top-choice school.

Tip: I often refer to the writing process with culinary metaphors — marinating on your ideas, preparing your raw ingredients, giving things time to simmer — and you're welcome to do the same if you need to buy yourself some time away from eager readers.

Writing the
Rough Draft

IN THIS PART. . .

Figure out the mechanics of creating a rough draft.

Tap into the mind of your audience: the admissions readers.

Identify the writing traits you want to avoid.

Craft your essay's opening hook (and an equally strong ending).

Implement the rule of "show, not tell" in your essays.

Get to the root of your writer's block and application anxiety.

Chapter **7**

Writing for the Tired, the Poor (The Admissions Office)

cross a deep, crocodile-infested moat and behind sound-proof titanium doors, they hold top-secret meetings. Each carries an ax. From time to time one of them chops an application into shreds, always with the sort of maniacal laughter you hear on old cartoons. They're the admissions counselors, and they delight in ruining your future.

Does this picture match the one your imagination creates? Be honest now. Okay, maybe a few details are different — perhaps your fantasy admissions office has a high-tech thumb-print lock and no moat — but I bet you think that you're writing college admission essays for trained torturers who are dying to reject you.

Not so. In fact your audience includes a group of overworked professionals who are dedicated to the institution they serve. Often, they're around or under 30, which means they remember all too well what it was like to be in your position. Their main goal is to gather a group of deserving students who will do well on their campus — in more ways than just academically. In this chapter I discuss how to reach that audience. I also reveal their biggest turn-offs, so you can avoid the ax.

Meeting Your Readers: The Admissions Committee

The Authority Figures deciding your future are a fairly diverse bunch. More than likely, your application will first be read by one or two regional admissions staffers (that is, counselors assigned to your region), and then by the official admissions committee, which includes admissions staff, faculty, and past or current students. The typical college admissions office is run by a director or dean, with a strong commitment to the institution and years of experience evaluating candidates. The following sections explain *how* the admissions staff will interact with your application and what you should keep in mind to make the best possible impression.

Understanding the counselors' duties

You may know no more about the job of an admissions counselor than that it involves an awful lot of power — specifically, the power to determine your future. But what does their role actually look like? The admissions office's tasks are many, including the following:

>> Attract a bright, varied pool of applicants.

>> Present the institution favorably so that those who are admitted choose to attend.

>> Stock the office with brewed-to-sludge-level coffee so that caffeinated counselors have the energy to stare at a computer screen and evaluate many thousands of applications.

>> Read a zillion essays, some of which are yours.

At most universities, two or more members of the admissions committee read every word of each application, including your essays. At the very least, one counselor will review your work. Though admissions counselors in general want to give you a fair shake, they plow through many, *many* essays every day.

In relation to the admission counselors who will read your essay, you have two main goals to keep in mind:

>> **Grab their attention and keep it.** Remember, your personal statement is your opportunity to breathe life into an application that is otherwise little more than facts and figures. Twelve years of experience have shown me that a compelling essay can get you into a "Reach" school (a school you're perhaps slightly underqualified for) and even result in scholarships. Refer to the

section, "Keeping Their Attention When Yours Is the 200th Essay They've Read Today," later in this chapter for more details.

>> **Make the experience of reading your essay worth their investment of time and energy.** If the admissions counselors can clearly see you've taken the process seriously, you can trust that at the very least, they'll treat your application with the same seriousness.

Factoring in your timeline

In addition to creating a more streamlined application process for yourself (picture this: by winter break of senior year, you've been accepted to one more colleges or universities you're excited about!), being aware of admissions plans also impacts how and when your readers process your application. Keep in mind that your application will arrive at one of two times:

>> **Early Decision/Early Action (ED/EA) applicants:** Due in autumn, usually by November 1. These admissions plans mean that you can apply to a college or university by a deadline that is earlier than the general deadline in order to also be notified of the admissions decision earlier. An ED application also signals to a college that it's your first choice because you're contracted to enroll if accepted, and can therefore increase your chances of acceptance significantly.

FOR ASPIRING ATHLETES — THE EARLIER THE BETTER

Recruitment for college sports has changed quite a bit in recent years, but one trend remains the same: If a college coach really wants to vouch for you, they may give you a much earlier deadline to submit your application — as early as August. And generally, you can't bypass submitting a completed application. This means that if you're hoping for a recruitment opportunity and believe you may be considered, you ought to have your essays ready.

For example, a student of mine who is a competitive rower was recently asked to submit her application to an extremely prestigious school with just a little more than *one week's* notice for recruitment consideration. In other words, if she hadn't already drafted not only her personal statement, but also her supplemental essays for this specific college during the month of July, she'd have risked losing her opportunity altogether. (Needless to say, even the most qualified and coveted athlete still has to submit a complete and traditional application.) If you're hoping or considering recruitment, that's all the more reason to write early and often.

The benefit of an ED or EA application is that the admissions committee reviews your application in a smaller applicant pool. You're catching the committee members when they're fresh and ready to begin assembling next year's freshmen class. For example, Boston University received a whopping 15,000 EA applications in the fall of 2020 — compared to more than 75,000 applications in January 2021 for Regular Decision. Clearly, if you can submit by an ED/EA deadline, you do have a better opportunity to stand out.

» **Regular Decision (RD) applicants:** Due in late winter or early spring. Deferred students from the EA/ED pool are reevaluated during this time. Your application may also arrive at the same time as your counselor sends the midyear report, with updates on your grades and GPA from the fall semester. Although many seniors believe that senior year grades "don't matter," for most universities that urban legend simply isn't true.

REMEMBER

Submitting at least one early application (whether it's an ED application, which is *binding* (meaning you agree to enroll, if accepted), or an EA application, which isn't binding and in most cases can be done for more than one school) is to your advantage. In addition to generally increasing your chances of acceptance, you'll also typically know by January 1 whether or not you've been accepted and can submit additional applications (or not) accordingly. Chapter 1 provides details about how you can develop your application timeline.

Strategizing for success

This section includes a sample plan you can adapt to help you stay on track. This sample is a pretty leisurely pace that allows for weekend getaways, a part-time job, and whatever else is on your plate during the summer. The overall framework may be helpful to keep in mind as you grease your wheels for the process that is about to begin:

❏ **End of junior year:** Take two weeks off after final exams. Then focus on Common App personal statement exclusively for approximately two to three weeks.

❏ **Month of July:** Finalize Common App personal statement, optional essay, and 50 percent of your Common App supplements by writing a little bit (less than an hour) every day or every other day.

❏ **August 1:** Common App goes live. Begin working on data entry and extracurricular pages. Check all supplemental essays to see if any of the prompts, especially those that you've already drafted have changed. Aim to have the Common App completely done with all essays by the first day of school.

ASKING FOR LETTERS OF RECOMMENDATIONS EARLY ENOUGH

Are you the kind of person who arrives at your destination 30 minutes in advance? You know what they say about the worm, right? If you want to stay two steps ahead before you take off for summer vacation, I recommend asking at least one teacher for a letter of recommendation. They may smirk a bit and tell you to remind them again in the fall, or they may thank you for the early request and tell you that they're already nearly full. Not only do teachers occasionally use their vacation time to write their letters (as the same time as you'll be writing your essays), but your recommenders may want to see a copy of your personal statement, list of colleges, and resume — and serve as helpful resources to bounce off ideas off.

Speaking of resumes, I recommend having one. You can find a template online (check out www.myperfectresume.com) and plug in activities rather mindlessly on an afternoon or two that you simply don't have the creative stamina for personal essay writing. Some schools invite you to upload this document directly to the application, and your teachers and counselors writing your letters of recommendation will certainly appreciate having a copy as a reference of some of your extracurricular activities and accomplishments.

Keeping Their Attention When Yours Is the 200th Essay They've Read Today

More colleges are embracing the concept of *holistic review*, or evaluating each candidate in terms of their qualities as a whole and why they may be an asset to a college institution. In other words, they're *not* judging you solely based on your GPA and test scores with annually increasing ruthlessness, and the personal statement and your other essays have never been more important. What you can offer through writing — a glimpse into your real self — is a key part of the holistic review process! (Chapter 1 delves more into the topic of holistic review.)

REMEMBER

That means that your writing should go beyond making a decent first impression. Make sure your essay is so good that your admissions reader stops in their tracks and forgets that their hand was halfway to the candy bowl. Instead, they'll grip the sides of their desk with both hands, disappear into your work for several absorbing minutes, and mark you as an Admit.

If you're thinking, "That's easy for you to say because you're a writer, and I'm anything but!" consider this visual. Imagine yourself turning one of your life experiences into a mini-TED Talk. Your personal statement is merely the transcription. In other words, you're not writing prize-winning poetry; you're writing *you*. (And very few of my students who get accepted to top colleges, often with a nod or two to their writing ability, consider themselves writers. They just took this process seriously.)

Consider these imaginary essay sentences and some possible reactions:

Blah Essay Sentence: I was born 18 years ago.

Reader Reaction: Yeah, you and just about everybody applying for the freshman class. Yawn.

Better Essay Sentence: My father had to snatch my mother's unfinished copy of *Harry Potter and the Order of the Phoenix* out of her hands just as she was being wheeled into the delivery room for my birth.

Reader Reaction: I remember that premiere! I stood in line at the bookstore for three hours the day that book came out.

Another Blah Essay Sentence: I have many varied hobbies.

Reader Reaction: I really have to get my resume together. I hear they're hiring at Disneyland.

Better Essay Sentence: Building the world's largest collection of harmonicas is only one of my hobbies.

Reader Reaction: Harmonicas? I'd like to take a look at this guy's garage.

One More Blah Essay Sentence: My friend is always there for me.

Reader Reaction: Congratulations. Everyone else's friends are totally absent.

Better Essay Sentence: When Godzilla bit my toe, my first thought was to call Emily.

Reader Reaction: Toe? Godzilla? What can Emily do?

Get the idea? Good essay sentences *connect* to the reader, the admission counselor, making them comment, speculate, or question. The "blah" essay sentences sound, well, blah. They're so general they could apply to just about anyone, and they give the admissions counselor no incentive to continue slogging through your paragraphs.

TIP

Don't think that you have to encounter Godzilla or do something as weird as collect harmonicas in order to write an interesting essay. Even the most boring life (and yours isn't boring at all, I'm sure) can become good reading material. It's all in the presentation! Check out Chapter 9 to find out how to add vivid detail to your essay. I show you how to write a strong first sentence in Chapter 10.

Avoiding Irksome Writing Traits

Don't try to psych out the admissions counselors by writing what you think they want to read. In this section, I discuss style and tone and reveal the most common turn-offs of the college admission essay.

My thesaurus and me: Unnatural vocabulary

You want to impress the admissions committee with your scholarly preparedness, but sounding like a talking dictionary isn't helpful. If you're tempted to look at your thesaurus for an impressive vocabulary word, take my advice: Don't!

In other words, when you write the college admission essay, don't plop words into your sentences that you're using for the very first time. Chances are you'll use the words improperly. Even if the words are in the right spot, you'll come across unnaturally.

Consider this example. Would you want to continue reading the first sentence of this paragraph? "As I ambulated through the fronds of semitropical vegetation, I. . .." You what? You looked up a smart-sounding synonym for every other word in your essay, right? You probably don't want to read more, and the admission counselor doesn't want to either.

Consider these two useful secrets about vocabulary:

>> **New words worm their way into your understanding** *gradually:*

- You first learn the meaning of the word from a list or from a dictionary. At this stage you know how to define the word on a test, but it's still a stranger.

- You next begin to hear the word in conversation or notice it as you read. The word is becoming an acquaintance now, more familiar each time you meet it, but it's not yet ready for an invitation into everyday expression.

- When the word is a true friend, you feel comfortable inserting it into your speaking and writing, where it meshes smoothly with other old friends, the words you've been using for years.

>> **Words have meanings (***denotations,*** in dictionary terms) and associations (***connotations***).** If you understand only the denotation of an expression but not the connotation, you may end up making some embarrassing mistakes.

For example, both "proud" and "haughty" have similar denotations; they describe the attitude of people who are fairly pleased with their own accomplishments. But "haughty" is an insult, and "proud" is more neutral. You can safely write that winning the contest made you "proud," but if you say that the gold medal made you "haughty," you're criticizing yourself.

Flowery language

Flowery language (you know, the overly verbose stuff that you'll be tempted to write to make yourself sound smarter) is as stiff and unpalatable as uncooked asparagus. Don't write your essay in this way, unless you want the admissions committee to appreciate your attempt at tapping into your Shakespearean qualities (believe me, they won't!). Some examples, with corrections, are as follows:

Stiff Sentence: It is now my understanding that the event that took place in my early childhood — the rattlesnake's entrance into my crib — played a formidable role in shaping my eventual character.

Better Sentence: The rattlesnake slithered into my crib and changed my entire life.

Another Stiff Sentence: Any 300-word essay that could be written by me must inevitably fail to communicate the entire nature of my character, but I will endeavor to comply with your request anyway.

Better Sentence: I can't possibly communicate my true self in 300 words, but I will try.

Last Stiff Sentence: It was the best of times, it was the worst of times, it was the age of victory, it was the era of defeat. . ..

Better Sentence: Forget about it! No better sentence exists. The preceding passage comes from Charles Dickens' *A Tale of Two Cities*. He was a genius, so he could break all the rules and create an unforgettable piece of writing. (Also, those paradoxes are real; they say something significant about the French Revolution era and aren't merely for literary effect.)

If you think you can pull off Dickensian style, go for it. (But be warned: The higher you aim, the farther you may fall if you don't hit the target.) For everyone else, the rule is simple: Write naturally. If you can't read your essay aloud smoothly or achieve a conversational tone and find yourself stuttering over certain words, you may have a problem with flowery language.

Having trouble achieving a natural style? Try "writing" your essay by speaking it into a voice memo or voice recorder. Then transcribe the recording. You may have to clean up the grammar a bit and rearrange a few things to achieve a logical flow, but chances are the tone will be realistic.

Grammar checkers and plug-ins may help you, but don't rely on them completely. Those squiggly lines and suggested corrections are sometimes wrong, based on a misread of your content or intention. Your best bet is to learn the rules and apply them with your very own brain, and at some point, enlist a great proofreader.

Untruths and exaggerations

Your essay may be beautifully vivid and relate a compelling story, but your words must also be true. Choose your topic (see Chapter 2 for help with this task) and write it accurately. Anything else is simply unacceptable. For example, if you won the math medal, say so. Just don't claim that you won the medal against insurmountable odds when your opponents were still struggling with pesky little problems like 2 + 2. Just tell it like it was. After all, the ambiguities of life and a dose of humility are far more interesting than the fibs you might concoct to build yourself up more.

Here is a primary example:

Exaggerating Example: "Time for you to put your natural skill into practice," said a voice from behind me. I'd been practicing my sutures on the training machine all morning, hoping that what would happen next would come to be: Dr. S. was going to let me perform a suture on a real patient." (Nah! If you're lucky enough to volunteer in a medical environment in high school, you can thank your lucky stars, but don't expect to be stitching anyone up. You'll learn the same way that every beginner does: through observation.)

The Believable Truth: I whirled around, still holding my laparoscopic instruments. Dr. S. squinted, and I realized he had been watching as I practiced sutures on a training machine. "Your work is impressive for only a college student," he said. I was floored by the compliment, mainly because I had actually been struggling with the suture." (I'm impressed with this, but I also believe it. Being compared to a college student is a flattering detail to include, but it's realistic — moreover, the student's admission that she struggled with her sutures feels likeably honest and shows that, even though it was hard, she was up for the challenge.)

I am a people person: Clichés

Every so often I point out a *cliché* — an old, worn out expression such as "so hungry I could eat a horse" — to a student and then struggle to answer the natural follow-up question: "What's wrong with using a cliché? It made my point. . .. Besides, I didn't know it was a cliché." Sigh. The student isn't completely wrong. Clichés became clichés because they once filled a need; they expressed a common idea in easily understood terms. The problem is that each time a cliché is used, it loses a bit of its meaning; now, people have heard them all so often that your use of a cliché simply comes across as lazy, unimaginative writing. The expression has become so childishly comfortable that people reading it press the automatic-pilot button and switch off their brains. They're not considering your ideas, they may not expect a lot of depth from you throughout the rest of your essay, and they may even be less inclined to admit you.

You may not recognize every cliché. So how can you avoid using clichés if you don't know what they are? Your best bet is to show your essay to a trusted adult, perhaps your parents or your English teacher, and ask the reader to point out any trite or tired phrases. Then put on your creativity cap and try again.

Table 7-1 lists examples of commonly used cliches and how they might worm their way into your essay writing. Be aware of them so you don't include them (or similar ones) in your admission essay.

TABLE 7-1   **Cliches to Avoid**

Line Which Includes a Tempting Cliché	Verdict
"When I first heard about my solo, I was scared to death."	"Scared to death" falls into the category of a cliché that just comes across as lazy writing — as does this cliché's best friend, "bored to tears" (which is what your reader will be if you write this way!). Instead, the student should include a sensory detail to help convey fear: a lump in one's throat or clammy hands, for example.
"I had the time of my life at the junior retreat."	Again, laziness is the real culprit here. You don't need a phrase like "time of my life" when writing about a meaningful experience. Instead, get to the meatier stuff about how the retreat changed you — and be specific!
"As a freshman, I was eager for a clean slate."	Of all of the clichés on this list, you may be able to get away with this one — it's somewhat subtle. However, I suggest you do away with it and be specific. This line doesn't answer how, why, or in what capacity the student was hoping to start over.
"Normally, I wouldn't be caught dead at an event like this, but Shira was excited about it so I went with the flow."	Bonus points if you caught both clichés here: "wouldn't be caught dead" and "going with the flow" are both way too stale to be useful to you. A solid alternative would be to say something more personal, like "Normally, I stuck with the soccer crowd, but when Shira proposed that I accompany her to the first Dungeons & Dragons meeting, I reluctantly agreed."

TIP

The main idea of your essay, not just individual phrases, may also be clichéd. In other words, a few topics have been so overdone that you're going to have to be an *excellent* writer to pull them off. These topics include essays on going on volunteer trips or recovering from a sports injury. But you don't want to present the admissions committee with the college-essay equivalent of the car chase that's in every action movie. The way to avoid this problem: Writing about your own experiences in a very specific, detailed, and personal way. The experience you describe may be a common one, but if you throw in enough detail and insight, your story will be unique because the details of your story do not match the specifics of anyone else's story. Chapter 9 discusses how you can be more specific in your essay.

Developing Your Voice on Paper

The admissions committee wants a sense of who you are and what you've been through. The committee members are interested in how you see the world, and your *voice* — or the tone and language with which you write — holds an important role in shaping how you come across.

So why type of essay should you write? A funny essay isn't preferable to a serious one. Nor is an essay bubbling over with optimism preferable to a wry one. The only type of college admission essay you can assume will resonate with your reader is a well-written essay.

When you read the sample essays in the Appendix, you'll notice that they have little in common other than the fact that the writers have figured out how their voice sounds on paper (which takes practice) and how to show a story that is important to who they are. The mood or perspective of each one varies widely, just like their topics. Because reading your essay should feel a bit like having a conversation with you, try not to actively think too much about tone. Just share your own observations and insights truthfully, and your own voice will emerge fairly naturally.

I GUESS THEY READ IT

A couple of years ago, I worked with a student I call Sam the Cynic. Sam was convinced that he had already thrown in the towel on his chances of being admitted to a four-year university — and to give him credit, he certainly hadn't done himself many favors on his transcript. But Sam had a very interesting personal story, one that shed some light as to why (until the latter half of his junior year) he hadn't had the bandwidth to fully commit to his schoolwork.

Did he want to apply to universities with a writing requirement? After I got past the defensiveness, Sam agreed he knew he would probably be more successful at a smaller school. "But there isn't a doubt in my mind they'll toss out my application," he chortled. "Come on. An essay's really going to make a difference?"

I smiled. "Let's pair a great essay with a semester of excellent grades and see what happens." Sam reluctantly agreed and began drafting a personal statement essay that went through many, many iterations until it was as close to perfect as he could get it. (He actually began to enjoy the self-discovery part of the writing process, which helped — though he still wasn't convinced of any future payoff.)

Three months later, Sam opened an acceptance letter to a private college in Southern California — which wasn't the only school that ended up accepting him, but was notable for one main reason. It was personalized and made reference to (drum roll, please) his personal statement essay. Sam had to admit that indeed the admissions committee must have read it.

REMEMBER

If you're not a naturally funny person, I recommend you stay away from writing funny. However, you don't have to be an aspiring comedian in order to insert an ironic comment or humorous observation. (My own husband describes me as "secretly funny," because even though my inner circle is familiar with my humor, I don't flamboyantly display this trait at dinner parties with strangers.) Similarly, your college writing may sound more like your private inner monologue (or your journal, if you've ever kept one) than the person who sits in English class.

WARNING

If you're writing about a serious topic or a conflict in your life that may still be lacking some resolution, your voice or tone may sound *so* anguished that your reader feels . . . well, concerned. (This can happen when you write a wildly unfiltered first draft.) Usually over the course of the revision process you're able to gain enough perspective and insight that the final draft sounds hopeful, not hopeless. If you're really struggling with finding that dose of perspective or resiliency when you write about a given topic and worry you're coming across as bleak, you may not have enough distance to be able to approach this topic from a growth mind-set. (Healing takes time.) In that case, you may want to try a different topic altogether for college essay purposes (I hope you'll talk through what you're feeling with someone you trust).

Chapter **8**

Building a Structure to Support Your Ideas

In your high school career, most of your academic papers have shared the same *structure:* a clear introduction that includes your thesis or claim, two to three body paragraphs in the middle, and a conclusion paragraph. In fact, more than likely, you may believe all essays follow this structure, which you may recognize as the Five-Paragraph Essay.

However, the structure of your college admission essay is different. Remember the following when you're writing your college admission essay:

» **The good news:** You get to break that structure when you write an admission essay (just as you would for other personal narrative writing or creative writing). College admission essays are *not* conducive to the religiously worshipped Five-Paragraph Essay.

» **The bad news:** You *have* to break the Five-Paragraph Essay structure, which might leave you spinning and asking, "How on earth do I organize this thing without the formula I've used for all of high school? Where do I start, and how will I know where to end?"

However, just because your college admission essay isn't a literary analysis of *The Great Gatsby* or a historical paper about the New Deal doesn't mean that it's going to be as free-flowing as the poetry you wrote in middle school. Your admission essay does need structure. But the structure of this essay isn't a prescription for a specific number of paragraphs or rigid template; it's a conceptual framework. You're probably not aware of the structure underlying most of the material you read. Nevertheless it's there, and if it's done correctly, it enhances the meaning of the writer's words.

In this chapter, I explain how structure works with (and when it's done poorly, against) your material. I show you how to match your essay topic with a suitable structure. Finally, I describe several structures and provide real student essay examples of the structures you're most likely to use.

Meeting the Major Players in the Structure Game

This section guides you toward structures likely to be useful for a college admission essay, matched to suitable questions and often accompanied by real student essays. As you read you may notice that some of the structures overlap. For example, a chronological order essay may survey some important events in your life. Don't worry about the labels. The point isn't to name the structure but to give you guidance on how use it.

Chronological order

When you write an admission essay, you naturally look back over your life and think about the events and people that shaped you. So *chronological* or time order is a good fit for lots of essays — especially for the ones that ask about events or people that shaped you. (Funny how these things go together!) This structure adapts itself to several different patterns:

>> **The origin story:** Thinking of an important aspect of your life — your obsession with eating leafy greens that turned into a gardening adventure — trace your involvement or the development of your interest way back to the beginning by describing several events very briefly.

>> **Single event:** Focusing on one event in your life — perhaps the time you attempted to lead your Boy Scouts troop on a hiking adventure and instead found yourself separated from the group and lost in the Santa Cruz Mountains — recount the event, hour by hour.

>> **Sequence of events:** For the "Reflect on something that someone has done for you" question (Common Application Prompt 4), describe what your chosen individual did for you (in order of how their actions unfolded) and then the impact on you, emotionally or otherwise.

In each of these essays you should devote a paragraph or two to interpreting or commenting the event(s) you're describing. As you write that paragraph, remember that you're asking your reader to accompany you through time to experience an event or period with you. The reader's logical question is "Why do you want me to be with you during this experience?" Make sure you answer that question.

Figure 8-1 is a chronological essay by a student who wants to be the next Steven Spielberg — and he may very well succeed. The writer concentrates on a single period in his life — summer study at a filmmaking academy — and focuses on the making of a short film. He begins with a brief reference to his lifelong passion for movies, but most of the essay deals with the few weeks of work on his own production. Notice that the writer takes care to explain what he learned from his brief course in movie-making.

Interrupted chronological order

All those movies about time machines reveal how fervently human beings would like to have the ability to interrupt the usual chronological order. You can't do it in real life, but you sure can tinker with time in your essay. *Interrupted chronological order* is helpful for essays about an event that changed you or an issue you care about, particularly when you want to relate a past event to your present situation or attitude. Interrupted chronological order has a million variations.

Here are two of the most useful:

>> **Flashback:** More than likely you've seen this technique on television. The present-day character stares blankly into space. The music swells, the picture fades, and suddenly a much younger actor is on the screen. In a flashback essay, start with the present and cut to the past event. End with the present or with an interpretation of the flashback.

>> **Bookends:** I call this structure *bookends* because you begin and end with two halves of the same event. The middle is usually the interpretation or background of the event. Suppose, for example, you're writing about the time you won a student election. You describe one particular part of the election in detail — your big speech calling upon the administration to abolish grades. You begin the essay with the first sentence or two of the speech and a quick peek at your audience. Then cut to your decision to run, the challenges awaiting candidates, the goals of your candidacy, and so on. End with the last few lines of the speech.

As far back as I can remember, I have always been captivated by movies, and how they are made. My parents have told me that watching movies with me, as a toddler, was almost unbearable because every ten seconds I would shout,"How'd they do that?" This interest in movies became a hobby of mine when my friends and I began making movies with our video cameras. The first films we made in sixth grade were usually simple five-minute stories that were always blatant copies of our favorite movies. Looking back on the movies we made in middle school, I realize they really brought me closer to my friends. Being a part of something like filmmaking was a great way to exercise my creative side, and make and strengthen friendships. And so, after my junior year of high school, I decided to take the next step from video to film.

I thus began this past summer studying filmmaking at the New York Film Academy. I went into the program with a lot of anxiety. I hadn't had to make new friends since my first summer at Camp Equinunk when I was ten years old. The notion of not knowing anyone, wandering the halls alone, and eating lunch alone concerned me; it shouldn't have, but it did. I also felt that I knew little about the technical aspects of film. Outside of my close circle of friends and my love for pointing the camera at things we thought were funny or entertaining, I was really just a beginner at film making.

The learning process of filmmaking was tiring yet rewarding and I did begin to make friends when the teachers divided the class into groups of four. Within each group, each person would direct his or her own film and the other three were to serve as an Assistant Cameraman, Director of Photography, and a Gaffer in charge of lighting. We rotated responsibilities after each Director's film was completed. As each became Director, he would learn to appreciate his dependence on the other three crewmembers for cooperation.

Unfortunately, the atmosphere in my group of young filmmakers was fiercely competitive. This is not to say I haven't endured competition in my life, after all, attending my prep school for fourteen years taught me a thing or two about it. When my turn to direct my final film had come and gone, you can imagine how horrified I was when I got back the film cans at the beginning of the editing process and found one of two and a half rolls had been double exposed.

Despite having received some sympathy from others who were busy working on their own films, it was too late to re-shoot my movie and I was left to work with what I had. The only thing that mattered was getting my clear, existing shots together, edited, and ready for the premiere with the rest of the students' completed films. After many hours in the dark editing room, I emerged a new man with a new film, much different from my originally planned concept. The next day, much to my relief, the film was very well received at the premiere.

FIGURE 8-1:
An example of a chronological order essay.

© John Wiley & Sons, Inc.

Despite the headache, heartache, and backache of the process, I came out of that program having achieved exactly what I had set out to do, and made the absolute best of an unfortunate situation. I made new friends, a movie, and learned the basics of the filmmaking process, and most importantly, I had learned a life lesson as well. Corny as it sounds, I learned the true meaning of teamwork and trust, and without these two very important things I might have become even more lost, scared, and frustrated. I am acutely aware of these things now more than ever, and happily, I am eager to make my next film.

FIGURE 8-1:
(Continued)

TIP

Regardless of what you're recounting in interrupted chronological order, you must still interpret the event for the reader. Here's what happened, you're saying, and this is why it mattered to me.

Check out the structure of the essay about track in Figure 8-2. The student begins seconds before he launches into a race. He cuts to a description of being chosen as track captain the year before, explaining the strategies he used to become an effective leader and strengthen the athleticism and camaraderie of the group. Notice that the last paragraph explains how he uses these skills in other areas of his life, and why the discipline of track was significant to his development.

Survey

The *survey* structure resembles a mosaic, a picture created with tons of tiny, tinted tiles. (I was going to say "multicolored," but I was having too much fun stringing "t" words together.) In writing, you can create a mosaic by briefly describing a number of objects, people, or events, giving equal weight to each. A survey essay, like a mosaic on the wall, should create a larger picture out of the smaller elements. So be sure that your survey essay has a main idea that you communicate clearly to the reader.

REMEMBER

The survey structure is useful when you want to discuss something or someone you love passionately. (I am *not* suggesting that you write about your latest romantic partner, by the way. Bad idea.) Perhaps you're nuts about toucans, those birds with the flashy orange beaks. You write an essay filled with lots of little toucan moments — the first meeting of the Toucans Lovers Society, which you founded; the way your pet Tookie used to sit on your lap while you watched cartoons; the Saturday morning walks in the park with Tookie; the time Tookie ate Grandma's ear; and so forth. The main idea is your devotion to a misunderstood but loveable animal.

"We're up, guys." The stadium is filled with a sea of spectators sporting shades of red. The coarse, hard rubber imprints on my fingertips as I get into the blocks. I can smell smoke from the starting gun. My mind is calm; my teammates are ready. On your mark. Get set. Go! Toe drag and arm drive. Adrenaline courses through me as I push off the block. Short, fast-paced steps turn into long strides. There is no stopping now. I cannot lift my head up until I am ten meters out. There is no thinking; there is only flow. Stress leads to tense muscles, which decreases energy in parts of the body that will slow me down. I close in on my teammate and yell, "Stick!" I hand off the baton and cheer as he takes off. Before I know it, our last leg for the 4x100 crosses the finish line in first place.

On the first day of track practice junior year, my coach announced, "Raboy, you're leading stretches this year; you're the captain." Speechless, I managed to remember enough of the stretches from last year to muster my way through. I had never created an exercise plan for others. I did not know what to expect, but everyone was counting on me. After a couple of days of my new exercise program, I noticed that my teammates were nervous, too. I opened up lines of communication and built trust by asking if certain exercises were effectively warming them up. I relaxed, cracked jokes and made sure everyone felt comfortable speaking freely. I also offered workout programs and shared my own healthy eating routines, such as oatmeal in the morning or avoiding processed junk food before exercising. I believed that if my teammates were encouraged to join me in focusing on self-improvement, they would perform better during practice.

The communication led to growth in ways I never would have imagined. Practice went from jogging amongst strangers to racing amongst brothers making each other better. The competition aspect of practice dramatically increased our speed, so much so that during time trials, I broke the 60-meter dash record for my school with a time of 7.24 seconds, and two of my teammates broke the 300-meter dash by a second. I learned the power of patience while helping the underclassmen with block starts and form correction.

Racing is about more than just guessing where your block pedal length is and running. It's measuring one step from the starting line away from the full starting block, two steps for the first pedal, and about three steps for the second pedal with the ball of the foot propped up. Precision is everything. I helped each runner with minute changes in block and pedal distances, pedal height, block posture, shoulders position over hands, and relaxing muscles in the blocks. It's hard to do something uncomfortable: as one of the runners put it, "This really hurts my fingers!" But after seeing the time decreasing and their techniques improve, they became less skeptical and much more motivated to learn the incremental changes in form.

FIGURE 8-2:
An example of an interrupted chronological order essay.

Figure 8-3 is a fine survey essay on photography. The main idea is that this is the writer's obsession, the combination of being attracted to both the very precise and the creative. But how cleverly she gets her point across!

It takes a true genius to turn an obsession into something memorable. The famous mathematician Euler turned the Basel Problem, an infinite series that tortured mathematicians for years, into something incredible and succinct: pi-squared over six. However, obsessions can also lead to insanity. Another mathematician, Gödels, spent decades preoccupied with infinity and incompleteness. His every waking thought was consumed by a concept so grand that the human brain cannot comprehend its complexity. He eventually went mad, refused to eat, and died of malnutrition — hardly a path to emulate.

In all honesty, I, too, am driven by my obsessions. I lose all sense of time when I am behind a camera. I willingly sacrifice the most precious thing in human existence — time — for the perfect shot. I have an insatiable urge for perfection; I am obsessed with capturing the moments in which joy, bliss, and fear cross my subjects' faces. This can take days or even weeks to accomplish. I'll play around with an algorithm I developed that intertwines ISO, aperture, and shutter speed depending on the lighting and location. I'll make subjects come in day after day until I am satisfied. Though there is little variation from photograph to photograph to someone who does not spend precious nights contemplating a 2.8 versus a 3.2 aperture for a black and white portrait, the difference, to me, is dramatic.

Photography combines my love of numbers and creative nature. The visual and tactile aspects, in combination with the computations necessary to capture a photo worth sharing, is a perfect mix of my favorite activities. I love thinking through not only the 2 numbers, but also the composure and layout of photography. The intellectual stimulation needed to take a great photo fires both my right and left brain, which is invigorating and satisfying, but also mildly infuriating. I could spend hours worrying over the minor imperfection in yesterday's work, only to realize it's 2 am and I have yet to eat dinner — hardly a sustainable way to live in high school.

Annoyingly, photography is an art form not easily taught, let alone perfected. Each individual approaches it in his or her own way. I can study every Magnum Photos cooperative legends, every Henry Carroll "Read This If You Want to Take Great Photographs" book, and every Pulitzer prize winning photograph in the Newseum, and end up more confused than when I began. I am often left, however, with a more secure sense of where I want to go with my photography in the future. The countless hours I have spent hunched over every book in the photography section of my public library allow me to admire the works of those who came before me, but also push me to follow my own path. They teach me that the days I sacrifice to do what I love are not lost to time, but saved from boredom.

My photographs are as close to perfect as I can get them, at least in my eyes. However, perfection varies according to the artist. Some prefer a lighter, more airy composition of whites and pastels. The great Irving Penn shot only in black and white, primarily fashion shots. More often than not, I shoot low f-stop with a high shutter — the result is single millisecond captured in time - the flap of a hummingbird's wings, or the smile on Usain Bolt's face during an Olympic race. Apprenticeship yields education, but also individualism. I can approach a subject just like Irving Penn, and never come close to his genius. But genius is created in many ways. So I will continue to obsess over what I love, until I find my pi-squared over six.

FIGURE 8-3:
An example of a survey essay.

Figure 8-4 is a different sort of survey essay, a hybrid of survey and chronological order. I include it here because the main point is a set of small events, not the order in which they occurred. The writer, who is extremely interested in Asian studies, talks about a summer in Japan. He briefly cites several experiences of that summer, showing their impact on his view of the world. Notice how the writer builds a picture of his evolution to an international point of view.

In the summer of 2001 I found myself living halfway around the world. I was finally in Japan. My first challenge was to adapt to another culture. Although this culture was not entirely new to me because of my prior studies and a previous visit in March of the same year, I was visiting it on different terms. My first trip was a nine-day trip in March as a tourist visiting Odaiba, Kyoto, and Yokohama. This time I was in Japan, living in West Tokyo, to experience life in another culture.

I was first exposed to Japanese language and culture in elementary school when a friend introduced me to Animé (Japanese Animation). I fell in love with the culture and language. Now, with years of continued interest and study, I have had invaluable life experiences that I will never forget and which will be there for me to build on.

During the first two weeks I was granted permission to attend a traditional Japanese school. As a native English speaking person, I took on the role of resident English specialist. I spent most periods helping students with pronunciation of English vocabulary. During classes I participated in discussions of American history, government, and current affairs.

Living with my host family, I realized that I had always taken for granted the amount of living space I had to myself. My host family's apartment was comfortable, but it was only about one and a half times the size of my bedroom at home. Suddenly I realized how attached I had been to materialism; bigger and more of something is not always better. My attempts in making Tokyo my own included several trips to Akiharbara — the consumer electronics district — and a personal introduction to the Vice Governor of Tokyo. Going into the city allowed me to meet people who had the same interests in things that I did: the advancement of technology. When I met the Vice Governor I felt like I had a personal welcome extended to me by a high ranking official who in most situations would probably not notice me, but being declared as an ambassador to Japan by the Mitsui Corporations, my visit meant all the difference.

Near the end of my visit my host brother took me to his friend's house on Oshima Island. Our stay was scheduled for five days but was cut short because of an oncoming typhoon. Having only experienced snow and thunderstorms the idea of a typhoon was more than overwhelming. Nevertheless on the last day before our return to Tokyo we climbed Mt. Mihara, a currently inactive volcano. Climbing a volcano was enough to make me nervous, and with a typhoon coming, I was on edge.

While ascending to the its summit, I expected to look outward from the volcano's peak and witness a beautiful view of this island and the its surrounding waters.

FIGURE 8-4:
An example essay that uses survey and chronological order.

However I had not expected was that I would also look inward and see myself from a new perspective. On Mt. Mihara, the importance of setting goals became critically clear to me. With this realization I became conscious that I had accomplished one of my first major goals in life. I had actually lived in Japan. I was not in Japan merely by chance. Although I received a lot of support, I worked very hard. Having accomplished one goal, I realized I could accomplish bigger and better ones. I felt tiny on top of this island with a population of less than 10,000, looking out at water. Although I felt small in a large world, I realized I could do more than I had previously imagined.

In preparation for college, I began to create new goals, such as maintaining good peer relationships and participating in extra curricular activities. But most importantly, I hoped to find a school that would help my growth and maturation within Japanese language and culture. Looking inward atop Mt. Mihara, I came to know that if I have clear goals and work hard, I can clarify my own vision and direct the path of my life.

Description and interpretation

What can you describe? Things, places, events, people, ideas . . . just about anything! And after you describe something, you can interpret its meaning by showing how it is relevant to your life. This sort of structure provides a strong base for essays about people or events that have influenced you, qualities that define your personality (describe the quality and then show how it plays out in your day-to-day life), values you cherish, and lots of other topics. This structure is very adaptable!

REMEMBER

When writing an essay with a description-and-interpretation structure, take pains with the description. Tuck in lots of sensory details — the sights, sounds, smells, feel, and (if appropriate) taste. Don't stint on the interpretation section either. Allow yourself to grow a bit philosophical, speculating on the meaning — to you and to the larger world — of what you've described. In other words, show, don't tell. Chapter 9 describes the idea of showing, not telling in greater detail.

Figure 8-5 is a terrific description-and-interpretation essay on the candy drawer, a staple of the yearbook committee at the writer's high school. The writer doesn't simply mention the candy drawer or use it as an opening anecdote; she uses it as a running theme throughout the essay. The candy drawer keeps the essay playful, at the same time as it provides useful imagery. The writer manages to showcase important lessons she learned about leadership, too — which is why at the end of the piece, the candy drawer is back to a well-stocked 99 percent!

100% filled. Traditionally, the yearbook editors fill a drawer with candy at the beginning of every school year. This year, as Editor-in-Chief, it was my turn to fill the drawer. Packed with Kit Kats and packs of microwavable popcorn, the stocked drawer means yearbook is ready to begin. I had already begun to pick everything from our color scheme down to the font of our folio. From the start, we feel as organized as our candy drawer.

75%. In the first month, my Co-Editor and I are already divided. My partner wants a school mascot illustration on our cover, and I advocate for anything but the overused visual of a panther. Since the cover causes the class to miss two deadlines, I propose a class vote. Although the editorial staff ultimately decides against the panther, I realize that I need to guide the class better.

50%. The smell of buttery popcorn that fills the hall during 5th period makes students believe that Yearbook class is an easy "A." They begin to leave class without completing their work, and while it is uncomfortable to give B to my peers who "go to the bathroom" for thirty minutes, my Co-Editor and I implement individual deadlines. Each week, students are given a few tasks to complete. After we assign accurate grades, the belief in an automatic "A" is debunked. The stricter grading system allows the class to complete another deadline and we throw a doughnut party to celebrate.

10%. More problems arise. The activity section heads, Emily and Kayla, who are responsible for thirty pages, cannot work together without complaining. Kayla whines that Emily designs pages without her input and Emily believes that Kayla never comes ready to work. Pages are incomplete and their section is as empty as our candy drawer.

99%. I have restocked the drawer and found a better system to ensure the class meets all deadlines. After assigning Kayla a laptop to bring home, she and Emily are able to work amicably together. We meet our first major deadline and our class waits excitedly for our proofs to arrive. Not only are doughnut parties and individual deadlines effective in motivating and managing a class towards one goal, but they also teach me that the candy drawer must remain stocked at all times.

FIGURE 8-5:
An example of a description-and-interpretation essay.

© John Wiley & Sons, Inc.

Cause and effect

Cause-and-effect college essays fall into two categories:

» Here's what happened, and here's what I did about it.

» Here's what happened, and here's what it did to me.

In each of these basic cause-and-effect scenarios, the "it" is a *situation* or *event*, also known as a *cause.* The effect is your reaction to that cause. You may build a fine cause-and-effect essay to answer several application questions, including "discuss an accomplishment, event, or realization that sparked a period of growth and a new understanding of yourself or others" (Common Application Prompt 5) or "recount a time when you faced a challenge, setback, or failure" (Common Application Prompt 2).

For an example of this type of essay, consider Figure 8-6. The student describes how her mother's requirement that she sign up for a high school sport became the impetus not only for developing athletic prowess, but also for discovering a new community of friends. The "cause" is described in detail and with humor (here, being honest about her resistance to sports only makes the effect — falling in love with cross country — all the more surprising). The "effect" is made clear through the details of her achievements and winning the coveted Coach's Award.

Growing up with a practically Olympic-level family, as a pudgy grade schooler I was shockingly unathletic. Whatever the sport, I could count on a spot on the B-Team and a trusty position on the bench. I told myself I would deal with this embarrassment until high school, and then I would be free to roam as a sport-less woman.

That is, until freshman year when, despite my protests, my mother required me to try out for ONE activity. She rattled a list of possible sports off a list while I grimaced and eliminated them all: "No…. Geez, no… Do I look like a field hockey girl to you?" Finally, my wary eyes circled in on Cross Country. Its "No Cut" policy suggested that failure was impossible, but I had no idea how wrong I was. On the first day of training, which included a three-mile run that the experienced girls could do in their sleep, I was barely able to shuffle my feet at a turtle's pace. Cross Country, it turned out, was like every other sport.

Though I continued to jog, rather than dash, around the track, countless drills and the decision to "just keep showing up" began to transform me into a person I didn't recognize. I managed to cut my 9:30 mile by three minutes. Mid-afternoon runs with my teammates became events I happily anticipated, the stitches in my side transformed into shortness of breath from laughter. My mindset shifted from viewing Cross Country as a backup sport to a community that consumed my life in the best possible way.

My mouth dropped open when my coach announced that I was awarded the near-sacred Coach's Award, an honor usually reserved for those with natural talent. After winning the shiny plaque, I have begun to approach my life differently. I applied my newfound determination to my hectic job at a cheesecake bakery and even returned to my previously abandoned sewing classes. Instead of being known as the family Couch Potato, determination has transformed into my dominant quality. I am now a person with abundant possibilities just waiting for me to say "yes."

FIGURE 8-6: An example of a cause and effect essay.

Structuring Your Meaning

You have all the structures from the preceding section plus a few more on a shelf in your mind, ready and waiting to be plucked from the shadows and established as the base for you to organize your thoughts. But take care; the right choice gets your point across forcefully, and the wrong choice weakens your material and confuses your reader.

The following sections examine how different structures can work for your essay depending on how you frame it and offer suggestions to help you make the final selection for your essay.

Understanding how different structures can work for your essay

Perhaps you have a topic in mind, but aren't sure of what structure would ultimately work best to convey your meaning. Here, I explain how various structures can be applied to your chosen topic and how to determine which approach is the best fit.

Suppose you're writing about a time you questioned or challenged a belief or idea, one of the essay questions on the Common Application. (As I discuss in Chapter 1, the Common Application, as its name implies, is a single form accepted by nearly 950 universities.) Consider this example of a possible topic for this prompt and the structures you use can vary, depending on how you choose to address the prompt.

You once held a viewpoint that was pretty pessimistic. You believed that people were inherently selfish. You argued vehemently in English class that *Lord of the Flies* is a completely accurate reflection of society's baser instincts — and that times of crisis reveal the worst in people instead of the best. Then you volunteered to distribute meals at a food bank during the COVID-19 pandemic, where you saw cooperation, organization, and generosity during one of the scariest moments in recent history. Though hundreds of people were waiting to be served, they respected the six-foot distance requirement, remained patient, kept their masks on, and didn't take more food than they were allotted. You even saw your own behavior: You (and the other volunteers) were willing to risk your own health, to an extent, by leaving your home during lockdown in order to help your community. After such an experience you'd have to question your conviction about selfishness, right? But how do you write about that process of reevaluating your thoughts in a coherent fashion?

Here are just a few of the structures available for your essay:

>> **Chronological order:** In strict chronological order, you start with your former belief that people are selfish (with examples from English class and wherever else you believe you gathered that idea from). You then introduce the pandemic, how you were moved to volunteer, and finally, how what you saw at the food bank led you to reexamine your belief. You might end with specifying your new view about human nature, something that shows your critical thinking skills and isn't black-and-white.

>> **Interrupted chronological order:** You begin with a vivid description showing up at the food pantry, expecting chaos. You give as many details as you can of what you actually saw and how impressed you were with how people conducted themselves. Halfway through the essay, you flash back to the English class debate — to the moment when you'd have bet your college savings on the fact that society's basic instincts are selfish and animalistic. End the essay with a critical examination of how you modified your beliefs and bring your reader up to speed on how you continued to volunteer at the food pantry for an entire year.

>> **Compare and contrast:** You first present the evidence for your belief in human selfishness. You plunge into how you arrived at that conclusion, with real examples. Next, you share and compare evidence from recent years where you began to notice (small or grandiose) gestures of generosity and kindness. Finally, you explain how you've reconciled this seemingly contradictory information, and what it means to you in your own life.

I could go on, but I think you can see the point already. Each of the essays I describe in the previous list has the same general topic and much of the same information. But each is likely to have a different effect on the reader. The first two structures are a stronger fit than the third, which is likelier to come across as more of an academic exercise than a personal statement.

The chronological order essay could work, although I have a preference for interrupted chronological order because it tends to be more interesting (interrupted chronological order also tends to offer the strongest essay structure for many, if not most, topics). Because it's a more recent and vivid lead (a *lead* is an opening line or anecdote designed to draw in your reader; see Chapter 10 for more about them), starting at the food pantry is likely to intrigue your reader more than starting with your younger self in English class, but the English class moment makes for a good flashback after the food pantry and showcases how you engaged with an experience that didn't compute with your previous beliefs.

Selecting the structure for your essay

So, when you do have an idea of the aim of your essay, how do you choose the correct structure? Keep these guidelines in mind:

>> **The essay should be focused on one main idea.** Before you choose a structure, be sure that you can identify that point. For example, in the food pantry essay in the previous section, your main idea is "I found myself defying my own beliefs and witnessing profound examples of human selflessness, which made me look differently at those around me." After you make that statement, starting at the food pantry before recalling your previous beliefs seems only natural.

>> **The essay should emphasize your main idea, not bury it in yards of ruminating detail.** That's why the best structure for most college admission essays is either interrupted chronological order or chronological order; you should anchor your ideas in *story*, rather than getting lost down a rabbit hole of analysis.

>> **The structure should reflect the way you want the reader to think about your material.** If you want the reader to travel through an experience with you (which is what you do want most of the time), select chronological order or interrupted chronological order. If you're writing a supplemental essay that is more intellectual in nature, you might go another route. If you're feeling creative and bold, you can consider the survey structure.

>> **The structure you choose should give a prominent position to the "why" portion of the essay, as in "why I feel strongly about this topic" or "why this topic matters to me."** Readers do tend to pay more attention at the beginning or the end of a piece of writing, so typically the beginning of an essay should offer details that may not be thoroughly explored until the *end* of the essay, where you'll feature your best insight. Make sure that no one who reads your work will find themselves asking, "So what?" The answer to that question — or why the information you included is meaningful and significant to you in your life and development — should be totally clear.

TIP

You don't need to impose a structure on your essay before you begin writing. Rather, look at your *freewrite* — your stream-of-consciousness writing where you say everything you could possibly want to say about your chosen topic (refer to Chapter 5 for more about freewriting) — and then consider structure when you're trying to turn that mess of details, observations, and information into a more formal draft.

Most of my students don't say to themselves, "I'm going to write about X, and I'll be using interrupted chronological order as my chosen structure." The rearranging and reworking into a coherent structure comes after you've done some messy early writing and begun to figure out what it is you want your essay to convey.

Embracing Uncertainty

When you're thinking about structure, you can easily envision that your essay has to end with clear answers or believe that you have to know exactly who you are and who you're going to be for the rest of your life by the end of 650 words. After all, you do want your readers, the admissions committee, to see how you've grown or matured. However, often the admission of what you *don't* yet know is just as impressive.

More than likely you're writing about an experience that is either ongoing or fairly recent. Admitting what you don't know — because no one knows everything (not even your Uncle Paul, though he'll forever insist he does) — is a sign of maturity and higher-order thinking. You don't have to tie your essay up with a bow at the end and claim to have arrived at all the answers. In fact, an essay that reads that way sounds a tad fishy. After all, most adults still see themselves as works-in-progress.

TIP

In order to successfully wrap up your essay, while also leaving room for ambiguity, acknowledge the gray areas. Maybe your personal statement focuses on overcoming an internal obstacle, such as your near-debilitating level of shyness as a kid — which mystified your hyper-extroverted parents. By the end of the essay, you're under *no* obligation to say that you're now head cheerleader and school president, and by the way, you're teaching a class on the psychological origins of social anxiety because you've totally figured it out. Instead, maybe your progress looks pretty modest (forming a supportive group of friends after joining the soccer team), so that's what you touch on. Maybe you've arrived at a level of self-acceptance that transcends the need for answers, so that you no longer ask yourself, "Why am I like this?" and instead focus on one small challenge at a time.

Here's the kicker: You can (and should) also acknowledge the work that still remains — what you're still wrestling with or where you notice an old challenge flaring back up again. For the sake of the essay on shyness, you may include a line toward the end like the following:

> I still have to remind myself to make eye contact and unclench my fists when I'm talking in front of more than one person. But this past Monday, I signed up to give the first presentation in Spanish class — something I once would have lost sleep over.

Using Structure to Explain Your Interest in your Major

More than likely you'll probably have a supplemental essay (a specific essay question from only one college) that asks you to answer a question that is far more direct or pointed than the open-ended personal statement prompts. Often, this question asks you about your academic interests and how you plan to pursue them at a given university or how you came to choose the major or field you hope to pursue. Many graduate schools also question why you want to enter a particular field. The following sections gives you the lowdown on structure for these types of supplemental essays. Chapter 17 provides more details about supplemental essays.

Pursuing your interests in college

Supplemental essays may ask you about what interests you plan to pursue in college. Here are some structures for this sort of essay:

>> **Survey:** Review several different factors that appeal to you about a given department or program. Then, explain how the combination of those factors are suited to your strengths and explain how you hope to apply yourself as a student there.

>> **Chronological order:** Perhaps start with a campus tour, if you've had the opportunity to take one, or another moment where you had an epiphany about the type of degree you want to pursue. Then, explain the follow-up research and interest you've taken in the school, all of which have contributed to the vision of how you see yourself contributing to and thriving on this campus (which you explain toward the end).

>> **Description and interpretation:** Say you're a student who I call *exploratory*, meaning you haven't yet committed to a major and are applying under "Undecided." (By the way, that's not bad as long as you position yourself as interested in multiple things, not interested in nothing.) Describe how you see yourself in college, actively engaged in multiple interests and figuring out how you want to channel your energy in the future. Then, interpret by tying that vision to the university you're applying to and how that setting or community is the optimal place for you to explore.

Answering the question: Why this field?

Some universities may ask you why you're choosing the major or career path you've identified on your application. If so, here are some structures for this sort of essay:

>> **Chronological order:** Show that your interest in this field has been a long time coming by going as far back to solving Rubik's cubes as a kid (if your interest is STEM) or submitting a haiku to a poetry contest in second grade (if your interest is in creative writing). Then, work your way to the present, ending with confidence in both your choice of major and that the school you are applying to would offer the best program for you.

>> **Survey:** Explain all the factors that draw you to the career. Remember to offer supporting details for why these factors appeal to you — you must go beyond "I am interested in Marketing because I value collaboration" and explain why collaboration (and each other factor you identify) is important to you. How do you know you work well with others?

>> **Description and interpretation:** Describe an interaction you've had with the field you're choosing (it doesn't have to be an internship where you were working in the field, but could also include more informal interactions, like watching a parent at work) and then explain how this shapes your vision and goals for your future. For example, if you were plagued by a series of health crises as a child and now want to be a doctor, you can recount the doctor whose bedside manner meant the most to you as a patient and then connect that memory to your future goals.

IN THIS CHAPTER

» Discovering the importance of specifics

» Making use of all your senses to get the point across

» Knowing which details to keep and which to toss

» Choosing strong nouns and verbs

» Finding the perfect metaphor

Chapter **9**

Showing, Not Telling, Your Story

Years ago, before taking my husband to see *Les Misérables* for the first time on stage, I recounted the entire plot of the French Revolution saga. I told him the story while we were hiking one afternoon, and when we finally got tickets to see the musical I worried that I'd killed his opportunity for a fresh, spoiler-free experience. Oh, well, I thought, at least he can lose himself in the production instead of struggling with plot points, because he already knows them.

The day finally came when we took our seats at the theater and waited for the orchestra to begin. And to my amazement, my husband hardly let out his breath through the entire first act. Suffice to say that watching the action unfold was a much more vivid experience than listening to my plot summary. Watching the production *showed* the story and brought it to life; I had simply *told* it.

Because you're ready to write the rough draft of your essay, you need to keep this important difference in mind. If you present the written equivalent of a plot summary, your audience will give you their polite attention. They're dedicated workers, and that's what they're paid to do. But if you draw them into your reality, making them experience the sights and sounds and feelings you experienced, you'll get much more than their polite attention. They'll be with you, hanging on every word. And the message you're trying to convey will come across clearly.

In this chapter I explain the best writing techniques that allow you to *show*, not *tell*, as you write. I illustrate why specifics are better than generalities and display the power of sensory details. Throughout, I pick apart some sample paragraphs to point out what works and what doesn't. When you've mastered these techniques, you're well on the road to a great rough draft.

Getting Down to Specifics

How hard do you work?

(1) Very hard

(2) Somewhat hard

(3) Not hard at all

Whatever your answer, I've learned almost nothing about you, because those three categories are meaningless. They're just too general. What you define as "very hard" may be someone else's definition of "not hard at all." (You may have noticed this sort of discrepancy when discussing the homework issue with parents or teachers.) Try again. How hard do you work?

(1) I spend 19 hours a day glued to my books, and another two hours typing homework assignments on the computer. I've learned to sleep with my eyes open and my brain on "full speed ahead." About ten years ago I took a three-minute vacation, but that's about it for goofing-off time.

(2) Two hours a night during the week is enough for me to finish all my assignments, except of course for the long-range stuff like term papers and art projects. I study a little on Sunday afternoons when the rest of the family is bowling, but when I'm really pressed with work, I hit the books on Saturday too. Friday night is my time, and unless you're wearing a flak jacket, don't ask me to do anything but party.

(3) I get all my assignments done in one concentrated burst of effort, usually the last three minutes of the bus ride to school. I find that a minute or so of the interval between classes goes a long way; I can usually whip out a science lab or an English paper after I hit my locker and before the bell rings to start class. When I go home, I download a couple of tracks from the bands that interest me, send instant messages to my best buds, and call it a day.

Now your answer means something. I may not agree with your schoolwork schedule (especially if your answer is #1 or #3), but at least I understand your work habits. The details make the difference between a clueless and a clued-in reader.

When you're writing the admission essay — or anything else, for that matter — one rule is vitally important:

TIP

In general, avoid generalities. To be more specific: Be specific!

Thus, you're driving a Honda, not a car. You're eating chips and hummus, not a snack. You didn't experience an injury; you split your knee open and had to have 28 stitches. Got the idea? Here are a few short examples:

Bad, general statement: My mother had a huge influence on my life.

Better, specific statement: Because my mother super-glued a pencil to my hand, I became a fluent writer.

Another bad, general statement: I enjoyed the science experiment I did in the fourth grade.

The better, specific version: When I blindfolded my guinea pig Porkchop and put him on a leash (not an easy task, given the fact that the average guinea pig has no neck whatsoever), I sent him through 12 different mazes. He found the lettuce much more quickly when the proper route through the maze was rubbed with a lettuce leaf first. Doing this science experiment added to my determination to become a laboratory researcher. Plus, I bonded with Porkchop and had a great time.

One last bad general statement: In my future career I hope to work for world peace, an important aim.

The non-beauty-contestant version: The School of Diplomacy and Really Hard Foreign Languages will prepare me for a career with the Bureau of Incomprehensible Treaties. I hope to learn negotiating skills and apply them in such intractable conflicts as the smelly-cheese dispute that nearly derailed the formation of NATO.

Time to see the principle of specifics in a real admissions essay. (Also time to see the consequences of ignoring the principle of specifics in a clunker written by yours truly.) Suppose that you have to write about a school assignment. You want to show that you work extremely hard and that you love to learn. Figure 9-1 contains a too-general version.

When I took European history, I learned a lot about the politics and history of the continent. The teacher often gave us photocopied notes, which were very useful when it came time to write papers. We had to write many long papers, but the hardest thing we had to do was to present our information to the class. On presentation days we had to give out notes that we had prepared and discuss the material with the other students.

The assignments for that class were always hard; I have read a lot of difficult books in my other courses, but in this class we had to talk and write about what we were reading, not just listen to the teacher. When it was my turn to make a presentation, I was too busy to start early. I stayed up all night working on the material. When the class began, I distributed papers about my topic to the class. They read the papers as I explained my main points.

I did a lot of work not only because I care about my grades, but also because I wanted to learn about the topic. I wanted to impress the teacher and my classmates, and I did. The assignment turned out to be one of the best I have ever done because I learned more from it than from anything else I've ever done for school.

FIGURE 9-1:
An example of a very general essay.

What's wrong with the essay in Figure 9-1? Just about everything. Okay, it's not terrible, but it's so general that the reader doesn't learn much. The reader, lacking facts, has to take the writer's word for everything. For example, the essay states that "I have read a lot of difficult books in my other courses." What books? How does the reader know they're difficult? Are we talking Dr. Seuss here or Sigmund Freud in the original German? Without a title or two, the reader can only trust the writer.

Now check out Figure 9-2, a real student essay about a school assignment. The writer gets his point across — the fact that he works really hard and enjoys an intellectual challenge more than sleeping — in a very specific way.

Notice some of the details the author of this essay included the following:

>> Tolstoy's *War and Peace*

>> Wagner pulsating in the background

>> amber light

>> 1½ pots of tea

>> clock striking four

>> list of 20 most influential people

As the clock struck midnight I grinned. I had completed the Computer Science project, and the rudimentary Spanish, Russian, and Math assignments. It was time to progress to the night's confection: my European History treatise. The project had been assigned four days earlier, on Monday, but I had not yet begun. I had trimester finals throughout the week, and had just returned home from competing in the Ivy League Winter Track Championship. My body yearned for sleep, but I worked hard to overcome my desires. I put on the teakettle and dove into the assignment, for I did not want to disappoint my fellow members of the colloquium.

I was to prepare a presentation on Sir Isaiah Berlin's The Hedgehog and the Fox. After reading Tolstoy's War and Peace for Russian class, I thought it would be interesting to read what the esteemed twentieth century historian had to say about him, so I had volunteered for the task. I read his treatise, with Wagner pulsating in the background and an amber light shining on my desk. As I delved into the book, a surreal sensation emerged of feeling like a twenty-first century Machiavelli, indulging in my texts about the past.

Two hours and one and a half pots of tea later, I had completed Berlin's work. The key concept was that the hedgehog knows just one thing, but knows it well, whereas the fox knows many things but lacks a depth of knowledge. Tolstoy had depth and breadth to his knowledge, fitting both classifications. Plagued with fatigue and sloth, I created a simplistic one-page pamphlet explaining what Berlin had said and its implications.

As I wrote, the theme of hedgehogs and foxes reverberated in my mind, and I started classifying people accordingly. I went through our texts and categorized the major figures. Drifting away from the assignment and into the world of intellectual history, I saw everything through the eyes of Berlin. From the darkness, I heard the grandfather clock strike four, and had little documented work with two and a half hours until I would have to wake up.

Recalling the first day of class when we had discussed who we thought were the twenty most influential people in history, I decided it would be sensible to use this list as my groundwork. Time was a luxury I did not possess, so I used the one tool that could provide me with enough information to make an informed decision: the Internet. As a historian and a bibliophile, I am weary of using the Internet for historical research, but it was the only tenable option.

Once I had categorized the twenty giants and justified my classifications, the time had crept up to five-thirty, and I had built a raw five-page pamphlet for the class. The next thing I can remember was being awakened by my mother at six-thirty, alarmed that my head was face-down on my desk, Wagner was playing on repeat-mode on my computer, eight tea bags were strewn across my desk, and one hundred pieces of paper were resting on the printer's till.

FIGURE 9-2: An example of a show-not-tell essay.

> The colloquium was appreciative of my work, but could not grasp why I would spend most of my night working like a Trojan for a simple presentation. When asked, I could not really answer them. It surely was not to get the 'A' on the assignment as many of my colleagues had suspected. I think it was a mix of my love for academia, my desire to please the class, and the warm feeling I got inside whenever my teacher saw me in the halls and told me "Good work."

FIGURE 9-2:
(Continued)

>> five-page pamphlet

>> mother's waking him at 6:30

>> head face-down on desk

>> 8 tea bags

>> 100 pieces of paper

>> "Good work"

How much more alive is this student's essay than the general one. You're there in his room as he grapples with the material. You see the scene — the tiredness, the dedication, the assignment, his thought processes — because he gave you a wealth of detail.

WARNING

I love this essay, but I am *not* advocating all-nighters. Your health is more important than any grades or admission offer. Go to bed at a reasonable hour. Pour those details in your essays during the daytime.

TIP

Aim for specifics regardless of the subject matter of your essay. If you're writing about yourself, as in Figure 9-2, hit the details. Also hit the details if you're writing about another topic.

Check out Figure 9-3, another real student essay, which describes "an event or realization that sparked a period of personal growth and a new understanding of yourself or others" (Common Application prompt 5).

Now, a less seasoned writer — one unfamiliar with "show, not tell" — might have dried up after a few sentences: "My family and I adopted a dog when I was younger. He turned out to be completely bonkers, but he taught us a lot about patience . . .. What else should I say?" In fact, it took several hours of interviews, discussion, and annotating rough drafts with "tell me *more*" to produce the level of detail that exists in Figure 9-3.

From his beginning with us, it was clear that Kopper wasn't like most other dogs. He shuddered when touched, constantly dribbled when anxious, and was perpetually miserable. Because it was my incessant begging that had brought Kopper into our lives, it was clear I would have to take on the bulk of the work. For a newly-graduated third-grader, the idea of caring for an entirely different being was daunting, but I convinced myself that the dog would be perfectly agreeable.

Although my family was subjected to countless warnings of Kopper's strange oddities, we unabashedly accepted him as part of our clan, never once thinking of exchanging him for another dog. His addition provided my family with a priceless anchor to the US, as he played a significant role in growing our roots in America despite feeling incomplete without our Irish relatives. Often, I felt lonely when seeing other kids bond with their American cousins. Kopper (and the responsibilities of his care) filled a missing piece to help complete our life across the water. Even though adding a dog created another layer to my family's chaotic dynamic, Kopper's unique charms filled me with enough joy and determination to give puppy-parenting my best shot.

Beginning with supplementary pet-training classes, we desperately tried to bring Kopper out of his stone shell. But his persistent kid-repellent was a shock, as he proved basically untrainable aside from learning to sit whenever he cornered my brother or me for a bite of food. Of course, Kopper participated in typical puppy behaviors, such as teething, growling, and an unhealthy obsession with playing fetch. Kopper's condition, however, peaked as he aged with increasingly serious anxiety and panicking frenzies. With the addition of — as strange as it sounds — prescribed Prozac, Kopper began slowing down to enjoy his life, though he is still triggered by cars and encounters with strangers.

Unfamiliar with even human mental health, tackling our dog's diagnosis was a rich education for my family. As we grew together, he even helped me resolve my own personal anxieties and insomnia. A few years ago, a midnight home invasion left me dreading every nightfall. Sleep fell more and more beyond my grasp at the thought of another break-in. It wasn't until my parents moved Kopper from his pen downstairs and allowed him to sleep upstairs in my room that my qualms were soothed, as I knew he would bark if something was amiss in the house. His comfort helped me recover some of the sleep I'd been missing, and I grew increasingly appreciative of Kopper's protective temperament. We now call Kopper the "third child."

Raising a naturally difficult dog brought forth in me a higher emotional connection and loyalty. (I still shake my head, flummoxed by his strange behavior, but doesn't every parent feel that way?) My family never once considered Kopper a lost cause, and he even managed to open our eyes to the stigma around mental health, no matter the subject. Kopper's influence developed beyond childhood companionship and instead taught me to find hope in the darkness.

© John Wiley & Sons, Inc.

FIGURE 9-3: A second example of a show-not-tell essay.

Notice the wealth of detail the writer provides the following:

>> The precise mannerisms of her dog which proved untrainable ("bonkers" doesn't really tell you anything, but the sensory details of his dribbling do)

>> The hole in her family, being so far away from their Irish relatives, and how a pet also became an anchor to the United States

>> Specific efforts the family took to train him

>> What finally helped: a doggy dose of Prozac

>> What the writer learned from dog ownership: loyalty, responsibility, groundedness

>> How Kopper the dog actually helped the writer to overcome her own anxieties and understand mental health better

By the time you finish reading this essay, you know something about this writer's values, and you may even wish you could sit down to dinner with this family: they're so loyal. You're also completely sure that the writer is probably a better friend and more mature individual for having raised such a high-maintenance animal. The specifics carry the message loudly and clearly.

TIP

In Figure 9-3, notice that the writer begins on a relatively light note. By the end of the essay, she has gotten to a deeper level of vulnerability when commenting on her anxiety after an attempted robbery. The progression worked — members of the admissions committee no doubt appreciate cute and quirky anecdotes, but their job is to get to know *you*, and so you *must* go deeper than a funny or surprising event in your life in order to get to the substance. Make sure you're clear about how this event was influential or even defining to your character and growth.

Another important reason for including specifics has to do with the nature of college or graduate school admissions. The average admissions counselor has read *thousands* of essays. The literal truth is that you can make no general statement whatsoever that they haven't already read (or heard during interviews). You favor world peace? Think your family is great? Appreciate your friends, want to see justice done, had a great experience with community service projects? Terrific. Join the thundering hordes banging on the admissions door. They all share similar sentiments. *But* — and this is a really big *but* — their experiences and insights aren't identical to yours, because every human being is unique. Your life and ideas — in the details — is different from that of every other person. So if you want to stand out from the crowd, *be specific.*

Using All Your Senses

Every September I give each of my students a raisin and ask for a list of descriptive details. The average student lists five to ten words, such as "brown," "wrinkled," "small," and "sticky." By the time each student has read their list, I've usually got 20 items on the board. (Yes, you *can* say 20 different things about a raisin. Try it.) The normal breakdown is as follows:

Visual details: 16

All other senses, including touch, smell, taste, and sound: 4

Before you hit the ceiling, let me explain the category of sound. How does a little piece of fruit make any sounds at all? Easy. When you squish, chew, drop, or shake the raisin, it makes noise. Not a lot of noise, but some faint sounds. Now back to the analysis. You don't have to be an advanced math student to realize that the sense of sight dominates the list of sensory details. And this tally is the result of describing an edible topic, making taste and smell obvious choices. If I ask the class to describe a corner of the classroom, the percentage of visual detail is even higher. In fact, I may get nothing but visual detail for that sort of assignment.

I'm not anti-vision. But what a barren existence I would have if sight were my only sense. I'd miss out on the cool breezes of summer and the soft nap of velvet (sense of touch). I wouldn't be able to relax with my lilac bath oils or curl up my nose at the container of leftovers in the back of my refrigerator (sense of smell). If I relied only on sight, I'd lose the tang of orange juice and the savoriness of my favorite pesto sauce (sense of taste). And I'd be sorry to say good-bye to the clang of Levon Helm's drums on my favorite Band song. I'd even miss the screech of my two preschoolers fighting (sense of hearing).

The following sections take a closer look at how you can focus on the other four senses besides vision and ways you find out some more sensory details to your admission essay.

Using the four senses besides vision

These four senses — sound, smell, touch, and taste — as well as good old, tried-and-true vision, wake up your writing. You don't live in a one-dimensional world, and you shouldn't write as if you did. And unless you take special care to give all your senses a shot, sight will edge out everything else.

You may be asking, right about now, why sensory details are necessary at all in your college essays. After all, the university is admitting you because you're a good student, not because you can describe the smell of Thanksgiving dinner. True. But in the essay, you're trying to present a piece of your reality to the admissions committee. And reality comes to you through your senses. (Note the plural.) So to convey your reality, you have to use visual, auditory (that's sound, for those of you who haven't swallowed a vocabulary list recently), olfactory (smell), tactile (touch), and gustatory (taste) senses.

Sensory details are particularly important for the Common Application essay prompts, although you may use a storytelling anchor for one or more of your supplemental essays, too. (Chapters 2 and 3 help you unearth the best stuff from your memory bank.) And when you tell a story, you need sensory details because the sum total of those details created the experience for you.

Discovering sensory details

In Chapter 5 I describe three great methods that may be used to gather topic ideas as well as details — visual brainstorming, listing, and free-writing. Here's one more helpful technique just for details: Spend a few moments concentrating on the memory or the incident you've chosen for your essay. Then mentally load an imaginary video clip of the incident, close your eyes, press play, and start your sensory list:

1. **With your mind's eye, watch what happens.**

   Play the clip over and over again until you've got the visual details down cold. Make a list of all the visual details you might mention in your essay.

2. **Play the clip again, focusing on the sounds.**

   Note everything that people say. Write down the exact words. Then note the environmental sounds such as the growl of your empty belly, the plunk of the bingo chips on the board, the hum of the paint-stripping machinery, and so on. Make a sound list.

3. **Replay again.**

   What do you smell? Food smells will be obvious, but most scenes feature other scents too — chalk dust in a classroom, clouds of diesel fumes off the interstate, and so on. Make an odor list.

4. **Pretend that you can play your clip in a futuristic, touchy-feely theater.**

   (You're pretending to have a video clip, so you may as well go all the way to touch, which theaters probably will have some day, at which point I'll stop going to horror movies.) What feelings is your body receiving? (Not emotions, tactile impressions.) Is it warm or cold? Humid or dry? Breezy or calm? Is something rough or smooth touching your skin? What do you feel inside your body? Is your stomach clenching? Do you have little goose bumps on your arms? Make a touch list.

5. **Check out the clip for any taste details.**

   Taste isn't going to be in every story, although it's in more than dinner scenes. Perhaps you're describing a situation in which you were nervous. Did your mouth taste dry, stale, bitter? If any taste sensations are relevant, put them on your list.

TIP

As you list all these details, you may realize that the English language has very few words for taste and smell. You may find yourself writing, "The orange tasted and smelled like an orange." You're not going to win a Pulitzer Prize with sentences like that. If you can't think of a good way to describe the detail, consider a metaphor or simile, as in "the orange tasted like the first morning of my vacation in California." If you can't think of any interesting way to describe the orange, just say you ate the orange and leave it at that.

(For more tips on descriptive metaphors and similes, see the section, "A Little Metaphor Won't Kill You," later in this chapter.)

Choosing the Best Details and Ignoring the Rest

After you've got a ton of sensory detail (see the preceding section for more information on why you need sensory detail), you're faced with a problem. If you tuck all those specifics into the story you're telling, the essay will be 453 pages long. Because your word limit is considerably lower (and because you also have to do a few other things in addition to college admission essay writing — pass math, for example), you'll have to winnow the list. In this section I explain how to choose the best details and ignore the rest.

Here's a paragraph about one of my favorite colleagues:

Mr. B. taught in a room with three chalkboards, ten student desks, and a bunch of bookshelves. The room faced south and east and had two large windows. The teacher's desk was made of gray metal. The sides of his classroom were lined with decrepit couches the school's thrift shop couldn't sell. Almost no one sat in the student desks because they all wanted to crash on the rug (another thrift-shop discard). That's where Mr. B.'s dog Rosie slept while he was teaching irregular verbs and the poetry of William Butler Yeats.

The point is fairly obvious, I think. All the details in the preceding paragraph are true. Some details apply to almost any classroom in the world. Most classrooms have student and teacher desks, and a lot of those desks are gray. But a few details show how Mr. B.'s classroom was different from all others. How many times have you heard barking during grammar class? When you choose details for your essay, concentrate on those that are unique, that show the special or distinctive aspects of your topic. Don't bother stating the obvious. In the sample paragraph about Mr. B., dump the chalkboards, student desks, bookshelves, and maybe the windows and the teacher's desk and keep the rest.

Try this pop quiz. Which details would you include from this list of observations about the five-year-old child you taught how to swim over the summer?

Wore a frilly pink-and-white checkered bathing suit to every lesson

Felt inevitably slippery, because her mother always coated her in sunscreen right before lessons

Splashes water when she practices frog kicks

Squealed with joy the first time she swam to the pool wall by herself

Has brown hair

Says "thank you" after each lesson

You can probably make a case for most of those details, depending on the situation. The two most general statements — "has brown hair" and "says 'thank you' after each lesson" — are probably automatic discards, unless you happened to teach a bunch of other children who never thanked you. And in my swimming experience, most children splash water when they kick, so the most distinct details are likely to be the bathing suit, the squealing with joy, and the slipperiness of the child when you were supporting her in the pool. Those details are vivid and not completely predictable.

TIP

In the pre-writing, gathering detail stage (check out Chapter 5 for more information), don't try to decide whether you need a particular detail. Just make a note of it and keep thinking. Later, when you're writing the rough draft, you'll have time to judge its worthiness. Also, you're in a good spot if you have 50 details and you need to choose 10. If you have 10 and you need 10, you've got to go back to the brainstorming stage.

Selecting Strong Verbs and Nouns

This section is short on grammar and heavy on writing tips. I supply only two definitions, one for each section.

Verbs

Verbs are the words in the sentence that express action or state of being, as in the following:

> Carmeline swished the damp mop over Engelbrot's bald head. (*swished* = verb)
>
> Engelbrot has been upset ever since that incident. (*has been* = verb)

Now that the term is clear, here's my point: Verbs are the most important words in your vocabulary. You want the souped-up, strong-as-a-weightlifter verbs, not the boring, found-on-every-corner words. Check out this example:

> Tourmaline went to the gem store.

Ho hum. "Went." *There's* a great verb. Haven't seen that one since two whole seconds ago! Plus, "went" is so general that it tells me practically nothing, just that Tourmaline was somewhere other than the gem store, and now she's not. How about these alternatives?

> Tourmaline ambled to the gem store.
>
> Tourmaline strode to the gem store.
>
> Tourmaline slithered to the gem store.
>
> Tourmaline boogied to the gem store.

I don't know which of these sentences is right, because I don't know how Tourmaline in fact got to the gem store. For all I know, the best possible sentence is "Tourmaline drove to the gem store in her very own Lamborghini." But I can declare confidently that any of the alternate sentences is more specific than the original, and specific is good. General is bad. In general, that is.

Here's another example:

> Tourmaline said that she would go.

"Said," in all its variations ("says," "say," "will say," and so on) is the first runner-up of the All-Time Boring Verb Contest. (Who won? Keep reading.) You can get so much more mileage out of other words for verbal self-expression, such as these:

Tourmaline declared that she would go.

Tourmaline conceded that she would go.

Tourmaline whispered that she would go.

Tourmaline bellowed that she would go.

Now for the winners of the All-Time Boring Verb Contest. Yes, two verbs tie for the trophy: "be" and "have." Okay, I know you need these verbs. They play a part in tons of sentences and often can't be replaced. But sometimes you can dump them in favor of much more interesting choices. Compare these two passages, in which the verbs are italicized:

The chair *is* metal and *has* curved legs. The seat *is* wood, and so *is* the back, which *is* shaped to support the spine.

Three-feet tall metal legs *curve* up from the floor. The wooden seat and back *mirror* and *support* the spine.

The verbs in the second passage are more interesting. Also, you saved five words and said the same thing, a real plus in the admission essay, because you're working with a word limit and tired readers.

REMEMBER

As you work on the rough draft of your essay, pay special attention to the verbs. Think of the verbs as the tires on a truck that carry your meaning to the reader. Go for the best tires you can afford; in the verb world, best means most specific.

Nouns

Nouns are words that name persons, places, things, or ideas. Read this sentence:

Carmeline values cleanliness, so she rubbed polish on Engelbrot's bald head.
(*Carmeline, cleanliness, polish, Engelbrot's,* and *head* = nouns)

If you're a stickler for terminology, *Engelbrot's* is a possessive noun because it shows that a person — *Engelbrot* — possesses a bald head. (Actually, he's a real chrome dome. If he stands in the sunlight, the glare from his forehead alone will blind you.)

Nouns, like verbs (check out the preceding section on verbs) can be general or specific. As always in writing, go for the specific over the general. Compare these sentence pairs:

Berylium contemplated the flower as she switched on her computer.

Berylium contemplated the dahlia as she switched on her sleek black Chromebook.

Nasturtium patted her pet and sustained an injury because the animal was not in a good mood.

Nasturtium patted her pet python and sustained a puncture because the animal was not in a good mood.

Xanthium cooked dinner and fell victim to an illness.

Xanthium cooked Tuna-Strawberry Surprise and fell victim to botulism.

In each pair, the second sentence contains more specific nouns — "dahlia" instead of "flower," "Tuna–Strawberry Surprise" instead of "dinner," and so on. The second sentence packs more meaning into its words. The moral of the story, one more time: Go for the specific over the general!

Adjectives and adverbs

I know, I know. I said only two grammar terms in this section, and here I am using two more. Sorry. *Adjectives* and *adverbs* are descriptive words. They're great, and you can't express yourself in English without them.

However, when it comes to your college essay writing, I allow you one or two adjectives and adverbs per essay . . . at the maximum!

Why aim to eliminate entire categories of language? Because the presence of vivid details in your college admission writing usually renders the need for adjectives and adverbs obsolete. The ban on adjectives, in particular, goes hand in hand with your writing maxim, "Show, not tell."

For example, say that you write, "I'm an incredibly determined student and individual." (Determined, of course, would be your adjective.) Is that going to impress anybody? It sounds like a strong statement, but what it actually offers is very little, other than bringing you to the verge of sounding braggy.

Say you write instead, "When our advisor first gave me the role of attorney on our mock trial team, I was overwhelmed, but I made a point to strategize with every single member of our team so I would be prepared for the case. I was often the first one to arrive and the last one to leave our meetings. I even read chapters from a reference book on the history of real estate law, although most of it read like a foreign language." Now I see you as someone with determination, because you offered clear evidence, and these examples give me a more vivid picture of who you might be when you are met with future challenges, too. By giving effective examples of a particular trait in action, you ensure that you no longer need self-describing adjectives (in this case, the word "determined") altogether.

WARNING

When you're aiming for specifics, adjectives and adverbs are tempting; however, don't get lazy and try to beef up weak nouns and verbs by slathering them with descriptions, as in this sentence:

He walked slowly.

Simply choose a better verb:

He strolled.

A Little Metaphor Won't Kill You

Describing everything literally — with the actual facts — gets your point across. Unfortunately, the literal truth may bore your reader to tears (or giggles, depending upon how late they're reading your essay and how loopy they're feeling). Sometimes the best writing veers away from facts and into the realm of metaphors and similes.

Don't let those English teacher terms throw you. A *metaphor* is just a poetic comparison. "Happiness is a warm puppy," as the Peanuts comic strip declares, is a metaphor, as is "You are my sunshine." A *simile* is also a poetic comparison, this time with the words "like" or "as," as in "tough as nails" and (a look I hope to help you avoid when you receive your admissions decisions) "white as a sheet."

Metaphors and similes can really liven up your essays. I once read a piece about a young man's experience attending a religious service of another faith. The essay was meant to show how this event deepened his appreciation of the many traditions that constitute American life. In the essay he described a partition that separated the male and female worshippers. His description included exact measurements of this wall — length, width, and height. (I have always wondered how he knew. Did he creep in after the service with a tape measure or check the blueprints?) His exciting sentence read something like this:

> The wall is 5'11" high, 21½ feet long, and 2" thick.

Yawn. Next, he changed the sentence this way:

> The wall is just high enough so that men and women can't see each other.

Much better! The description now gives the purpose of the wall as well as a fair idea of its dimensions. Okay, you don't know how thick it is in version two, but do you really, really care about thickness? I don't think so. The final version hit the metaphorical level nicely:

> The wall is a boundary between the world of men and the world of women.

REMEMBER

Poetic descriptions are great, but don't overload the reader with your brilliant creations. A little poetry goes a long way, at least when you're writing an admission essay. I've read some essays that make me imagine a writer who declares, "I sat through three months of sonnets last year and I'm going to use that stuff if it kills me." If you have ten details, one might be a good candidate for a metaphor or a simile. Not nine! Take the essay in Figure 9-3 earlier in this chapter. Did you notice the last line about how she found "hope in the darkness"? You may not have even registered that as a metaphor. Such a line is subtle enough to make for a nicely poetic ending, without forcing you to think about the writer's literary prowess.

TIP

Metaphors and similes tend to catch the reader's attention because they change the pace of your writing. The reader is zipping along and suddenly stops to ponder the comparison. Milk the reader's reaction for all it's worth by placing the metaphor or simile at a pivotal point in the essay, a time when you want the reader to pay special attention. Such a point might be a detail that emphasizes the theme of your essay. (For more information on themes, see Chapter 2.)

WARNING

Lots of metaphors and similes express the most common human emotions and the most universal life experiences. Unfortunately, many of these comparisons have turned into clichés — overused, stale phrases such as "raining cats and dogs" and "as happy as a clam." (Does anyone know where that last one comes from? All the clams I've seen seem fairly neutral in their emotions.) Take care to avoid clichés in your essay. (For more about clichés, check out Chapter 7.)

Calibrating Expectations: "But 650 Words Is So Short!"

When I finally reveal the news — that your personal statement for the Common Application must be 650 or fewer words — students usually balk. "What? That's less than a page! And I'm supposed to include a vivid and detailed portrayal of who I really am?!"

If your reaction is similar, you're probably used to the moseying approach when figuring out what you're trying to say. With other types of writing — an academic paper, for example — you get about six sentences of a winding introduction before *finally* presenting your first meaningful sentence, which is your thesis. The rest of your paper may meander a bit, too, especially if you have a tendency toward flowery language (refer to Chapter 7 for more). In other words, you're used to writing with quite a bit of fluff, or unneeded filler material.

However, that strategy doesn't work for college application essays, at least not in your final draft. By the time you get to a finished product, *every single word* has to be there deliberately, because it does something to drive your essay forward, or else it gets cut. I've helped many students reduce their word counts from 2,000 words to 650 words in a single sitting, and often (actually, almost always!) the 650-word essay is *much better*. The finalized, shorter version of your essay will be dense, to be sure, with absolutely no fluff, which usually makes for much stronger writing. Plus, the details you leave in need to be the good ones, or they won't get your point across.

Figure 9-4 is an example of a well-written essay that is fewer than *400 words* (the writer wrote it for the University of California, which, unlike the Common Application structure of one main essay at 650 words, requires four essays of 350 words each). Still, after reading this response, you'll know *plenty* about this student's route toward exploring journalism, because she made every word count.

As you freewrite (like I discuss in Chapter 5), map out details, and figure out what you want your essay to say, you'll probably write something *much* longer than 650 words. In fact, you need to write freely, because later in your writing process you'll be glad that you did. During the revision process, you will likely cut around half of your essay as you differentiate between purposeful writing and fluff or filler sentences. If you've fixated on writing fewer than 650 words from the start, you may then find that with edits you don't have an essay yet at all — so write without limit. Cutting during revising is much easier than trying to come up with new content later. Lowering your word count is the easy part, and like I said, usually makes your writing better.

In elementary school I would write stories, compose songs, and report on robberies and murders I'd invented in faux newspaper articles. I consumed *The Boxcar Children* and *Anne of Green Gables* books as fast as I could carry them home from the library. In high school, I grew fascinated by the ways authors carefully chose their words. I wanted to be able to write the way that Toni Morrison did. I kept a running list of words to incorporate into my own writing and filled the walls with story ideas on Post-It notes.

I joined the school paper during my sophomore year to explore a new style of writing. I became a copy editor and then editor-in-chief, eager to increase our readership. Through the paper, I found opportunities to learn more about my city, interviewing candidates for city council and learning about the history of local places such as the grove of Eucalyptus lining our main street. I wrote about issues concerning the student body, even covering an instance of anti-Semitic vandalism that was eventually picked up by CNN. I learned how to interview teachers and administrators and ask direct, sometimes difficult questions. I was invigorated to see that my writing led to change, including the reopening of bathrooms closed by the administration as a response to misuse. Intimidated by the football field, I eventually learned the difference between the offense and defense as I covered the most important game of the year.

When I was denied a writing internship at our local newspaper, I took the opportunity to accept the alternative: a photography internship. The editor of the paper continued to read my writing, allowing me to work in the archives, and months later, I finally earned an official position. Now, I have a monthly column where I write about events in the community from a teenage perspective.

Journalism has been a pathway for me to learn about local politics, helping me develop my interest in advocacy and social justice. I hope to continue to use my voice on behalf of the causes that are important to me.

FIGURE 9-4:
An example of an effective essay in less than 400 words.

© *John Wiley & Sons, Inc.*

I revisit word count reductions at various points throughout the book, such as the Red Pen Exercise in Chapter 14, but that shouldn't be something holding you back in the drafting stage. When you're drafting, incorporate the spaghetti-at-the-wall strategy: Say everything and see what sticks. (How's that for a metaphor?)

IN THIS CHAPTER

» **Understanding the role of opening lines**

» **Grabbing the reader's attention**

» **Establishing the tone of the essay**

» **Directing the reader to your topic**

» **Side-stepping pitfalls in your lead**

Chapter **10**

Leading with Your Best Shot

Scroll, scroll, keep scrolling. You might scan a sentence of description there, then watch ten seconds of a trailer there. When you're trying to figure out what to watch, how much time do you give each option on your screen? Half a minute, maybe? Inevitably you don't like what you see, so you click to something else. Two seconds later, another decision. Interesting or boring? Stay or go? Or, do you just decide on an episode of your favorite TV show that you've already seen 12 times?

The readers of your college essays aren't quite as twitchy, and they know that they owe you a thorough review of your application, regardless of how compelling (or entertaining) they find your writing. However, they *are* human, and they're overworked. They'll give you a fair shake, but within the first paragraph of your personal statement, they could be reading with one of two attitudes: "Hmm, this looks interesting" or "Oh, man. Wake me when this one's over." Which attitude are you hoping for? I thought so. In this chapter I show you how to create a lead (the journalists' term for the opening sentences) that grabs your reader's attention. I also show you how the lead sets the stage by establishing the right tone and orienting the reader to the contents of the essay.

Taking the Right First Step: What the Lead Does for Your Essay

If you've had a chance to tour a college campus, you probably started off in the main quad. You'll know you're there because it's far and away the most scenic part of campus — the one the college or university features on its website and the one that lets you know, as you gaze around and take in your surroundings, that you're *here*. That main campus quad is the physical lead to the college experience (the equivalent to the first few sentences of your essay). A good essay lead (like entering a campus quad) does the following:

>> **It catches attention.** In addition to being beautiful and central, the quad is usually where you have the best visibility and access to wherever else you might be looking for on campus. Your essay lead should similarly make your reader feel intrigued and interested to know more.

>> **It sets a tone.** Whether the buildings are brick- and ivy-covered or modern and sleek, you'll know something about the school's reputation and how the community perceives it through the aesthetic. The lead to your essay also sets the stage for a specific mood or emotion to come through.

>> **It orients the reader.** When you enter the quad, you're basically at the starting point on your map. The opening lines of your essay should be vivid and specific enough that your reader can picture the moment and location in time, instead of wondering, "Huh? Who? What's happening?"

The following sections take a closer look at the lead of your college admission essay, including what it should accomplish and how.

Capturing the Reader's Attention

Your essay's lead pulls your reader in. Here are some ways you can do the same:

>> **An interesting comment or observation:** When I lived in New York City, I used to follow a blog where New Yorkers could submit comments or conversations overheard in the city. I was always guaranteed a laugh, just by reading a couple of sentences — and wished I could hear the rest of the conversation.

Of course, sometimes the comments that grab your attention in public settings are a bit too off-color or inappropriate for college admission essays. In this case, think more about how to intrigue your reader about the theme or experience your essay will focus on. Take the opening line from a student's essay about participating in a theatrical assembly on drunk driving: "As we brushed our teeth and washed our faces side by side, it occurred to me that my sister had no idea that the school administration had selected me to 'die' that afternoon." (The correct reaction to this is *What?*)

» **An interesting anecdote:** One thing that I miss about living in New York and San Francisco is taking extensive walks around an urban city. (Urban walks are much more interesting than suburban ones.) When I returned from one of my walks, I had plenty of stories to tell, including the following:

- My conversation with a man who had a giant snake around his neck

- An encounter with a French couple in matching outfits in search of the buffalo reserve

- A sand castle contest at Ocean Beach

» **An intriguing moment:** Once more into the city streets. Here are some only-in-the-city glimpses:

- Dancing. All kinds of dancing. Breakdancing, interpretive dancing, sponta- neous bursts of movement. Almost always, I want to know what music the dancer in question is listening to (if it's through headphones) and whether they're having a great day or trying to shake off a bad one.

- A tourist hopping over a fire hydrant. Was he practicing for the Olympics? Auditioning for a musical comedy with a street scene?

- An escape artist having himself buried alive in a city park. (Don't worry — he got out unscathed.) Why would anyone ever do something like that? And how much did they pay him?

» **Previews:** Sure, they annoy some people, but the chance to snatch a glimpse of movies you haven't seen yet is usually tempting. Feel free to jump to a highlight moment of the essay — the moment that you'll spend much of your essay reflecting on — you can tell the reader how you got there later. (Chapter 8 teaches you more about how to write out of chronological order.)

If these factors catch people's attention in real life, think what they'll do for your college admission essay. You don't need a city dweller's daily quotient of zaniness to create an interesting lead for your essay. Any topic, even those that seem to be the verbal equivalent of a sleeping pill, can be made interesting with the proper approach.

In the following sections I illustrate several techniques based loosely on the these four elements. Each super-glues the reader's mind to your essay.

Sharing an anecdote

If your essay is based on a story from your life (*a* story, not *the* story of your life — don't begin with your birthday unless you have an excellent reason to do so), you'll naturally begin with part of the event. Lead with the first thing that happened (chronological structure), or if you want, play around with time travel, a later part of the story (interrupted chronological order). For more information on structure, check out Chapter 8.

REMEMBER

Even if you're not primarily interpreting a memory in your essay, you can still insert a little story — an *anecdote* — into the lead. This technique is a favorite of after-dinner speakers for very good reason. If the anecdote is interesting, heads immediately rise from the apple pie to listen attentively. A good story or anecdote sends the crowd into five-year-old story time listening mode.

Regardless of whether the story makes up the bulk of your essay or only one paragraph, it should be interesting. Look for a small detail that brings your reader into the reality of the story. (Chapter 9 gives pointers on choosing details.) For example, suppose you're writing about how social you are. Check out these two sentences and my imagined reader responses:

> **Bad, boring detail:** I'm a social person. (Yawn.)

> **Better, interesting detail:** When Mr. Cook asked if anyone in our senior leadership class would be willing to speak to a family considering enrolling their daughter at our school, I felt several of my peers' eyes land on me followed shortly those of Mr. Cook. "Well," he said, "How about our unofficial mayor?"

REMEMBER

Apart from the interest factor, if you lead with an anecdote, you must also be sure that it relates closely to the ideas you're going to discuss in the essay. I still remember an essay that began with a story about two tigers, a plum, and a kid on a vine trying to escape. To this day I have no idea why the author inserted that particular anecdote into his essay, because the rest of the essay talked about the importance of relaxation in life. Maybe he was trying to say that you should eat the plum before the tigers do? Or that you're going to get eaten by a tiger anyway so you may as well relax and enjoy the time you have? I don't know the meaning of that story, but I do know that if a reasonably intelligent reader can't figure out your meaning, you're in trouble. Remember that your audience has no desire to reread your essay several times in an attempt to make sense of your anecdote.

Intriguing the reader

This sort of lead is the verbal equivalent of a quick glimpse of an unusual or mysterious sight. It's a bit risky, but it can be dynamite if you do it correctly. The lead sets the reader up with a question or a teasing statement. The body of the essay is the pay off — the answer to the question or the meaning of the "tease." Where's the risk? If the payoff is inadequate, the reader will feel let down. (Think of a knock-knock joke with no punch line.)

Take care to avoid clichéd questions such as the following:

What is the meaning of life?

Have you ever wondered about the meaning of life?

Why should you accept me? (A cliché peculiar to the college essay.)

How do I love thee? (Just kidding. This one comes from Elizabeth Barrett Browning, one of my favorite poets.)

The teasing statement doesn't have to be a question; it can be anything at all that relates to the topic of your essay. Here are a handful of examples:

I met Beethoven last week. (Essay about learning to appreciate music.)

No one ever has to tell me twice that I'm not wanted. (Essay about prejudice and discrimination.)

Most of the great mathematicians I know walk around in T-shirts, even during snowstorms. (Essay about becoming totally involved in one's work.)

Previewing the coming attractions

You've been to the movies, so you already know this technique: a swirl of images and brief moments of dialogue, designed to give you an idea of what the movie's about, ideally without spoiling so much of the plot that you feel as if you've seen everything. In the admission essay, a "preview of coming attractions" lead is a set of quick references to the subject matter, as in the following sentences:

I'm not sure how slippers arrived to Latin America. I like to imagine that someone, fed up with his mother's nagging to please quit walking around barefoot, decided enough was enough and introduced the slipper. (Essay goes on to describe a series of culturally relevant questions the writer has grappled with.)

While both of my parents worked, my brother and I spent much of our childhood under the care of a series of tap-dancing babysitters. (Essay about the influence of diverse caregivers.)

I've done three terrible things in my life and learned from all of them: I accidentally cut off all my sister's hair when she was a toddler, I stole a library book on purpose, and I slacked off when we studied genetic engineering. (The essay goes on to describe these three events, with the emphasis on the last one and the author's newfound seriousness about science.)

Previews work best if the material in the essay itself is interesting. If you've got only boring stuff to work with, who cares about coming attractions? Also, be careful to write a specific, not a general, lead. Nobody wants to read an essay that begins "I am conscientious, kind, and thoughtful." (Okay, maybe your mom does, but unless she's on the admissions committee, her interest isn't helpful. See Chapter 6 for tips on your parents' involvement in this process.) For the "conscientious, kind, and thoughtful" lead, substitute with a detail of *when* and *how* you put these traits into action — in other words, show, not tell, which I discuss more in Chapter 9.

Setting the Right Tone

At the *sound of the tone* . . . you hang up. But first you recognize a certain quality in the voice coming through the telephone. *Tone* is the English-teacher word for the mood that the voice reflects. Tone is created by several elements in your writing, including word choice, word order, and content. In the *For Dummies* series, for example, the tone is conversational, humorous, and informative, a little hip and sarcastic. In most of your schoolbooks, the tone is serious and informative, a little boring (sadly), and carefully neutral.

The tone of your lead should match the tone of the rest of the essay. The reader has the right to expect that whatever tone you began with will be the tone you continue with in the essay. One exception to this rule is a deliberate switch designed to surprise the reader — a tough-to-pull-off but extremely effective tactic.

TIP

The tone should also match the seriousness of the topic. If you're writing about the family members who were lost in the Holocaust, you can hardly begin with a humorous anecdote about dropping your suitcase on your toe as you checked into a hotel before your visit to the concentration camp site. Similarly, if you're writing about the time you failed a biology test, don't use a tone that signals a major world tragedy.

WARNING

If you choose a humorous tone, remember that humor is serious business — hard to write (unless you're Dave Chappelle) and tough to mix with factual information. Not that I'm ruling out humor. Humor can be great, but you want to be sure that what you include is universal humor (that is, content that your reader will find funny, *even if they weren't there*) and not simply individual humor (you simply cracking yourself up). But if you choose a humorous tone for your essay, run the finished product by a couple of trusted advice-givers. Ask them whether you hit the mark or fell on your nose. Chapter 6 offers advice as to how (and when) you should elicit feedback, and from whom.

Taking a Closer Look: Five Strong Openings

If you're still struggling to conceptualize how an opening anecdote might work, remember that you're trying to foreshadow the growth and/or conflict you're going to unpack throughout your essay. One way of generating moments (other than the exercises in Chapter 2 and 3) is to think of what character traits have most defined you and then brainstorm moments when you had to

» Make a decision

» Face a challenge

» Recognize an influence

» Put your best skills into practice

» Display your dominant qualities

Your openings may be a vivid description of you doing what you love, if that's what your essay is about, or what you do best. Here are a few examples:

Example 1: My hair is blue, black, and a little bit brown — kind of like the hair version of a bruise. I'm standing under fluorescent lights, a wooden cylinder in one hand and a piece of slimy latex in the other. Trembling, I think, "Why must I insist on putting myself into situations that involve public speaking?

That slimy latex refers to a condom. And the idea of a fairly shy, poetic-type student with bruised hair finding herself elaborating on safe sex in front of a group of her peers? It's pretty irresistible. What interesting territory!

Example 2: An eight-year-old boy looks up at me, visibly surprised by my effort to say "six feet apart" in Cantonese. It is April 2020 and my first week serving meals in Chinatown, organizing lines of hundreds of people. It has been weeks since I have seen this many people in one place, but hunger outweighs the risks of the virus.

This opening accomplishes two things worth noting:

- It shows you how a brief line of dialogue or visual detail can naturally weave your reader into a scene.

- It introduces *high stakes.* An anecdote where the stakes are high — that is, where there's a lot to lose — is often a surefire way to draw in your reader. With a unique angle and high stakes, no topic is off-limits or too ubiquitous to write about.

Example 3: The sound of Bob Dylan's Highway 61 Revisited plays quietly in the background as I sit at my desk. And it catches my eye. It's been in the corner of my vision this whole time, but I tell myself: just one more page of Calculus. The brazen progressions draw me closer. And as Dylan asks, "How does it feel?" I can't bear it anymore: just a ten-minute guitar break. I snatch up my Les Paul and vigorously run to turn the amp on.

This student did a great job revealing his obsession with music. I told him he had to write an essay without once using the words "love" or "passion" with regards to music — instead, he should "show, not tell" how much he loved it. When I asked for descriptive details, he commented, "Jam sessions take over me all the time." And then he wrote this opening.

Example 4: "I can order," I insist to Emmy. I approach the glass case, stick out two fingers, and timidly say, *"Cha siu bao."* The bakery clerk responds, "Two for $5" in English, but they look different. They are too small, and I do not know how to ask for larger, so instead I grab my wallet. As I start to pay, Emmy stops me and asks for one *cha siu bao*. The woman immediately reaches in the back and grabs one larger, normal-size bao. Although I grew up eating these barbecue pork buns, I realize I've been paying tourist prices because my kindergarten-level Cantonese skills could not convince her that I was a local Chinese girl.

This subtle moment of tension sets the stage well for an essay on the student's identity. The writer could have easily told the reader how she felt (using words like "self-conscious," "different," or "misunderstood"), but the anecdote effectively shows how the issue of identity arose in the writer's simple, day-to-day exchanges, like a stop at the bakery.

Example 5: Usually, the last thing I think about before nodding off to sleep is socks. I pick a pair in my head and then plan what I'll wear the next day around the selected pair.

This is one of my favorites: simple, yet so telling. Don't you just read that and think, I *have* to know who this girl is, the only teenager on the planet obsessed with socks? The essay turns out to be mostly about her identity as a Latina and how her obsession with socks was a true indication of her American-ness, but this lead is killer.

You might also notice that each of these leads grabs your attention by plunging you in the middle of a vivid narrative. Some writers don't work this way, to be sure. Example 5 isn't exactly a narrative moment, but it's a surefire way to pull in your reader.

Avoiding Common Pitfalls

Browse through this book and read the first couple of sentences of each student essay that are sprinkled throughout. Which leads appeal to you? Why? Your answers may not match mine. No problem. You should be trying to write a lead that matches your own personal taste. Remember, you're trying to sound like yourself in the essay, not like me. You're a unique individual, and your essay should reflect that fact.

WARNING

I can't tell you what's right for you. However, I can point out a few style elements that are *wrong* for you and everybody else. Avoid these pitfalls as you write your lead:

» **Don't announce.** A lot of teachers instruct their students to "announce" the main idea of a homework essay, as in this lead: "In this essay I will discuss my brother's senate campaign and my role in it." Sigh. I really hate this sort of opening paragraph, even in school assignments. In a college admission essay, it's deadly. Take this as a good general rule: Talk about the topic, not about the essay. Also, try for a little subtlety!

» **Don't address the reader directly.** I've seen a number of student essays that attempt to emulate the title character in Charlotte Bronte's *Jane Eyre*. Every chapter or so Jane speaks to "Dear Reader" or just "Reader." Okay, Bronte got away with it, but she was a genius. Don't begin your admission essay with "Dear Reader, please admit me," as one student did.

» **Don't go for shock value content.** Surprise is okay, but shock isn't. Don't lead off with gory or gross images. Actually, don't put gory or gross images anywhere in the essay. Stay away from profanity and bathroom humor. That may be your thing, but a college admission essay isn't the right audience.

» **Don't begin with a cliché.** Actually, don't end with a cliché either, and try not to put any in the middle of your essay. The admissions officers have read thousands of essays that begin with these or similar statements:

My friend _____ is always there for me.

Nothing is more important than my family (or education).

When I _____, I understood the purpose of life.

>> **Don't try to sound older than you are.** If you're applying for admission after a lifetime of learning, you may certainly declare that fact. But if adolescence is still a fairly sharp memory, stay away from blanket statements about your life as a whole. I once had to dig my fingernails into my palms to avoid laughing at a young man who told me, "I was born in New York, I've lived in New York my whole life, and I'll die in New York." He was ten years old at the time.

>> **Don't start with a dictionary definition or citations.** Stay away from starting your essay with something like, "Webster's Dictionary defines 'gratitude' as . . . ." Your job in your opening (and throughout your essay) is to be specific and personal, which should automatically preclude external citations. Quotes might be okay once in a while for an analytical paper or the opening of a speech, but for college admission essays, you should be the one articulating themes and ideas, not a famous person.

Parting with the Traditional Thesis

Your college admission essays don't need specific claims or arguments in specific locations. Instead, your writing usually involves a progression toward understanding that only reaches its crescendo at the end. Sometimes, this structure looks like a story, followed by reflection about that story and its meaning in your life. Sometimes the progression is more subtle. In any case, the last thing you want to do is plug in a little claim about yourself toward the beginning of your essay. (Chapter 8 offers a more thorough understanding of various possible essay structures.)

Imagine if you wrote a college admission essay like a history paper: "I realized that I found myself standing at the edge of the dock for political, economic, and social reasons which I'll now unpack." ICK! If you feel tempted to map out what's coming in some way or another, you may ask yourself: Am I dropping a hint in order to create a good lead (See the section, "Taking a Closer Look: Five Strong Openings," earlier in this chapter for examples) or am I simply giving my meaning away too early, like a bad movie trailer? If your answer is the latter, you may simply be having a hard time breaking the model of your academic papers.

REMEMBER

You may not know exactly what the takeaway is from your essay until you've written extensively about your topic. That's another reason why trying to write under the word limit is incredibly unhelpful. You have to write your way into figuring out what you're trying to say before you can eliminate the fluff. Because you don't know where you're headed until you get there, the ending of a college admission essay, and not the beginning, is often where you'll finally reveal your best insight. Chapter 12 discusses powerful endings. (*Hint:* They also don't require a thesis.)

Chapter **11**

Constructing Good Paragraphs

I f you've ever seen *Inglourious Basterds*, you know how well director Quentin Tarantino creates perfect paragraphs in his scenes. (If you haven't seen it or haven't seen it in a while, check out the film for some great examples of pacing that can help you as a writer.)

In one particular scene, Christoph Waltz, who portrays Hans Landa, a Nazi attempting to track down Jews hiding in Nazi-occupied France, arrives at the home of a French farmer whom he suspects is hiding a Jewish family. (It doesn't spoil anything to tell you that this family is right underneath the floorboards during this conversation.) Landa exchanges pleasantries with the farmer and then asks for a glass of milk. Guzzling the milk provides a perfect pause before Landa moves into a series of more pointed questions. At one particularly dramatic moment, he asks for more milk — another pause signaling a change in topic. If you transcribe the interview, the paragraph breaks are clearly marked by physical gestures that require a break in speech. New topic: more milk. Dramatic emphasis: farmer lights his pipe.

Tarantino seems to have a perfect sense of timing. No surprise there; after all, he's a famous film director. The progression of this scene demonstrates that he knows when to incorporate an effective pause and when to group related thoughts together.

As you craft, and eventually edit, your college essays, you too have to become the director that decides when your reader should take a pause. Even though this might seem like an arbitrary or unimportant decision, you'd be surprised what a difference a well-chosen paragraph break can do in terms of the progression of your overall essay. Paragraphs that begin and end at logical or suspenseful moments in your writing can, like Tarantino's pacing, mean the difference between a highly polished essay and one that feels out of control or all over the place — like an unedited movie.

This chapter explains the why, when, and how to place paragraph breaks in your essay.

Punctuating Your Points with Paragraphs

In the introduction to this chapter, I hint at the two most important reasons to create a paragraph break: logic and drama. Time for more detail on the Big Two.

REMEMBER

I describe logic and drama as two separate categories of paragraph breaks, but in practice they overlap. Dramatic paragraph breaks must occur at logical spots in your essay — moments when emphasis changes, the speaker or topic shifts, or a new stage in the story arrives.

Including some logic

Move this book out, slightly beyond the focus range of your eyes. What do you see? Clumps of gray print, also known as paragraphs. Even before you read a word, you have an idea how many ideas are contained in this chapter, just by estimating the number of paragraphs. In general, one important idea equals one paragraph.

Move the book back in and start to read. You see immediately that a paragraph break stops the flow of words, not greatly, as a new heading or a new chapter does, but briefly. If you're reading aloud or speaking, a paragraph break comes across as a short pause, longer than a quick breath at the end of a sentence or the even quicker breath of a comma.

REMEMBER

The paragraph break shows you that it's time for something new — another example, a change of story line, a shift in location or person, or a further link in a chain of thought. If you're writing the essay based on an outline, each new letter or number in the outline turns into a paragraph in your text.

Figure 11-1 shows an example of an outline for an essay about your desire to be your school's mascot.

FIGURE 11-1: An example outline for your essay.

© John Wiley & Sons, Inc.

Your essay will have at least one paragraph on the process of trying out for mascot (though there might be enough content there for two). The next paragraph(s) shift in both tone and pacing, describing the process of accepting and eventually embracing your new role as freshmen orientation leader.

Adding some drama

When I watch anything in the drama or mystery genres, I always know when a cliffhanger looms because the story has built to a dramatic moment. The detective gathers the suspects and declares, "The murderer is in this room. . . ." Of course, I lean forward in excitement, even though I know I can count on the credits cutting in right at that very moment, sometimes preceded by a teasing note: "To Be Continued . . ." If it's a movie that has to be wrapped up at the end, the same rule still applies, only instead of cliffhangers you'll notice the scene abruptly changing at an especially exciting beat. The break arrives at a dramatic moment because the pause heightens the tension. So too does this rule apply for essays.

Say you're writing an essay about how you faced a crisis of misunderstanding. You discuss your happy, pre-crisis life in the first paragraph. The second paragraph follows you into the principal's office, where she states, "I can't believe I'm saying this, but there's a problem with the history paper you turned in." The reader is all but drooling to read the next paragraph. Who can stop there? Yet before your revelation that the problem must have to do with James, whom you made the *very big mistake* of allowing access to your rough draft when he was having trouble with his own essay, you break to the next paragraph. End scene!

REMEMBER

Dramatic paragraph breaks work only if you insert them sparingly. If every paragraph ends on a high note, the effect is lost. With too frequent use, dramatic paragraph breaks turn ho hum. The reader gets to the big moment, sighs, and thinks, "Here we go again." Not the reaction you're hoping for! So think of this paragraphing technique as a chili pepper. For the Tex-Mex deprived, chili peppers are very spicy — good for an occasional intense sensation, but not acceptable in big bunches.

TIP

The most dramatic technique — and here I'm talking once per essay, if at all, because this technique definitely isn't for frequent use — is the one-sentence paragraph. The shortness of the paragraph grabs the reader by the throat and says, "Look at me!" Hence you should place this kind of paragraph break only at a truly crucial point in the essay.

I once read an essay in which a veteran soldier describes some of the terrible things he saw in battle. Near the end of his account he writes of his postwar years, during which he has turned to religious texts for help in understanding the meaning of his experience. One paragraph ends with his statement that the meaning must be in the holy book somewhere. The next paragraph, in its entirety, is "I can't find it." The essay goes on in subsequent paragraphs to describe his work with various veterans' groups. Wow! That one-sentence paragraph blew me away. My eye went back to it over and over again. Also, that tiny paragraph summed up the theme of the essay — the search for meaning in the context of war.

Creating a Strong Scope Sentence

One way to check the logic of your paragraph breaks is to identify the main idea of each paragraph. The main idea is generally expressed in a single sentence, which your English teachers call the *topic sentence.* Because most students associate topic sentences with the first sentence of each paragraph, I refer to them as *scope sentences* in this book because they can be placed anywhere in each of your paragraphs. The scope sentence is the umbrella that covers all the ideas in the paragraph; just as you want a strong umbrella to protect you from the weather, you want a strong scope sentence in each paragraph of your essay.

You should be able to underline the scope sentence of each of your paragraphs — and you may print a copy of your draft so that you can underline a physical copy or mark your paragraph's main ideas. If you have two candidates for a scope sentence and can't decide between them, you may have two paragraphs mistakenly glued together. Consider breaking them apart with one scope sentence left in each. If you can't find any scope sentence at all, you probably have a disorganized paragraph. Identify the main idea and add a good scope sentence to the paragraph.

But what is a good scope sentence? What's the difference between a hearty and robust scope sentence and one that needs to eat more spinach? A tight fit. A good scope sentence covers all the material in the paragraph, but it doesn't flap around loosely, spreading itself over tons of ideas that aren't in the paragraph. For example, suppose you have a paragraph describing an antique rolling pin that once belonged to your grandmother. (Don't laugh. The rolling pin was the subject of one of the best admission essays I ever read. The author related that rolling pin to the Italian heritage she received from her maternal relatives. I think she became an English major at Harvard. Good for her.) Examine these two paragraphs, neither of which is from her essay. (I made them up.)

> The slender wooden tool resembles a clean, perfectly smooth log. It has no handles. Perhaps Grandma didn't want anything extra separating her from the feel of the dough, or perhaps Grandpa, who fashioned the rolling pin, didn't know how to make a handle. Either way, the pin represents function at its purest — all you need, and nothing more, to stretch the delicate dough.

> The slender wooden tool resembles a clean, perfectly smooth log. It has no handles. Perhaps Grandma didn't want anything extra separating her from the feel of the dough, or perhaps Grandpa, who fashioned the rolling pin, didn't know how to make a handle. All tools should be simple.

In each paragraph the scope sentence comes last. (Scope sentences can be placed anywhere in the paragraph. Check out the next section, "Placing Scope Sentences and Details," for more info.) In the first sample paragraph, the last sentence stays focused on the rolling pin. It sums up the idea in the paragraph: that the rolling pin is simple, but it does the job well. A fine scope sentence. In the second sample paragraph, the scope sentence is far too broad. The writer hasn't been discussing all tools — just the rolling pin. Not a good fit. Granted, later in the essay the writer may go on to make broader, more general points . . . perhaps that the best things in life are simple. But this paragraph isn't about the best things in life; it's about a rolling pin. So the scope sentence should also be about a rolling pin.

Take care not to write a scope sentence that is too narrow. In the sample paragraph about the rolling pin, a too-narrow scope sentence might refer only to Grandpa. Grandpa is in the paragraph, but he's only one half of one sentence. A scope sentence about him would leave out the pin description and the musing about Grandma's preferences in dough-stretching equipment.

Bottom line: Your scope sentences should fit everything in the paragraph and nothing outside the paragraph.

TIP

When you've finished your essay, place it slightly beyond the focal length of your vision and check the paragraphs. Are they all more or less the same length? If so, you may want to consider altering them a bit, for the sake of variety. A longer or shorter paragraph here and there breaks the monotony.

Placing Scope Sentences and Details

Refer to the preceding section with its two sample paragraphs about a rolling pin. Each paragraph ended with the scope sentence. Your scope sentence may fill the last spot in the paragraph, or it may land somewhere else — say, at the beginning, more like a traditional topic sentence. Similarly, your details may roam around a bit. Check out the following sections for three sample paragraphs, each of which presents a different alternative. Then run your eyeballs over the section "One more word about details" for tips on organizing the rest of the paragraph.

Starting with a scope sentence

A scope sentence in this position begins the paragraph with a bang. If you want to orient the reader immediately, clearly revealing the most important point of the paragraph, go for a first-place scope sentence. However, be aware that everything after the scope sentence may feel like a letdown. Also, because a vast majority of paragraphs begin with the scope sentence, your reader may be tempted to jump from Alp to Alp, reading the topic sentences of each and skipping everything else. (Not a bad reading tip, by the way, when you're actually in college and facing more reading than you have time for.) Here's the paragraph. I italicized the topic sentence to make it absolutely clear (don't italicize it in your finished essay).

Over and over again, my mother's honesty has helped and challenged me in my relationships. In fourth grade, I accidentally (or perhaps not) stole a marble from a corner store, revealing the procured marble only as we pulled into our driveway. My mother's horrified glance in the mirror prompted my immediate guilt, and we drove back to the store to return the marble. In eighth grade, when I wanted to quit baseball, my mother encouraged me to speak to my coach directly about why I was having trouble with the commitment, instead of using the excuse that I didn't have time. Last week, it was the stare she gave me when I told my dad that I 'might' apply to his alma mater. "You can tell him the truth," she said.

See the set up? The first sentence (the scope sentence) tells you what to expect: a series of examples to show how the student's mother has pushed him towards honesty.

Finishing with the scope sentence

If you're building up to a big payoff, a last-place scope sentence is best. This sort of paragraph brings the reader along slowly and gives the reader a chance to come to the conclusion (the main idea of the paragraph, which is in the scope sentence) at the same time the writer gets there. The reader feels smart, and a smart-feeling reader is a happy reader. Check out this version of the paragraph, in which all I did was move the scope sentence to the end of the paragraph.

> In fourth grade, I accidentally (or perhaps not) stole a marble from a corner store, revealing the procured marble only as we pulled into our driveway. My mother's horrified glance in the mirror prompted my immediate guilt, and we drove back to the store to return the marble. In eighth grade, when I wanted to quit baseball, my mother encouraged me to speak to my coach directly about why I was having trouble with the commitment, instead of using the excuse that I didn't have time. Last week, it was the stare she gave me when I told my dad that I 'might' apply to his alma matre. "You can tell him the truth," she said. *Over and over again, my mother's honesty has helped and challenged me in my relationships.*

Not vastly different from the example in the prior section, but an interesting variation. Try one in your writing!

Putting the scope sentence in the middle

Scope sentences may land in the middle of the paragraph, though this position is rarer than the other two. The middle spot is good for variety, for when you want to keep the reader alert and hunting for your message. The downside is that the reader may hunt but not actually find the main idea, and you risk losing clarity. Read this paragraph for an example of the scope sentence in the middle of the paragraph (the scope sentence is italicized).

> In fourth grade, I accidentally (or perhaps not) stole a marble from a corner store, revealing the procured marble only as we pulled into our driveway. My mother's horrified glance in the mirror prompted my immediate guilt, and we drove back to the store to return the marble. *Over and over again, my mother's honesty has helped and challenged me in my relationships.* In eighth grade, when I wanted to quit baseball, my mother encouraged me to speak to my coach directly about why I was having trouble with the commitment, instead of using the excuse that I didn't have time. Last week, it was the stare she gave me when I told my dad that I 'might' apply to his alma matre. "You can tell him the truth," she said.

Would you have found that sentence without the italics? Maybe yes, maybe no. And now you know why few writers make a habit of placing the scope sentence in the middle of the paragraph — the scope sentence is often best used as an anchor at the beginning or end of your paragraph. But as a change of pace, try the middle position.

One more word about details

The details fill up all the space in the paragraph not taken up by the scope sentence. Fine. But what should you put where? Which detail goes first, which second, and so forth? Sometimes the answer to those questions is a simple statement: It doesn't matter. But more often you'll end up with a stronger piece of writing if you consider the internal logic of the paragraph and place the details accordingly.

Suppose, for example, you're describing your grandmother. You might follow a kind of geographical order, describing her dyed blue hair first and working your way downward to her gigantic, size 15 feet. Or you may choose to work by the clock, mentioning your earliest memory of Grandma and moving forward in time — or backward to family stories about her life before you were born. A point of view approach also works, as in this paragraph:

> Everyone in my family talked about Grandma at her funeral. My grandpa thought Grandma was "the finest person I have known," as he said in a voice filled with tears. He didn't smile once for the first year after her death. My brother told a story about picking a bouquet of weeds for Grandma, who accepted them as if they were the finest orchids. She didn't even scold him, he said, for trampling the real flowers in her garden during his bouquet-gathering expedition. My mom's comment was the only one to make me cry. She said she saw my grandmother whenever she looked at me.

Notice that the details are grouped by person: Grandpa, brother, mom. The writer might have chosen a different order — perhaps brother, Grandpa, mom — and still ended up with a fine paragraph. Whatever the order, the groupings give the paragraph a logical structure, allowing the reader to grasp the ideas more easily. Don't be afraid to move a few details around and see how the impression of your writing changes — you can often vastly improve an essay by switching the order of your sentences or even your paragraphs. By the way, the first sentence of the sample paragraph is the scope sentence, which sets up the main idea of the paragraph. For more about scope sentences, read the section, "Creating a Strong Scope Sentence," earlier in this chapter.

As you write your admission essay, think for a moment about where you place the details. Random order may be all right, but if you can come up with a structure that makes sense, go for it.

Setting Up a Transition

When you began drafting your essay, you placed each idea in its spot for a reason. If the design of your essay is effective, the ideas flow logically from one to another. Now that you're writing, you should help the reader "go with the flow" by providing transitions. *Transitions* are like little hands that reach between paragraphs for a good, strong clasp. Sometimes the transitions are repeated ideas — one at the end of a paragraph and the other at the beginning of the next paragraph. Often the transitions are words that illustrate the logical connection, such as "on the other hand," "afterwards," "because," and so on.

The following sections take a closer look at a couple different strategies about transitions you can incorporate into your writing.

Using linked transitions

As you consider how you to create smooth bridges between your paragraphs, one option available to you is the linked transition. That's when the ending of one paragraph and the beginning of the next paragraph share a common theme or idea, ensuring that your paragraphs feel cohesive and connected. Say the first paragraph of your essay includes an early childhood anecdote about your love of performing. Your second paragraph may begin with a phrase like "Although I no longer spend my weekend evenings belting out songs from *Wicked* in the mirror, I do find myself . . . ." The reference to what was shared in the first paragraph allows you to lead into the next phase of your essay.

Figure 11-2 is a real student essay by a young man who is destined to win the Nobel Prize for Robotics, if such a prize is ever given. This essay about his "disaster bot" provides good examples of linked transitions. (To help you identify these transitions, I italicize them.) Notice that paragraph one ends with the idea of perfection. Paragraph two begins with a statement about perfection. Similarly, paragraph two ends with a statement about disappointment, and the first sentence of paragraph three mentions "disillusioned," "confusion," and "panic" — all ingredients of disappointment.

The advantage of a linked transition is that the reader can easily grasp the connections between paragraphs. However, a linked transition does carry one important risk. If you repeat too many words or reuse the same terms, your reader may wander off mentally, sure that the meaning you're trying to impart has already been received. If you use a linked transition, take care to keep the links short, and vary the wording as much as you can.

I have built four completely functional robots to this day. As proud as I am of them, the focus of every one of my conversations dealing with robotics always revolves around the HMW#2, my disaster bot. It was built for my independent study course on robotic locomotion. The purpose of this bot was simply to move with the aid of four legs, but I set out to do much more than that. My intentions were to amaze and astound my mentors and even myself. The completion of the bot was meant to be my big accomplishment. It represented my mastery of motors, sensors, pics (programmable integrated circuits), and miscellaneous electronic components. Unlike the soporific act of memorizing Spanish vocabulary words, which I was never good at, building a robot requires creativity and intuition. I can actually remember drawing diagrams and schematics for the construction of the bot months before I even looked at my soldering iron. I was making sure that there would be absolutely no uncertainty about anything. It was supposed to be *perfect*.

Everything did, in fact, go *perfectly* according to plan. I completed the robot just a few days before it was due, and it was absolutely beautiful. It was capable of transportation by the method of flipping itself in all directions, responding to voice commands (with the help of Voice Direct by Sensory Inc.) and avoiding all foreign objects with its numerous infrared proximity detectors. For the next couple of days, I reveled in my accomplishment. On the night before my big presentation, I decided to give my creation an exhaustive test run to ensure that there were no bugs. Sure enough, there was one. I found that there are cases where the legs get caught on each other, resisting further movement. After forgetting to turn the robot off, I pulled each leg free from the others. By doing this, I managed to turn the servomotor towards its opposite direction while it was still operating. Apparently, this forced a current back up through the wires from which the motors were receiving their power. This current fried everything in its path and debilitated the pic. When I realized what I had done, I dropped a tear for the first time in a decade. This was the single biggest *disappointment* in my young engineering career.

After many *disillusioned hours of confusion and panic*, I was reminded that nothing comes without failure. As a future engineer, I had to comprehend the fact that failure means nothing if I don't learn from it. What I took away from this project was a deeper knowledge of circuit design, servomotors, integrating microphones and speakers, soldering circuits, and the value of failure, all of which only come from hands-on experience. I later salvaged what I could for my presentation. I separated the voice command system to display the outputs to LEDs in place of the pins on the pic and I also implemented a few proximity detectors into circuits that make use of the unharmed motors. But more importantly, I was able to explain exactly what caused the bug and how to fix it. I displayed a new altered design of my robot that was now really perfect. Luckily I was not evaluated purely on the quality of my robot, but on my newly acquired knowledge as well. I am currently in the middle of rebuilding this bot, which I respectfully call the HMW#2-rev.II.

FIGURE 11-2:
An essay example with transitions underlined.

Adding transitions later

Word and phrase transitions do a fine job marking out the logical path that you want the reader to take, especially toward the end of a college admission essay, where you're likely to include some reflection on the significance of a given event in your life (you almost never need transitional words or phrases In the middle of a narrative-style anecdote). Here I offer examples of transitions you can add into a draft later, though you should do so sparingly, because they can easily make your writing feel overly formal and analytical rather than personal.

You're probably familiar with these examples of transitional words/phrases. Your initial draft may not contain any of these words or phrases, because when you wrote it you were probably more focused on churning out your best content than bridging between paragraphs to ensure continuity. However, after you're certain that you have your sentences and paragraphs in the order that you want them, you can always go back and add in a transition or two to make your essay more effective.

RELATIONSHIP: additional idea

TRANSITIONS: also, moreover, in addition to, besides, furthermore, likewise, not the only, not only

RELATIONSHIP: contrasting idea

TRANSITIONS: on the other hand, in contrast to, however, despite, in spite of, nevertheless, nonetheless, otherwise

RELATIONSHIP: comparison

TRANSITIONS: than, equally, as ___ as, similarly, similar to, like

RELATIONSHIP: cause/effect

TRANSITIONS: because, hence, thus, so, accordingly, consequently, as a result

RELATIONSHIP: time

TRANSITIONS: previously, after, before, since, still, yet, up until, then, later, before, earlier, finally, in the end

RELATIONSHIP: example

TRANSITIONS: for example, for instance, illustrating, showing

Don't overuse transitions in your writing. After all, you aren't writing an academic paper, so your total allowance of "therefore" is zero — don't use it in your personal statement unless you have a very good reason! (On the other hand, your supplemental essays, or individual essays for one school, might be more academic or professional by nature, and so you can be a bit more formal in your writing. Check out Chapter 17 for more on supplemental essays.) If the connection between one paragraph and another is already clear, don't plop in a word transition also. Overkill isn't an attractive quality.

Chapter **12**

Going Out with a Bang: The Conclusion

Typing away, you glimpse the light at the end of the tunnel. You're almost finished! The last line . . . just one more line . . . and you can rest easy knowing you have a complete draft of your essay. Maybe a couple of sentences. A paragraph. No more than a paragraph, right? How hard could a little paragraph be? Okay, maybe you'll go for a walk and write the conclusion later. After all, you're nearly done.

So near and yet so far. Is that how you feel as you attempt to conjure up a conclusion? If so, you have a lot of company. Most people find those final couple of sentences quite a challenge. In fact, any number of terrific pieces of writing have crashed nose first into the conclusion barrier. The resulting wreck is seldom a pretty sight.

Fortunately, if you keep a few simple guidelines in mind, the best conclusion for your essay will practically write itself. This chapter supplies those guidelines and provides tips for the most common essay questions, along with two real student essays displaying strong conclusions.

Repeating Yourself and Other Non-Answers to the Conclusion Question

More than any other part of the essay, the conclusion attracts mistaken ideas. I don't mean that writers insert false information in their conclusions. Rather, I'm referring to the fact that lots of writers *think* they know what should be in the conclusion, but they're mistaken. Indeed, the art of writing a conclusion is surrounded by more myths than ancient Greece. So before I explain what a good conclusion *is*, I must discuss what a conclusion is *not*.

Not a reworded introduction

Contrary to what you may have learned in elementary school, a conclusion isn't a restatement of your introduction, with slightly different wording. For example, suppose you're applying to the University of Colorado and writing in response to Personal Insight Question 6 about an academic subject that inspires you. You chose Computer Science. You first took this elective reluctantly; your first choice, Business, was out of the question and only open to seniors. Your first paragraph explains how you fell in love with coding, discovering that only in this realm did you truly feel both creative (designing a new app) and absolutely precise (even the tiniest error in code will render your work defective). You explain how you used your knowledge of coding to create your own website for your dog-walking business. Your last paragraph returns to the reasons why you love coding. Good idea? Actually, that's probably a pretty bad idea. You've explained your interest in coding already.

REMEMBER

Some teachers tell their students to rewrite the introduction and tack the new version of paragraph one onto the end of the composition. I imagine that they do so because young kids can't write a true conclusion, and the teachers believe that any ending is better than just stopping short — and I come across plenty of high school students who still use this approach for school papers, because they haven't learned a better one. But when you're out of middle school, you must aim higher. Forget the reworded introduction!

TIP

One structure I describe in Chapter 8 relies on bookends — two halves of one story framing the essay. One half of the story begins the essay and the other half ends it. (The middle discusses the issues raised by the story or relates other events.) This structure isn't repetitive because although you're telling the same story in both the introduction and the conclusion, you're relating different parts of the story in each spot. The essay focuses on one event, but everything in it is stated only once.

Not a miniature essay

A conclusion is *not* a restatement of all the points you made in the body of your work. I've seen "conclusions" that are nearly as long as the entire essay. Here's a (fictional) restatement ending for the Computer Science essay, with extra, not-included-in-the-essay comments from me in parentheses:

> You might think that Computer Science is boring, but in fact it is not. (A point you made in paragraph two.) I've been attracted to creative pursuits for most of my life. (As you explained in detail in paragraph one.) Computer Science, and specifically coding, gives me constant room for improvement and experimentation. (That's already in paragraph 3.) After building my website, I wasn't immediately approached by new clients (paragraph four's main idea), but I am not discouraged. (Check out paragraph five.) I have begun offering my services to Student Government and journalism to help them improve their own websites. (Paragraph five told about these steps as well.)

Anything new here? Nothing at all! Many students get a bit flustered when they realize that their ending is simply a restatement. (I refuse to dignify that sort of writing with the term "conclusion.") Afraid that the point hasn't come across, the writer goes through the whole thing again, hoping that one last round will make everything clear. But if your essay is reasonably well written, the information in each preceding paragraph *is* already clear. And if the essay is floundering around in complete confusion, a restatement at the end won't solve the problem.

Not an announcement

One truly deadly ending goes something like this: "In this essay I have shown that I am highly suited to be a Computer Science major in college." Yikes! Personally, I hate this kind of ending for any paper, though I know that a few of my colleagues in academia favor a version of the "announcement" conclusion for some research papers. Good for them. But for a college admission essay, this ending is totally inappropriate. Remember that you're showing off your writing skills for the admissions committee. They're hoping to see something a bit more creative. Besides, if you truly have made the point, the admissions committee will know *without* an announcement.

Not a new topic

Some writers avoid repetition, restatement, and announcing by going to the opposite extreme. They plunk down a completely new idea in the conclusion — something brought in from another universe for the sake of novelty. Referring to the Computer Science essay example, you can imagine the reader's confusion if the last paragraph suddenly veered off into a lengthy description of why you also like Business, and will take that elective as a senior, after all. If you've had a sudden brainstorm, write another essay. But as you conclude the one you've just written, stay on topic.

Concluding the Essay Effectively

If you plowed through the preceding section, you know what you shouldn't put in your conclusion. But what *should* you write? Before you pick the words, keep in mind the tasks the last paragraph of your essay must accomplish. Specifically, a good conclusion:

>> Ties up loose ends

>> Places the topic of the essay into a larger context

>> Gives the reader a feeling of completion

>> Provides the last link in the chain of logic you've forged

>> Creates a lasting memory for the reader

Not every conclusion performs every single one of these functions, and some of the functions overlap. To help you understand the role of a conclusion, in the following sections I tackle the characteristics of a true conclusion one by one, showing you how to achieve each in your essay.

Tying up loose ends

If the bulk of your essay is a story, the conclusion is the spot to let the reader know how the story ends. Perhaps your essay is about your experiment in novel writing, which occupied countless hours during your sophomore year. In the conclusion you say whether you actually finished the novel, how your writing was received by its intended audience, and what you learned from your year as a budding Dickens. Your conclusion ties up the loose ends and gives the reader a feeling of completion. The reader's reaction is "Ah, so that's how it all worked out! He finished it after all. And he gained confidence in his writing skills. Great!"

Or perhaps your essay is a reflection on the meaning of your brother's bout with illness and how his struggle affected you. The conclusion gives the reader an update on your brother's condition and your current thoughts on the experience. Those current thoughts place the event in the wider context of your life, and update the reader to the present moment. Another way of thinking about this: the ending of your essay should feel like we are hearing an update from you in the present moment, not the person you were at the beginning of your essay.

Here's the tying-up-loose-ends technique in action, in skeletal form ("bones" only, no details) in response to the "tell about a significant experience" question:

Introduction: Description of family's escape from war-torn area, mother and father in separate refugee camps, children divided, two left behind when soldiers prevented them from crossing the border.

Body: Details about the family's life before the war, the strong bonds between family members, the values shared by all, their reactions to the early stage of the crisis and increasingly difficult conditions.

Conclusion: How the family reunited and resettled, the current status of family members, reflections on the effect of these experiences.

For a glimpse of this sort of conclusion in a real student essay, check out Figure 12-1. (This essay is only 350 words, because it was written as a supplemental response about how the student took advantage of an educational opportunity, so the conclusion is short as well.) Notice how the conclusion resolves several issues raised by the body of the essay. By reading the conclusion, the reader finds out the following:

>> The student did successfully achieve a degree of Spanish fluency by the end of the trip

>> Measures she has taken to continue developing her skills back in the United States

>> That she hopes to somehow incorporate Spanish-speaking into her future career

Only a few sentences long, the conclusion nevertheless packs a lot of information into a small space.

I love walking down the street in my hometown and understanding Spanish conversations or reading the English and Spanish versions of street signs. During my sophomore year, I applied to a program in Mexico, volunteering for three weeks while staying with a host family and taking Spanish lessons. Upon my arrival, my host family asked me questions in a flurry of rapid-fire language. I responded with "¿Qué?" until my roommate from the program, a native Spanish speaker, quietly informed me that the way I was asking for clarification was impolite. As she conversed with our family, I stood there, embarrassed by my error, realizing that perhaps my five years of Spanish wouldn't serve me as well as I had hoped.

My first night in Mérida my host family took my roommate and me out to dinner. In the classroom, errors are expected, but here I stood out as yet another foreigner. During our dinner, I fumbled, conjugating verbs off the top of my head as I tried to explain cross country to an audience who hadn't heard of competitive running.

It wasn't until my roommate fell sick and was confined to her room that I had my first real conversation with my host mother. I began to realize that people didn't mind that I was conjugating verbs incorrectly, and I could order for myself in restaurants and ask my host family questions about Mérida. In the days that followed, I arrived home each evening to tell my host family about my adventures of the day, giddily explaining how we found our way home after taking the wrong bus. As the program continued, I knew which tenses to use in different situations and my vocabulary grew exponentially.

By the end of the trip I was able to hold conversations in Spanish, ask for directions and navigate the city by myself. I continue to practice my Spanish by watching TV shows and listening to podcasts to increase my proficiency. I hope my language skills will help me access new cultures and bridge divides in my future career.

FIGURE 12-1:
An example of a tying-up-the-loose-ends conclusion.

Creating a wider context

In a properly focused essay, you zero in on a narrow topic — the time you potty-trained the local zoo's yak herd, perhaps. But what's the meaning of that experience beyond the fact that the zookeepers don't have to shovel all day and the fact that you had to wash your hands a lot last summer? And do universities care?

Yes, they do. Universities, when they're doing a proper job, prepare students for a meaningful role in society. So, by definition, the institution you're applying to needs to think about the meaning of your years on its campus — not just "What will you learn from us?" but "What will you contribute (and I don't mean only money) after you leave us?" Consequently, they're interested in your ability to look beyond your own concerns toward the wider context — your view of the world beyond yourself. One way you can provide this information is by writing a wider-context conclusion. A *wider-context conclusion*, as its name implies, begins where the rest of the essay left off and expands outward. If your essay is about your family, the wider context may be the way families like yours are perceived in the community. In an essay about your learning experience, the wider-context conclusion may broaden outward to a philosophy of education. (*Note:* Sometimes "tying-up-loose-ends" conclusions also place the issue or event in a wider context. Check out the preceding section for details.)

Here's a summary of an essay responding to a typical "tell-us-about-your-ambition" question, such as Rice University's supplemental essay prompt on why you want to study in the academic area you indicated on your application.

Introduction: Student explains she was raised in a city and witnessed shortcomings of health clinics, appreciates kids, doesn't want to be on call 24/7, but knows patients need coverage. Shares insight that group medical practice solves problems and gives population a needed service.

Middle: Conveys understanding that rural areas are underserved, health of the poor has not been a national priority, next generation of doctors should do their part to improve health care itself, not just heal individual patients.

Brief Conclusion: Explains how Rice is the ideal setting to pursue these goals.

Coming full circle: Completing the experience

You may have heard the expression "coming full circle." The full circle (as opposed, I imagine, to a half or semi-circle) is a complete figure. The beginning and end come together seamlessly, and nothing more is necessary. In an essay, a full-circle conclusion encloses everything you've written in a neat package. The reader has a feeling of fulfillment, an "I know it all now" sensation. This sort of conclusion often resembles or overlaps the "tying-up-loose-ends" conclusion because it brings the topic to a close for the reader. (Check out the section, "Tying up loose ends," earlier in this chapter for more information.)

The easiest way to write a full-circle conclusion is to end where you began the essay . . . in time, in ideas, in location. This technique is fairly easy to apply; if you're writing about your room, for example, you may begin and end at the most important feature — your 40-pipe, ultra-loud, antique organ. If you're writing about the neighbors' attempts to have your 40-pipe, ultra-loud, antique organ blown up, you may begin with the visit from the Environmental Protection Agency's Noise Squad, cut to the importance in your life of the instrument (your first lessons, your carving of replacement pipes, your discovery of Bach at high volume, and so on), and then back to the Noise Squad, whose measurements showed that the organ was not as bad as a freight train engine but louder than a heavy metal concert.

REMEMBER

Coming full circle does *not* mean repeating yourself. End where you began, but don't overlap. Check out the section, "Repeating Yourself and Other Non-Answers to the Conclusion Question," earlier in this chapter for reasons why repetition isn't okay.

Forging the last link in a chain of logic

By "forging" I don't mean cranking out your very own twenty-dollar bills in the basement. I refer to the hammering the blacksmith does on a piece of hot metal, the turning of a lump of iron into a yard of chain. You don't have to sweat over a hot fire to create links; you just have to think logically. And when you get to the last link, the final step should be a cinch. When have you taken the reader with your reasoning power? The answer to that question is your conclusion.

REMEMBER

The essay structure most often taught in school is simple. In paragraph one you make a statement, and in the rest of the essay you back up that statement with proof. The structure I discuss in this section is different. Instead of backing up, you lead the reader forward to a new idea.

A chain-of-logic conclusion flows naturally from the ideas that precede it. You're saying, "If this is true, then that is true. And if that is true, this other idea is also true. . . ." Here's a chain-of-logic conclusion for an essay about food allergies:

> **Introduction:** Description of your food allergies and how they dominate much of your life.
>
> **Body:** Examples of how the fear of accidentally ingesting a nut or egg became debilitating — until you finally made the decision to take back control.
>
> **Conclusion:** Here you explain that a fearless life is far more appetizing than pizza.

The preceding example is a win-win, in that it includes both a chain-of-logic *and* a tactfully chosen metaphor. Depending on the drama of your subject and the impact of your concluding thought, a chain-of-logic conclusion may make a strong impression on your reader. The next section goes into detail on this function of a conclusion.

Making a strong impression

Composers of Broadway musicals speak of the "eleven o'clock number" — the showstopper at the end of the performance that sends audience members out into the night, humming and tapping their feet. Your admission essay needs an eleven o'clock number too: a strong last paragraph that makes an indelible impression on the reader.

Fortunately, human nature makes the task of writing a memorable conclusion easier. Why? Think about all the speeches (or class lectures and church sermons) you've attended. You probably tuned in on full power at the beginning. Most people are optimists, and unless proven otherwise, they live in hope that the speech will be at least moderately interesting. Sadly, unless you were listening to an exceptionally fine orator, you may have faded a bit in the middle. But everyone perks up toward the end, giving the speaker one last bit of attention. The same phenomenon holds true for essays. Even readers who skim the middle on automatic pilot switch to manual control for the last paragraph. So you've got a good audience for your parting shot.

TIP

Take advantage of that increased concentration. As you plan your essay, identify particularly strong points or interesting details and save them for the end, as long as you don't wreck the logical structure by doing so. To be more specific:

>> If your essay is primarily a story, interpret the story in the conclusion.

>> If your essay contains a lengthy description, choose a great sensory detail or a metaphor for the last paragraph.

>> If you've broadened the focus of the essay to a wider context, consider concluding with an interesting anecdote illustrating that context.

>> For an essay with a survey structure (check out Chapter 8 for more on structure), in the last paragraph interpret the overall meaning of the items surveyed.

>> If you have one line that's a real zinger, place it at the end.

Figure 12-2 is another real student essay with a great concluding line. The very last line — a zinger — communicates the meaning of the baling twine, a motif that she has used throughout the essay . . . all in a single sentence!

My summers, for as long as I can remember, have been spent at the ranch. I fell in love with the fresh air, the animals — even the manure. I became, admittedly, a "barn rat," spending as many hours there as humanly possible and doing odd jobs just to extend my time. Now, I am a year-round staff member and horse owner.

When I first began taking lessons at the barn, my trainer Mimi explained: "If it can't be fixed with baling twine, it can't be fixed at all." If there's a fence broken, a halter snapped, or the need for a last-minute art project, anyone can easily run to the hayloft and take some strands. For those whose horse experience goes as far as Mister Ed, baling twine is a plastic-like type of thin rope designed for bundling bales of hay, but in our case, it serves nearly every purpose.

The extent of our resourcefulness isn't limited to pieces of twine. Last year, while feeding the horses, the shell by the transmission of the four-wheeler broke off. My coworkers and I expected our boss Breen to make a small repair; instead we got a cutting board taped to the seat. The "if it ain't broke, don't fix it" mentality has morphed into "even if it is broke, barely fix it" and this is exemplified all across the ranch. At this point, I have learned to embrace the creative solutions that are part of the barn's culture. Even my horse's water is held together with strips of a garbage bag and I hung her toys and salt lick with the crowd favorite: baling twine.

During our horseback riding camps in the summer, the campers often suffer minor injuries at the hands of rusty gates and art projects. To my knowledge, we ran out of band aids in 2007 and our new retort when confronted with a scrape is "rub some dirt on it". With zero cases of tetanus ten years later, I don't anticipate Breen wanting to allocate any more money in the budget for medical supplies.

You would be surprised by how many times you can refill an empty bottle of soap before it no longer has any suds or how toilet paper rolls can double as ornate flowers with a few snips of the scissors. This minimalism, however, isn't a result of sheer laziness, but rather, out of the shared belief that everything must be utilized to the maximum extent. The ranch is one of the greenest places around, both literally and metaphorically.

When I find unique uses for household products and create tools out of nothing, it does not feel like some animalistic resourcefulness channeled from my inner Neanderthal. I do, however, experience the sense of going back to my roots. Even in my own home I find myself creating guinea pig toys from toilet paper rolls, stuffing an ill-fitting helmet with coffee filters, and I haven't purchased band aids since 2007, either.

When the WD40 has run out, the plumber is three days behind schedule or my printer won't print the last page of my final essay, it is this sense of self-sufficiency that I draw upon. I know that when confronting a dilemma, however big or small, I can not only make do with what I have, but even improve upon it. Sometimes it feels like I, too, am held together by baling twine.

FIGURE 12-2:
An example of a conclusion that makes a strong impression.

THE SEARCH FOR MARVIN GARDENS

One of the best conclusions I've ever seen was written by John McPhee, a nonfiction writer whose work has appeared frequently in *The New Yorker*. McPhee's essay, "The Search for Marvin Gardens," has an interlocking structure. In a series of short segments he recounts playing the board game Monopoly. As you may know, the properties for sale in the traditional game are named for streets in Atlantic City, New Jersey. McPhee's paragraphs on the game are interwoven with paragraphs describing the actual streets and other locations from the game, including the local jail. One property — Marvin Gardens — proves elusive.

The narrator can't find that street, though it appears on the board game. For the second half of the essay the narrator asks everyone he meets in Atlantic City about Marvin Gardens. No one knows where it is. Finally, in the last paragraph, the author discovers that Marvin Gardens is a planned community outside the city limits. The reader shares the narrator's relief that the puzzle is solved. That last paragraph is a good payoff to several pages of rising tension.

Chapter **13**

Overcoming Writer's Block

You can write a homework assignment, a grocery list, an email to a friend, and millions of other things. No sweat. So why are you stuck at the starting line for the admission essay? Or perhaps you've made a fine opening move, but now you're stalled three paragraphs into the best piece of writing you've ever done. No matter what you do, you can't seem to go forward.

Congratulations. You've joined an extremely large club whose membership at one time or another has included some of the best authors on the planet: The Blocked Writers (TBW, for short). Of course, TBW is a club no one wants to be in. Hitting writer's block gives you the same sensation as the tenth month of pregnancy. Enough already! What's inside you just *has* to emerge, and you're willing to do almost anything to get things moving.

Chin up. Writer's block isn't fatal, and in this chapter I show you several strategies that help you leap over whatever barrier is confining your ideas.

Understanding Your Block

The key to surmounting the two-story-high, three-foot-thick wall of writer's block is to understand what the bricks are made of. Are you worried about failure, thinking too much about the final outcome, trying to write and edit at the same time? Or have you become mired in details? These are some of the many factors that may bottle up your writing. Each of these factors presents a different problem with a different solution.

In my experience, writer's block in the context of the admission essay stems from one of these two issues:

>> The emotions surrounding the application process itself

>> Faulty approaches to writing

In this chapter I address both types of problems. For the emotional stuff, check out the section, "Confronting Your Application Anxieties." For writing-approach blocks, turn to the section, "Leaping Over Writing-Related Blocks."

Confronting Your Application Anxieties

I've observed closely and learned a fair amount about the anxieties of my students as they fill out their applications, and here I've tried to sum up the insights that you might find helpful. I can give you some hints on how to handle your emotions, but if you're feeling down and self-help measures aren't making a difference, talk with a counselor or a trusted friend. Needing some assistance in handling the transition between one level of schooling and another is common, and sometimes the anxiety about this transition comes out in the form of resisting (occasionally, even sabotaging) the application process.

TIP

If you've hit the wall with your essay, see if any of the following descriptions match your mood. Often the answer arises the moment you recognize the problem. At other times the solution is a change of attitude — easy to prescribe, harder to accomplish. (Harder, but not impossible.) I place outlook-adjustment tips in each of the following sections. If you recognize your problem and take a stab at fixing it, but you're still stuck, move on to the section, "Leaping Over Writing-Related Blocks," later in this chapter. The proven techniques there may smash through emotional blocks as well.

Overcoming a fear of failure

If you don't run the race, you can't lose it. Of course, you can't win the race either, but sometimes that particular truth seems like a side issue. The most important thing, for some people, is not to fail. Adding to the pressure is the tendency of many applicants to see the admissions process as a judgment on their entire lives thus far. Are you a good person? Is the sum total of your years on the planet successful? With stakes like that, is it any wonder why many opt out of essay writing?

REMEMBER

But the admissions process is *not* a divine judgment. In fact, it's not even a perfect system: The vast majority of candidates who are rejected by colleges are deserving of admissions. The admissions process is a well-intentioned but flawed attempt to select a small number of applicants — from a pool of *many* qualified people — for an incoming class. No more, no less. It doesn't judge *who* you are, and it doesn't even do a very good job of judging *how* you've lived your life or spent your school years thus far. Beyond a certain, basic level of competency for each school, the admissions process is just a matching game between an institution and a set of students.

If you fear failure, take a long look in the mirror. Repeat after me, filling in the blanks appropriately:

> The University of _____ *won't* evaluate my worth as a person. I'm more than my application, and I'm pretty brave for giving these competitive applications a shot while knowing the odds. Regardless of the outcome, I will still be proud of my achievements.

TIP

Go through this little ritual each morning until you believe what you're saying. And you *should* believe what you're saying, because every word is true.

Also, keep in mind that the only way to fail the essay question is not to write an essay at all. Every essay, no matter what level of writing skill you've achieved, tells something about you. And that's the job of the essay. So if you write it, you automatically pass.

Coping with perfectionism and paralysis

If you're a perfectionist, you might know the frustration of reading back something that falls flat compared to the vision in your mind. You can't quite pin down that vision; the flow of your sentences is clunky and doesn't sound the way you had imagined. At some point, though, you have to commit to your words, real words, instead of chasing ethereal ideals. Don't let the frustration inhibit your writing. Keep going.

Chapter 2 discusses why college essay prompts tend to emphasize overcoming adversity as a key theme in many prompts — because the challenges you've faced have likely sparked your growth far more than when things are easy-breezy. The same is true for the writing process itself. The only way to get better is to have the bravery and grit to wrestle through each stage of the process, instead of averting your eyes and slipping into avoidance.

Still, some students want to shred every sentence the second they compose it. Others find themselves projecting final draft standards onto what should inevitably be a messy first draft, full of half-realized ideas and seeds of potential. Some have the impulse to be especially flowery out of a desire to sound impressive (more on avoiding this tendency in Chapter 7). Here's an example of a student's line, first unedited and then simplified: "Throughout my entire, yet brief, life, I have witnessed the excessive exuberance of Jewish music that is present at every occasion" became "Every major milestone in my life has been amplified by the presence of Jewish music."

No matter which of these tendencies you most identify with, remember that fixating on perfection will only ever paralyze you, keeping you from moving forward. You might also remember that, although you may be able to meet your own standards in an analytical essay about Toni Morrison's *Beloved*, a truly personal essay with no prescribed structure is bound to frustrate you. Take these feelings as something that comes with the territory instead of an indication that you're doing something wrong — and *don't* let them stop you from continuing to write.

Reclaiming power

Applying to college or graduate school or seeking a scholarship puts you in an unequal power relationship. The committee deciding your fate holds all the cards, and powerlessness never feels good. In fact, many of the world's wars have begun for exactly that reason: one group or another feels an acute lack of power and challenges those who appear to have all the advantages.

I don't mean to suggest that you're waging war on the admissions or scholarship committee. (You could try the rebellious approach: "To whoever is reading this, I don't care what you think of me, anyway!" but you can imagine how far that approach would get you.)

Because that option's a nonstarter, perhaps you've decided to turn all those war-like urges on yourself. By blocking your writing talent (and you *do* have writing talent — everyone does), you at least gain power over one aspect of the process. You tell yourself, "I don't have to do this," and you stop trying. Briefly, you may feel as if you've regained control.

The solution here is to redraw the battle lines. You'll *never* be in control of the outcome of your applications. Too many variables, many of which have more to do with the university's needs than with your background and achievements, influence the committee's choices. Instead of banging your head against that brick wall, move your expectations over a notch or two. If one school doesn't admit you, another will. Instead of narrowing your view to a tiny slice of academia, cast a wider net. In your application list, include universities that are likely to feel honored by your interest. You'll undoubtedly enjoy a wonderful career and a great life after graduating from any number of schools.

Embracing change

Your experience of writer's block actually has very little to do with writing and everything to do with what happens when you're *done* writing. Not only does college essay writing demand rigorous self-reflection (much of which is the focus of this book), but the process also encourages you to look into your future. Depending on your point of view, this is exciting — and perhaps terrifying.

Consider Blanca: She was a straight-A student with leading positions in several major extracurricular activities. She filled out all the applications and completed drafts of all the essays. She checked over her applications a dozen times and received praise on her essays — but she never submitted any of them. Her mother's sleuthing realized this, about a month after it was too late. Everyone asked her the same thing: "Why didn't you send in your applications?"

It took her a long time to come up with the answer, but after some heavy-duty counseling, she identified the issue. She had entered her school's nursery division at age two. For the next 15 years she felt cozy, smart, and loved, surrounded by many of the same friends and teachers she had met in toddlerhood. As college loomed, her self-doubts mounted. Suppose that the next step was harder, suppose that no one liked her, suppose that her family forgot her, suppose that . . . well, you get the idea. She was dreading the move to a new school, so she opted out of the process altogether.

If your essay is bogged down, reflect for a moment on your fantasies about the coming year. If fear of moving on is your problem, you'll immediately see, as did Blanca, that staying put is *not* an option. No matter what your plans for the next school term, you can't remain in high school after graduation. Of course if you're out of school and working, thinking of returning to full-time study, you can keep the status quo. But do you really, truly want to do so? Are you letting fear govern your actions?

A *gap year* (or semester) — taking a break from formal schooling before you begin your higher education — may be a worthwhile consideration, but considering that decision is beyond the scope of this book. If you're thinking of taking a gap year, before you make any decision, discuss it with a college or guidance counselor. If you do decide on this option, I recommend applying to college with a traditional timeline and *then*, upon acceptance, you can notify your future college or university that you'll be deferring your enrollment by a semester or a year. In other words, don't use this path as an excuse not to apply.

If you're admittedly terrified of the future, make a scare list. Sometimes, simply seeing your looming fears in writing can make them seem much smaller or less likely, but you may also talk to your friends, family members, or a counselor — anyone in your life who has been in your shoes before — about their college experiences. You may also use your fears as information to help shape your approach to applications: If your biggest worry is feeling homesick and you truly feel intimidated by a cross-country move, for example, you may want to put your focus on in-state college options.

Along with your scare list, try making a list that focuses on ways you can bound to be better. Jot down everything about the new stage in your life that you're likely to enjoy, pointing out things you're excited to try, see, or do in college that may not have been available to you in high school. Read that list from time to time, focusing on the positive aspects of your future. After you've worked your way through your "scare" and "better" lists, go back to your essay. You may even write about the experience you've just gone through.

Overcoming self-doubt

I like humility. It's a good virtue, and if more people chose the humble path, the world would be a better place. But when you write a college essay, even if you're writing about a weakness or setback, do so from a place of pride in what you've already overcome. Some degree of self-appreciation is fine and necessary.

Humility is sometimes a mask for another feeling, one that doesn't fall into the virtuous category. That feeling, which everyone has from time to time, is self-doubt. Okay, self-doubt *can* be a fine phenomenon; if someone's got a finger on the nuclear trigger, I'd like them to ask, "Am I capable of making this decision?" before pressing anything. But self-doubt at the wrong time becomes a dead end.

Ponder your feelings. Are you reluctant to speak well of yourself because you're afraid you don't deserve the attention of the reader (that is, the admissions committee)? Do you suspect that you're not worthy of admission? If I've described you correctly, it's time for an attitude adjustment. You're writing for the admissions committee of a school, not the guardians of the pearly gates. Regular people, just like you, attend the school. They may be smart, but they're not necessarily smarter than you are. And if they're smarter than you, you'll learn. That's why you want to go to school, right?

Gaining perspective

The best word for sentence three of paragraph two is "the." No. It's "an." "An" is definitely the right choice! Um . . . "the" looks better now. (Sob.) I don't know which to choose! They'll hate me if I pick the wrong one. They'll *reject* me if I pick the wrong one. And then I won't go to college and I won't have a career and no one will love me, ever.

Sound familiar? If so, lighten up. You're writing an essay, not a peace treaty ending 600 years of armed conflict. No one word — or sentence or even paragraph — will make or break your essay. Come to think of it, it's pretty rare that an essay, all by itself, will dash your chances of admissions (though an essay can work in the opposite way — to help secure admissions for a student whose other credentials might be lacking a bit). But if you get yourself into a make-or-break frame of mind, you won't be able to write anything. The anxiety will fill your mind and force all the words in your head to vanish.

TIP

Apply a little logic to the situation. Simply write, assuming that everything that lands on the page is "good enough for now." Then put the draft away for a while. Take it out when you're calmer. Now edit your work. Make the essay the best writing you're capable of creating. Refer to Chapters 14 and 15 for help when editing your essay. When you've finally submitted your applications (see Chapter 16), hum that old tune, "Que será, será, whatever will be, will be."

Leaping Over Writing-Related Blocks

Even if you weren't confronting a college admission essay, you might stub your toe on a writing block somewhere along the way to a finished product. Writing isn't brain surgery, but getting those words onto the page isn't the easiest task in the world either. I once read an interview with a fine author of many nonfiction books and articles. He claimed that he had to tie himself to the desk chair with a belt whenever it was time to begin a new piece!

You (probably) won't have to go that far to overcome blocks that arise from the writing process. Mostly you need to identify the problems and then change your technique slightly. Think of the small adjustments that a hitter makes when facing a new pitcher in baseball. If you're not (gasp) a baseball fan, think of the way you subtly change your argument when you begin to anticipate the parental response, "No, you can't have the car tonight." In this section I explain how to tweak your writing techniques.

Rising from the fog of details

You're writing a poignant essay about your adoption of a homeless tarantula, waxing poetic about Spidey's first minutes in his new home. Suddenly, you stop. Spidey's initial ascent up the orange-striped wall . . . was the wallpaper at your old house really orange? You search your memory bank, but nothing pops up. Hmm, maybe the wallpaper was purple? Or chartreuse? The essay languishes, a victim of your quest for an accurate wallpaper description. By the time you remember that you were right the first time, it's too late. You've lost your train of thought and can't finish the essay.

REMEMBER

Don't get me wrong. Details are great. You can read about details in Chapter 9. But if you allow yourself to agonize over one particular fact, you're in trouble. Think of the issue this way: Your brain has room for only one job at a time: wallpaper remembering or essay writing. I think everyone out there can identify the right choice.

Here's what to do when you hit a detail-snag: Insert a quick note to yourself. Then *keep going*. Returning to the tarantula example:

> Smoothly sliding each of his legs over the orange (?) wallpaper, Spidey immediately made himself at home. [FIND OUT ABOUT THE WALL PAPER]

Editing while writing

In Chapter 5 I explain why editing while writing or preparing to write is a bad idea. (Briefly, the two tasks rely on different mental processes, which clash.) Unfortunately, lots of people do attempt to combine these two functions while working on the rough draft. Some, for example, stare at a sentence for ten minutes trying to find the perfect verb. That's editing, not writing. So by the time the Platonic Ideal of Verb Land shows up, the essay is on life support, because the editing has overshadowed the writing.

Chapter 6 goes into detail on how to send your inner editor away while you're preparing to write. The techniques I describe depend on one basic principle: Don't stop to analyze when you're creating. Just keep going and leave the critical judgment for later. So in the "which verb is best" dilemma, the solution is simple: Put a verb in — any reasonably sensible verb — and move on. And that's the answer to all the blocks you may encounter while working on the rough draft: Just pour it out onto the page. Later you can punch it into shape. And later you *should* punch it into shape. (Part 4 provides more editing tips.)

Stopping and starting with ease

It's 3 a.m. and you're on a roll. The rough draft is zipping along smoothly. The only problem is that you have a Spanish test at 8:30 a.m. You'll have less than five hours of sleep if you can get to school by teleporting, and even less sleep if you go to school by 21st-century transportation. You're afraid to stop because you'll lose the thread of logic, and you know from experience that starting again is really tough. However, Señora Woods has been sending increasingly cranky notes about "lackadaisical preparation for tests." What to do?

Short-term answer: Go to sleep *now*. Long-term answer: Do your writing at a reasonable hour and give your body the eight hours of rest that it needs to function. But when you stop work, use these tricks to make the restart much simpler:

>> Before you turn the computer off or put the paper away, jot down all the ideas floating around in your head for the next paragraph or section. Don't try to put those ideas in order, and don't worry about spelling or syntax. Just write enough to remind you of what you would write had you had time to continue.

>> Stop in the middle of the section, preferably in the middle of a paragraph. Although the normal human tendency is to keep going until you hit the end of a section, that's a bad idea. If restarting is a problem for you (and it is for most people), you'll find it easier to start with something you were already working on than to approach a completely new task.

>> As you approach quitting time, look over your notes or outline. Identify the least difficult section of the essay. Stop before you get to that section. When you take the essay out again, you should be able to convince yourself that restarting is a cinch because you know you're facing an easy part.

In case you're wondering whether this book is totally theoretical, I should mention that I myself use these tricks. I have to pause in the writing of *College Admission Essays For Dummies* because I have to meet a student on Zoom before I pick up my two kids from preschool. I plan to pause in the middle of Chapter 14, the chapter on polishing your essay, because the revision process is my forte. After my family has had dinner and I've taken care of laundry and dishes, I can sit down at the computer again knowing that "all I have to do" that evening is make some headway on the revision chapter.

4

I'd Like to Finish Before Retirement Age: The Final Draft

Understand how to go from a college essay rough draft to a polished final product.

Apply the revision exercises that will help you finalize your essays.

Verify your admission essays are structured and worded for maximum effectiveness.

Edit your essays for both content and the mechanics of grammar and wording.

Gain a thorough walk-through of the submission process to ensure you've completed all steps.

Chapter **14**

Leaving a Good Impression

When you're in the thick of writing, you can easily get so absorbed in your storytelling and insights about yourself ("Sleepaway camp really *was* the first time I felt a sense of a larger community — wow!") that you forget to zoom out and make sure you're in control of the bigger picture. Now's the time to take yourself out of the details for a moment so that you can assess how the actual material you're writing compares with your vision, your outline, or the message you intended to send.

For each essay that's part of your application, ask yourself some important questions:

» Have you thoroughly addressed the prompt?

» Have you considered the entirety of your application and what kind of impression yours creates?

» Will the admissions committee be able to identify your values and interests and understand more about your life?

If the answers to these questions please you, you've increased the chances that your application will do its job — to present your true self to the college or university. In this chapter I show you what to look for — and what to look out for — as you prepare for submission.

Considering How Multiple Essays Work Together

You've probably been fixated on your personal statement for some time. The good news is you have not just one, but several opportunities to introduce yourself in writing to the admissions committee and make a strong impression. In addition to your personal statement, you have an optional essay on the Common App to address additional circumstances — especially those that have affected your academic performance. Plus, you may have supplemental essays for individual schools, which tend to be focused around your academics, your interest in the college, your sense of community, and what you'll bring to a college campus (among other things — refer to Chapter 17 for more on supplemental essays). Applications other than the Common App tend to follow this format, too: one central essay, followed by optional and/or short-answer additional responses.

This volume of writing, although draining, gives you ample opportunities to share aspects of yourself with the admissions committee that don't

>> Exist elsewhere on your application, either on your transcript or extracurricular sections

>> Overlap with each other

In other words, you have several distinct opportunities to make an impression.

For example, say you've written your Common App personal statement about your experience participating in an annual competition to write, direct, and perform the best ten-minute play in a 24-hour period (yes, for you Californians, I'm talking about Theatreworks 1440 Countdown). Aspiring to be a director is a huge part of your life, and one of the key points of this essay is recognizing room for growth in your leadership style (see, imperfection is good). There's no other atmosphere where you'd rather refine your skills than in the world of theater.

You then realize that one of your Common App schools asks you to write about a leadership experience as a 200-word supplement. You also have the optional Common App essay where you considered writing about the 20 hours a week you devote to theater during certain times of the year, all while earning consistently strong grades. That would be a total of three essays about theater, in some way or other.

There's nothing wrong with writing three essays that include some overlap — especially if you're applying to a specialized program that requires immense dedication. If your goal is to showcase your theatrical background because that's who you are — mind, body, and soul — then you may want to write about theater in three different responses. After all, you may have different productions you can highlight, challenges or skills you can talk about, and unique ways to craft three responses that are loosely connected to theater without being repetitive.

However, if you haven't had a chance to reflect on other aspects of your personality or background, then you may consider whether or not you want to come across as a theater kid and perhaps not much else. Maybe theater offers the most obvious examples of your leadership experience, but actually you took a strong role at that summer camp where you worked. You can choose to write about the summer camp and at some point in the essay compare being a leader at camp with directing school productions — your more obvious forte. You'll remind the admissions counselors of your directorial strengths without letting them completely overwhelm all the other experiences you could write about.

Getting Your Point Across

What's the point of your essay? I know, I know. The point is to get the admissions committee to scream, "Yes, yes, yes we want you!" as they throw scholarship money in your direction. But that's the long-range goal. The immediate issue is a little different. When you first set out to write a college admissions essay, you chose a moment in your life, significant ideas, or people to describe. Now, as you polish the draft, you need to recall why you chose that particular topic. Then you must make sure that the reason is clear to the reader.

Getting your point across firmly and accurately is crucial. Imagine the admissions counselor closing the folder after reading your personal statement. Do you want that reader to muse, "That's nice, but why are you telling me this?" I don't think so! You have to hammer the idea home, but gently. How about I call it a velvet hammer.

TIP

Work the main idea into the essay subtly in a couple of interpretive sentences that make your meaning clear without being forced or obvious. Check out these examples of gently making your point:

> When my cousin Isabella killed the banana slugs, I turned my frustration into resolve. I now have a deep commitment to protecting nature and have fostered a more environmentally-friendly approach to my daily life.

> When my cousin Isabella disrupted the forest's ecosystem by killing banana slugs, I vented my frustration to my father. "Don't be sad," he said. "Take action. Make a commitment to protect nature in all its glory." That moment was one of several interactions that led me toward the ambition of majoring in environmental science.

> By majoring in environmental science, I'll be able to serve the very same redwood forest where I once stood with Isabella.

WARNING

Compare the previous list to the following "hammers" — avoid them at all costs:

> I told you the story of cousin Isabella and the redwood trees so that you will understand my deep commitment to protecting nature in all its glory, including insect life.

> I have shown that I am committed to protecting nature in all its glory, including the lowly insects.

> The story of Isabella and the redwoods makes it clear that I love nature and should major in environmental science.

> In the essay I have proved my commitment to the protection of nature.

Nothing like overkill! In each of these clunkers, the writer has talked down to the reader, treating them as a child who must be taught what to look for. Not a good attitude!

For an example from a real student applicant, take a look at Figure 14-1, an essay written by a student with a truly horrendous commute to school. The writer was initially unsure about discussing the endless daily ride he endured for three years, even though the trip was a major part of his high school experience. But he eventually realized that his travel to school demonstrated his ability to manage time. A sentence in the paragraph emphasizes the message of his essay: "I have learned how to use my time to my advantage."

TIP

As you reread your rough draft, ask yourself what the title or pitch of your essay would be if you were delivering it as a TED Talk. (*Tip:* You won't need titles for either your personal statement or other college essays, but sometimes forcing yourself to place one at the top when you're still in the drafting stage can help you to clarify your mission.) After you've defined the TED Talk-esque message of your essay, find the sentences that convey the idea to the reader. If you can't find those sentences, write some and insert them in the proper place.

When I first decided to attend my high school in tenth grade, I thought I had made the perfect choice. This school would offer me one of the best academic experiences possible, and by taking advantage of the sports and other extracurricular experiences, I would become a well-rounded student. I was aware that entering as a new student, I would have to make new friends, get accustomed to different workloads, and get a general feel for the school. However, the one thing I didn't foresee were the problems that come with having a two-hour commute to and from school.

When I first considered my commute to school, I thought that two hours merely seemed a long period of time and that it wouldn't be of any consequence. However, after serious contemplation, I realized that over the course of a week I would spend a total of 24 hours traveling to and from school. Needless to say, I began to feel a bit apprehensive about my daily commute. After my first two weeks of traveling to school, I was exhausted. I was going to sleep after midnight due to homework and would then have to wake up at 5:30 to get to school on time. I would get on the train, where I could neither find a place to sit and rest nor anywhere quiet enough to do my work. Because I had to transfer four times, I was constantly stopping whatever I was doing to change trains. I no longer thought that it would be feasible to play a sport or to be involved in any other after-school activities. Though at first my situation seemed hopeless, over time things began to improve.

As the months went by, I learned that my cursed commute was actually a blessing in disguise. Once I had learned to tune out the noise and chatter around me, I found myself with a four-hour block of time every day. I had always liked to read for enjoyment, and soon discovered that by using my train time for reading, it was quite possible for me to finished an entire book within a day or two. I was able to borrow four library books on Monday and return them all by Friday. I quickly realized that not only could I read for pleasure, but I could also finish my reading homework. I learned how to study on the train, which proved an invaluable skill. Instead of staying up until midnight studying, I could go to bed at ten and finished studying on the train the next morning, refreshed and rested. After I figured out how to write neatly on the train, I could do all my assignments on the train except those that had to be typed. When I learned how to sleep on the train either sitting down or standing up, my routine became complete. I was now able to function fully on the train, able to study, read, sleep, or complete homework.

Since I entered my high school, I have learned how to do more than just deal with my train ride. I have learned how to use my time to my advantage. By using my train ride effectively, I am able to take on more work and participate in more activities than I would have if I had lived a half hour away. Given the chance, I wouldn't change anything.

© John Wiley & Sons, Inc.

FIGURE 14-1:
An essay example that gets the point across clearly.

Verifying That You've Answered the Question

Most application questions are so vague that almost any essay will do. After all, when the college asks you to "write about something that you feel is important," whatever you choose to write about answers the question, at least in theory. But some application questions, such as the following, are quite specific:

>> Describe the world you come from and how you, as a product of it, might add to the diversity of the University of Washington. (University of Washington)

>> Tell us more about the topic that most engages your intellectual curiosity. (Wake Forest University)

>> Briefly discuss your reasons for pursing the major you have selected. (Purdue University)

>> Great art evokes a sense of wonder. It nourishes the mind and spirit. Is there a particular song, poem, speech, or novel from which you have drawn insight or inspiration? (Boston College)

>> As you prepare to join a new college community, reflect on your role as a community member throughout the past four years. What legacy do you hope to leave behind? (Bryn Mawr College)

These questions — and many others like them — don't accept one-size-fits-all answers. Before you check your rough draft, reread the question you're supposed to be answering. What information is the college after? What do the admissions counselors want to find out about you? Now go back to your essay. Have you actually provided that information? Have you answered the question they posed? If not, you have to revise.

TIP

Sometimes revising an essay to suit a particular question is a matter of changing or adding only one or two sentences. Imagine that you've written a general essay about taking your little brother to the beach. The question asked you to write about a risk. But all you've got are a couple of paragraphs about sibling bonds and the effect little Riley's innocence has had on your worldview — you're excited about what you wrote, but it feels pretty off track. Where's the risk? Well, you tell me! You chose that topic after reading the question, so you probably have a risk somewhere in your mind on some level of consciousness. Now you need to make it explicitly clear. Perhaps you thought that adopting a similar attitude of innocence might make you unpopular with the "cool" group in your school. Or perhaps you were worried that you couldn't supervise a six-year-old on a crowded beach.

Identify the issue and then add a few sentences clarifying the risk. You can do this at the end of the essay, or embed some of your thoughts throughout your response. Presto! Question answered.

WARNING

If you're adapting one essay to several different questions (Chapter 1 tells you how), be especially careful in checking your rough draft. Be sure that the essay relates clearly to the question asked by each college.

TIP

Even when you're answering a very specific question, you still have to make the admissions committee understand why you wrote the essay, even if the word "why" never appears in the application question. (I know; you wrote the essay so you can get into college, but the admissions committee needs to know the personal significance of the topic you selected to answer their query.) Check out the section, "Getting Your Point Across," earlier in this chapter for tips on explaining the significance of an issue or event in a general essay. In an essay answering a specific question, remember that even a very narrow request requires choice. For example, in order to share a "song, poem, speech, or novel from which you have drawn inspiration," you must first select a work of art. Well, why *did* you pick that particular work? How are you connected to it? Why do you find it inspiring, and when in your life has it been most valuable to you? Again, tuck this reasoning into the essay.

Conveying Strength

I hope it's not insensitive for me to imply that some young adults have a flair for the dramatic — as in, some days you may feel like the world is your oyster, and other days you may feel like you're swallowed by despair or have a hard time mustering up confidence. This sections helps you become more aware of the tone and impression created by your writing.

Projecting confidence

"Say what you wanna say," belted out Sara Bareilles — and, well, me, on occasion, when I'm trying to coax a student into writing a declarative statement instead of a noncommittal one. The tendency to sidestep a firm opinion especially comes up when students are responding to questions about their strengths.

Nothing's wrong with having some humility — or the realistic understanding that your peers, too, have plenty to offer a college campus. Still, when you've been asked a question outright, you want to make a clear and committed statement and stand behind it. Here are some tentative statements written in answer to real application questions, along with an improved, stronger version of each:

Prompt: Write about a book that affected you.

Tentative: I enjoyed Charles Dickens' *Great Expectations,* which may be one of the best novels ever written.

Confident: When Pip receives notice that he has "great expectations," I was hooked. Dickens' novel is one of the best ever written and certainly the best I've read.

Why version two is better: The writer describes the feelings more concretely and specifically and eliminates qualifiers.

Prompt: Describe something you've done that you consider creative.

Tentative: I thought I might turn my campus into something that looked like a tented caterpillar, a project that was more or less inspired by the artist Christo and seemed creative to me.

Confident: My creativity was stretched to the limit when I erected a giant tent over the campus, a project inspired by the artist Christo.

Why version two is better: You must make a definitive judgment to answer that question, and you must also evaluate your own actions. Version one gives the impression that you aren't up to either of those tasks.

Prompt: Translate a visual image into words and explain your rationale.

Tentative: Picasso's painting *Guernica* makes me think about the horrors of war, though other viewers may have a different impression. Everyone sees art in a unique way, and no one can say that one way is more correct than another.

Confident: Picasso's painting *Guernica* presents the horrors of war.

Why version two is better: You're not answering a question about everyone's views of art, and inserting a statement about others' opinions takes the focus off your own ideas. The focus of your essay should be on your ideas.

Prompt: What characteristics of our school influenced your decision to apply?

Tentative: I think I might enjoy the annual leadership symposium, though I'm not sure whether or not I'd actually attend, depending upon the amount of work I have to do.

Confident: When I visited Villanova University, my tour guide explained that she had just attended the annual leadership symposium. I was newly enrolled in my high school's leadership class and was incredibly excited to hear about this offering at Villanova and hope to attend someday as a Wildcat.

Why version two is better: Version two expresses your views with assurance. Although you're not signing a binding contract that you'll be at the symposium, you're expressing every intention of being there, and tying the event you've expressed interest to your background.

REMEMBER

Sounding confident isn't the same as oversimplifying a complicated situation or emotion, or worse, projecting arrogance. Suppose that you're writing about an issue that matters to you (a real question). After examining all the facts, you see that several solutions are possible, but no solution is perfect. Or, perhaps you have mixed feelings about a person who has had an impact on your life (another real question). In your essay, acknowledge all the ins and outs of the topic you're pondering. Be honest about your conflicting impulses — doing so takes confidence — and chances are the admissions committee will appreciate the degree to which you've tried to grapple with its complexity. In other words, you don't need a false sense of bravado.

Winning without whining

You want to endear yourself to your reader rather than expend essay lines whining about how horrible you feel about writing an essay. The admissions counselors are well aware of the limitations of the college application process. They understand that they're not getting a complete picture of each and every person who knocks on their college door and that the limits of each freshmen class means rejecting a lot of wonderful candidates. Limitations aside, the admissions counselors *are* taking the time to consider you for admission, so let them in to see who you are.

In your essay you may certainly talk about the hardships in your life, and if those hardships have had a significant impact on you, you probably should make them the topic of your essay. Just strive to keep your own trials and tribulations in perspective. Check out the next section for tips on how to do so.

Steering away from a whine is easy. Here are a few "before-and-afters":

Whine: I've got 12 pages of history to read, a term paper to research, and 15 math problems for homework. Plus I've got to write this essay.

Non-whine: Everyone told me about the challenges of senior year in high school, but I never understood the concept of time management until I sat down to read 12 pages of history, research a term paper, solve 15 math problems, and finalize my college applications.

Why version two is better: The second sentence hints at a context — time management. The essay goes on to discuss *how* the writer packs all those tasks into one day. Thus the reader sees a point, not just a complaint.

Whine: I've been through more hardships in my seventeen years of life than anyone ever should — definitely more than any of my friends

Non-whine: My mother often remarks that I've handled more challenges in my seventeen years than many of the adults she knows.

Why version two is better: Don't let me be the one to minimize your — or anyone's — hardships. I don't call this one a whine, but maybe you agree with me that claiming your unique set of challenges weighs more than anyone else's is pretty presumptuous. Version 2 focuses on handling the challenges and also moves into showing and not telling by letting your mother be the one to comment about how much you have coped with.

Whine: The issue that matters most to me is the environment. My generation will have to pay the price for the stupidity of the older generation, which treated our air and water as garbage dumps.

Non-whine: The issue that matters most to me is the environment. My generation will have to face the consequences of decades of mismanagement of the earth's air and water resources.

Why version two is better: The people reading your essay may not enjoy a blanket statement condemning them for stupidity. Version two doesn't assign blame. The essay focuses on a description of the problem and possible courses of action to remedy the situation.

WARNING Stay away from spiraling into righteousness indignation or predicting your own failure. That's basically the equivalent of saying to someone you want to date, "I know you won't go for someone like me, anyway . . ." (I know it's a protective instinct, but it makes things uncomfortable for the person you're interested in — in this case the college admissions counselors.)

Keeping perspective

As you check your rough draft, allow your global consciousness to dominate for a moment. If you're presenting injustice, hardships, or tragedies, try to examine them in a larger context. Be conscious that whatever you personally have struggled with, you're likely in good (and plenty of) company.

I once read a student paper referred to "that tragic day when someone scratched my BMW." You can bet I advised this student *not* to submit a comment like that to his English teacher, who, even though he had been driving for several decades longer than the student, didn't own a BMW. But even if teaching salaries were suddenly increased by a factor of ten, it's hard not to wince at that kind of remark. I had to bite my own tongue from lecturing about the millions of people around the world who go to bed hungry each night.

REMEMBER

Of course, keeping perspective can be a pretty tall order. You can only understand one reality completely — your own. And the things that have hurt or challenged you are real and important, regardless of whether or not some other people would love to have your troubles instead of their own. In your essay, you should explain what has been difficult in your life, and especially, how you dealt with your problems. Just don't present the topic as if it were a matter of life and death — unless of course it *is* a matter of life and death.

To help you achieve the right tone, here is one last "before-and-after" example:

Narrow perspective: My entire world crashed the day my father lost his job.

Better perspective: When my father lost his job, my family had to make a number of stressful adjustments.

Before you tell your reader to take that leap with you, examine all the factors in your life that your father's unemployment disrupted. You may also take a look at the aspects of your life that *weren't* impacted by this event. (In other words, interrogate the facts and make sure you have a good sense of perspective.) By going with the second statement, you can show and not tell how your life was changed by your father's job loss and then, if it then still feels appropriate to use a strong metaphor like your world crashing, your reader will have a much better understanding of the truth in that statement.

Checking the Essay One Last Time

I promise. This is it! After you read this section, you can be sure that the content of your essay is exactly as you want it. (Chapter 15 offers strategies for completing the final round of edits for wording and grammar.) Take a moment to consider the relevant questions from this list during your big-picture assessment of your essay:

>> Does the essay represent aspects of your experience that you want the college to understand?

>> Does the essay show the admissions committee who you truly are?

- » Have you answered the question they asked?

- » Is the point of the essay clear?

- » Is everything in the essay true?

- » Does the essay contain specific details?

- » Does the essay represent your views accurately?

- » Have you communicated the complexity of your thoughts?

- » Does the essay sound like you?

- » Have you avoided false modesty, complaints, unwarranted criticisms, blanket statements, and flattery?

I hope the answer to all these questions is "yes!" If so, congratulations. If not, Chapter 15 addresses the revision process as well as how to re-enlist your support system, should you find that you need third party input.

Chapter **15**

Smoothing the Rough Edges: Polishing the Essay

Perhaps you've reached a point where you've been working on the same draft (or set of drafts) for weeks, or more, and are at a loss as to what to do to make it better. Or, you may feel like you've hit a wall. You know your essay doesn't feel "done," but nothing comes to mind that you should add or remove. In this chapter, I show you how to make the small but important alterations that tame awkward sentences, enliven monotonous paragraphs, and put you on the path to making your rough draft a final draft. You can apply these strategies to your personal statement as well as supplemental or other essays.

Trying the Red Pen Exercise

When you either have your essay nearly memorized to the point that you can't possibly see it through fresh eyes, or you've been staring at the same document for weeks and still can't decide whether your draft is finished, the Red Pen Exercise is my favorite trick.

The *Red Pen Exercise* is a fast and efficient editing technique to help you see your essay from a fresh perspective. What it comes down to is reading a hard copy of your essay, out loud, with a red pen in hand.

To do this exercise, just follow these steps:

1. **Take a break from your essay.**

   This exercise is most effective when you haven't read it in at least a few days

2. **Print your essay.**

   You're going to be marking the hard copy with corrections, so you need a printed copy. If you don't have a printer at home, you can pop into your school library or local public library to use one. (Your local shipping or copy store probably also has a printer you can use.)

3. **Grab a red pen.**

   The color does matter. Make sure it's red. Blue is acceptable if it's ballpoint, but don't use pencils, crayons, highlighters, or other inferior writing tools. This exercise is serious business.

4. **Read your essay aloud.**

   Any time you pause, stumble over your words, or notice an issue such as redundancy or floweriness, underline, circle, or cross out the text and write the correction you want to make in red pen. (You can do this in the presence of a benevolent listener or alone. If you want company, refer to the section, "Re-Enlisting Your Support System," later in this chapter for guidance on who to pick.)

5. **Incorporate your changes into the electronic version of your essay.**

   Viola! You have a much more polished — perhaps even *final* — draft!

The awkward bits and final touches become so glaringly obvious when you complete this exercise that you may wonder how you didn't see them. However, subtleties can easily slip by you when the your essay remains static on a computer monitor.

The only way to reveal them is by printing your essay and reviewing a physical copy *and* simultaneously forcing your ear to hear the flow of your writing out loud. Suddenly, you'll be able to analyze your work as if it weren't your own — a bit more impartially and with an eye toward finalizing.

Writing Anew

If you're not sure if your essay is your best work and feel you may need a bolder editing option, then you may want to consider this approach. The "writing anew" sort of revision is a bit more ambitious: You have to be willing to do more than just tinker and tweak your existing draft ad nauseum, but it can also lead to big payoffs.

Okay, ready for it? Put your piece away where you can't see it.

Now rewrite your essay from scratch without consulting or peeking at your existing essay. You can try following the exact same structure, you can write from a different starting point, or you can add a section in the middle that you hadn't experimented with before. How you do it isn't as important as sitting down and rewriting the whole thing as best you can.

REMEMBER

When you're writing anew, you may find that from all of the writing practice and ideas you generated while working on your first version your new version comes out a bit more polished from the get-go. (Kudos to you if you can even recreate certain sections of your essay from memory!) Even if your second version doesn't come very naturally, you can try editing it with the Red Pen Exercise (I explain it in the preceding chapters) before comparing it to your original version.

When you're finished, you have two essays to review, compare, and cherry-pick the best content. Maybe you'll take a single sentence from your newest attempt, realize that it's absolutely brilliant, and insert it into the original draft. (Often, an insight will jiggle loose as soon as you break free from the structure of rereading the same thing over and over again.) Or maybe you'll end up combining aspects of each version of your essay. At least you'll have exhausted your curiosity as to whether you could have written the piece better.

Now is the time for final experiments, and you may be surprised by how well small change works. Breaking your rigid attachment to one specific draft can help you see it more objectively and know whether or not your draft works well as it was already written.

Avoiding the Perils of Overediting

Feeling a bit nervous is a normal instinct (especially when phrases like "final draft" or "submission-ready" start getting tossed around). Those nerves occasionally lead students to make impulsive or emotion-driven changes to their essays, simply because they're struggling with the idea of handing their personal writing over to what they imagine as the judging eyes of strangers. Take heart and consider Amanda's example if you find yourself editing from a place of fear.

Amanda fidgeted while I read over the final iteration of her application to Brown: her personal statement, optional essay, and Brown supplemental essays. I saw that she had removed most of the vulnerable details from her optional essay where she had written about her struggle with anxiety and how she had overcome a challenging period at the end of her sophomore year. Anxiety is far from an unprecedented topic. But her editing conveyed fearfulness. "I took out some stuff," she said bluntly.

I responded to Amanda's editing with a reminder: The details you provide are at your discretion and should be based on your comfort. But if you tell only half the story, *that's* when people are far less likely to understand you. Overediting your thoughtful essay at the last minute until you're left with a colorless, ambiguous essay isn't the right move. In fact, Amanda's willingness to paint a clear picture of both her anxiety and her resiliency brought her parents (and even a few peers) to tears by the end of her essay, which she was eventually invited to read aloud at a school function. Amanda didn't just write an awesome essay; she managed to unite a graduating class.

REMEMBER

Getting a little jittery before you paste your final essay into an application and prepare to actually submit it is natural. Sometimes this feeling brings out the best editing, and sometimes it can lead you in the wrong direction by driving you into self-doubt. If you're feeling tempted to water down your essay or omit details that once felt important, take a moment and run your current version by someone you trust and ask how the essay would read without that material (refer to the section, "Reenlisting Your Support System," later in this chapter for more information). At that point you'll have a better understanding of whether or not your polishing is effective.

WHY I WANT TO ATTEND THE UNIVERSITY OF COLORADO CALIFORNIA

Okay, you're in "no matter what, don't do this" territory here. As you check the rough draft, take extreme care to use the correct name of the institution you're actually sending the essay to. Because computer word processing programs have made cutting and pasting material super easy, a fair number of applicants (who never, by the way, turn into accepted and enrolled students) forget to change the name of the college when they recycle a short answer or an essay paragraph. You may certainly reuse material, and if you're applying to five or six different places you'll probably have to do so, unless you're willing to give up sleeping and eating for a month or so. But the details, the names, the reasons why you want to attend — these should be tailored to each college.

Creating Stylish Sentences

Most students don't consciously think about stylish sentences or creating varied sentence structures when they write an essay. But you probably do have a few favorite sentence patterns that, if you're not careful, you might overuse in your college essays. The Red Pen Exercise (which I explain in the section, "Trying the Red Pen Exercise," earlier in this chapter) can also help you with sentence variation. Here I give you other tips and examples to help you identify when the flow of your sentences is choppy, repetitive, or awkward.

Consider this example:

> See Spot run. Dick and Jane run after Spot. Spot pulls out a cell phone. Spot calls the Society for the Prevention of Cruelty to Fictional Animals. The society responds. Dick and Jane are arrested. See Dick booked. See Jane fingerprinted. See Spot celebrate. Spot is a happy dog.

Not counting the subject matter, don't the sentences sound awkward? Choppy, like little slaps of sound? The sentences don't flow smoothly, leading the reader from one to another. Plus, they resemble a second-grader's first efforts at telling a story — not a bad effect if you *are* a second grader relating your very first story. But if you're writing an admission essay, you're in trouble.

In this section I show you how to avoid two pitfalls of sentence construction — monotony and awkwardness. When you're done, you'll be able to write, "See the successful essay get results!"

Monotony

In the preceding section, I write about Spot and his attempt to foil Dick and Jane's chase. The story itself isn't uninteresting (especially the part I left out, when Jane went wild in the police station and threw the fingerprint ink at Dick, who had masterminded the Spot chase). But the sentences leave a lot to be desired in length and pattern. When writing your essay, make sure your sentences aren't dull and boring.

Length

Sentences may be two words long (*Barney shaves.*) or run for a complete and breathless page. (For an example of one of these verbal marathons, thumb through any Victorian novel.) I'm betting that you have few sentences of extreme length (either very long or very short) in your rough draft. Good!

The ends of the sentence–length spectrum are tough to handle. However, if all your sentences are more or less the same length, you risk boring the reader by creating a monotonous sound. The solution is simple. Combine a couple of shorter sentences into one, longer sentence, taking care not to break any grammar rules. Or, chop a longer sentence into pieces (again, following grammar rules) so that you have a few short sentences tucked here and there in your essay.

The key concept here is *variety*. Some examples:

Monotonous sentence length: I was inspired by Spot's campaign against leash laws. His courage to resist restrictive laws captured my imagination. Spot was willing to stand up against the Establishment. Could I live with myself if I did nothing?

Why it's monotonous: All the sentences have nine words, no more and no less.

Possible change: Inspired by Spot's campaign against leash laws, I pondered his courage to resist restrictive laws. Spot was willing to stand up against the Establishment, an act that required great personal courage. My conscience spoke. I had to act.

Why it's better: Long and short sentences are mixed: 15, 16, 3, 4 words.

Monotonous sentence length: The raft drifted downstream swiftly. I hung onto the sides. Suddenly, I saw rocks ahead. The raft tipped sideways onto one boulder. I lost my left oar. The boat sped up immediately. It was clearly out of control. Rocks rushed by my frightened eyes. I struggled to hold on. Finally we reached calm waters.

Why it's monotonous: The shortest sentence is five words long, and the longest has seven words. Snooze-inducing sameness!

Possible change: The raft drifted downstream swiftly as I hung onto the sides. Suddenly, I saw rocks ahead. When the raft tipped sideways onto one boulder, I lost my left oar and the boat sped up immediately. I had no control! Rocks rushed by my frightened eyes, but I struggled to hold on. Finally we reached calm waters.

Why it's better: The sentence lengths range from 4 to 19 words. Variety is the spice of life!

Pattern

You should experiment with sentence pattern as well. Grammarians determine the pattern of a sentence by examining where the major elements of the sentence are — the subjects and verbs, the clauses and phrases. Before you have a nervous breakdown, note that you don't have to place a grammar label on *anything* in the essay in order to fiddle with sentence patterns. Just use your ear!

Read the essay, aloud or silently, and listen to the sentences. Does a certain set of sounds repeat? Do you hear the same type of word, in the same order, over and over again? If so, stir things up a little by moving a couple of things around. Some examples:

Boring pattern: I became interested in penguin habitats about a year ago. I worked in the local zoo, and I volunteered for the penguin house because I like cold weather. I read many books on penguin behavior and biology. I also discussed the birds' habitats with the chief keeper. I learned quite a bit about these animals, and I want to major in penguin biology in college.

Why it's boring: Do I really have to explain? All the sentences are "I + verb," or, in non-grammatical terms, "I + what the 'I' in the sentence is doing" (the action or state of being, in other words).

Possible change: Working in a local zoo about a year ago, I became interested in penguins. Because I like cold weather, I volunteered for the penguin house. Books on penguin behavior and biology and conversations with the chief keeper educated me about these birds, and I'd like to learn more about this subject in college.

Why it's better: The "I" shows up only three times, compared with eight in the original passage. Also, one sentence begins with a verb form ("working") and another begins with "because," a word that joins two ideas. Much more creative!

TIP

Chances are a few sentence patterns are your favorites, and unless you force yourself to become conscious of them, you'll work them to death. To find your favorites, reread a couple of your old school assignments or other written work. Check for phrases or patterns that pop up frequently. Those are your "default" writing habits — what you'll place on the page automatically.

You don't have to eliminate all your writing patterns. In fact, your default value habits may be terrific. The point is that you shouldn't overuse any pattern in your work. After you identify a pattern, reread your essay and be sure that you've included sufficient variety.

Saying It Once and Only Once

Here I discuss an important, crucial point about how you express yourself when you're writing or speaking aloud or on paper, particularly in the college admissions essay, which you write when you're applying for admission to college. No one, not one single person in the world, likes or enjoys wasting hours and minutes of precious time that is so valuable these days in their busy, event-filled lives.

Are you still awake? I just inflicted 68 words on you to say:

> Don't repeat yourself, especially in a college admission essay.

Which version do you prefer? I'm betting that the short one drew your love, and the long one your yawn. Just think how wonderful life would be if everyone said it once *and only once.* Political speeches would be five minutes long. Parents wouldn't spend an hour explaining why you can't have the car keys for a trip to the mall. School assemblies on "The Many Ways the World Is Round" would be over in time for recess. And your little brother would stop asking, "Are we there yet?"

I could go on, but you get the point. Say it once, and then stop. Also, don't use 15 words to do a 10-word job. Some guidelines for spotting repetition:

>> **Beware of double descriptions.** I call this the "tense and nervous" syndrome. "Tense" and "nervous" are similar in meaning — so similar that you probably don't need to say both when you're describing one feeling. Can you find the doubles (or sometimes triples) in these sentences?

> Robert Matses built many roads, highways, and parkways. ("Highways" and "parkways" are roads. Just say roads, or get more specific, as in "Oyster Brook Parkway," "Blue Creek Highway," and so forth.)

> We were prepared and ready for the ninth race. ("Prepared" and "ready" mean the same thing. Use one or the other.)

>> **Watch out for unnecessary descriptions.** The name I've chosen for this problem is "island surrounded by water." Unless you're talking about a traffic island surrounded by cement, the water part is pretty much a no-brainer. Check out these unnecessary descriptions:

> On my tenth birthday when I reached ten years of age, I won a prize for bug collecting and identification. (On your tenth birthday, you can't reach the age of 22. Dump "when I reached ten years of age.")

> In my school the English department, which teaches literature, grammar, and writing, is wonderful. (What else would an English department teach? Toe-nail clipping? Drop everything between the commas or make another more specific statement about the curriculum.)

>> **Dump unneeded declarations of opinion.** My term for this problem is the "In my opinion I think" issue. Okay, if you're citing a bunch of ideas you got from someone else and you need to draw a distinction between the opinion of others and your own thoughts, "I believe" or a similar expression is okay.

Most of the time the reader knows that the statement represents your opinion. Why else would you make it? Read these examples:

In my view, Hamlet is a tragic hero. (Just state that Hamlet is a tragic hero and then go on to make your other points.)

Attending the University of Wooster will, in my opinion, help me to face life's challenges. (Delete "in my opinion." The whole statement clearly represents your view.)

» **Be stingy with words.** Don't say, "He is a man who smirks." Just state, "He smirks." Avoid "there is" or "there are" sentences, unless you can't say what you want any other way. Check out these sentences:

Before: There is a swan floating on the river.

After: A swan is floating on the river.

Before: Five students from my college are presently applying to your graduate program.

After: Five students from my college are applying to your graduate program. ("are applying" indicates that the action is in the present)

Before: It was here, at Sadmouth Academy, that I heard my first blues recording.

After: I heard my first blues recording at Sadmouth Academy.

Before: I then proceeded to learn jazz guitar.

After: I then learned jazz guitar.

» **Don't add a string of qualifiers.** "Sort of," "kind of," "a little bit," "rather" . . . these words may be useful, but they just take up space. Also, they make your writing sound shaky and tentative, as if you didn't have confidence in your own words or in yourself — not exactly the impression you want to give the college of your choice.

Here are some examples of unnecessary qualifiers, with instructions on how to strengthen the sentence:

I became a little bit interested in the arts. (Drop "a little bit." Either you're interested or not. And "interested" is neutral. You're not saying that you ate and slept in the studio for six months.)

My education more or less began at that moment. (Dump "more or less" and explain in what sense your education began at that moment.)

I think you might be rather intrigued by my solution to the problem. (I would delete this entire sentence and simply present the solution. You don't have to tell the university how to react if you've explained the situation well, and if you haven't, attempting to control their reaction won't work. Also, "might" and "rather" soften the meaning of your words, but if you stand behind your statement, you shouldn't need to decrease its impact.)

Reenlisting Your Support System

Perhaps you've been working on your essays mostly independently or maybe you did some brainstorming with a trusted mentor to come up with topics or outlines before doing your revisions alone. Even if you've been getting steady guidance throughout drafting your essays, the polishing stage can still be tricky. (Chapter 6 discusses the types of support you can enlist during the application process.)

REMEMBER

Enlisting one or two trusted individuals like your English teacher, college counselor, or parent to give some advice on your nearly finished essay as a second set of eyes can be helpful. You'll especially want to take note if the feedback you receive has certain patterns — for example, neither of your chosen readers is quite sure what your second paragraph is trying to say. Chapter 8 explains how to ask for help.

The following sections are a couple of reminders for when you're enlisting help while finalizing a draft.

Having realistic expectations

Even if your essay is wonderful, amazing, thought-provoking, and written well (I'm sure it is), most people who you ask to review it, especially English teachers, won't return your shared draft with a declaration that your writing is perfection incarnate. In fact, a teacher, mentor, advisor, or parent is almost guaranteed to find some piece of critical feedback to give you (I should know; I read around a hundred essays every year and have yet to turn around a draft with zero feedback).

REMEMBER

Don't expect your reviewers to return your essay with no feedback. If you get more feedback than you had expected, don't take it personally. You've trusted this qualified person(s) to help you. After all, you want your essay to be as strong as possible.

To fight the feeling of overwhelm if you believed your essay was finished and your reviewer(s) seem to disagree, you can keep your review circle narrow. Ask only people you respect the most to give you fair and honest feedback (such as your favorite English teacher). This process is yours, and you get to decide what feedback you agree should be implemented and what you can pass on. You're still in charge.

TIP

If you want to ensure that the feedback you receive is manageable and concrete, simply ask your reviewer(s) to tell you what they understand about you after reading your essay. If their takeaways align with the themes you intended, you know you've done that part of the job well.

Keeping it tasteful

Although the admissions committee is likely to include mostly twenty- and thirty-somethings (see Chapter 7), stay away from using the same language in a college essay as you might with a twenty-something you know in real life (an older sibling or cousin, for instance). Offensive language and tasteless comments have no place in your admissions essay. It includes not only slang, but language that is sexist, prejudiced, or bigoted in any way (unless the whole point of your essay is to respond to a situation of discrimination or bullying). This is a G-rated book, but without thinking for more than three nanoseconds, you can probably come up with a fairly long list of avoid-at-all-cost words. (And if you can't, good for you! Profanity is pretty lazy — think of a better way to get your message across.)

REMEMBER

Be especially careful with humor — a real minefield when it comes to taste. A good general rule: If you can tell the joke to your great-aunt and your little brother or sister, it's probably okay. If you can't, don't place it in your essay. Also, don't place any jokes in your essay unless the joke makes a point worth conveying to the admissions committee.

IN THIS CHAPTER

» Clarifying the submission process and how it works

» Tackling any final considerations and concerns before you submit

» Clicking the "submit" button

Chapter **16**

Navigating the Submission Process

As I mention repeatedly throughout this book (perhaps ad nauseum), most of my students finish their essays the summer before senior year. Sometimes, this fast-track timeline means that they're done with everything — including supplements and filling out the data entry portion of their applications — by the time they start school in the fall.

So when is the best time to submit your applications? Even though the submission process can be confusing and a bit tricky, you don't need to be stressed. In this chapter, I have your back. Here I explain the ins and outs of the submission process, help you figure out what you need to do to ensure you're actually finished, and point out any last-minute to-do items before you hit the "Submit" button.

Getting the Lowdown on the Submission Process

Once upon a time, applying to college involved ball point pens, stamps, and coming to know everyone at the post office on a first-name basis. Though college applications are certainly challenging today, the submission process might be the one step that has gotten easier. Today, the process is mostly a matter of reviewing key details of your application and understanding which steps are your personal responsibility. The electronic submission process allows you to submit your applications online and subsequently check the status of your application online to make sure that the universities in which you're applying have received all required documents.

The following sections break down what you'll do during the submission process, including ensuring your essay meets word count, pasting your essay into your application, and addressing any additional short answer questions.

Eyeing the characteristics of the process

Although the submission process may vary depending on the school you're applying to, Table 16-1 lists some standardized basics about the submission process, including the four main items you'll need for your application to be complete.

TABLE 16-1   **The 4-1-1 of the Submission Process**

Submission Item	How to Submit
Application (includes your personal statement, extracurricular information, GPA, and other basic information about you)	Through Common App or another application platform (if the school you're applying to doesn't use the Common App)
Recommendations and transcripts (when required)	Your school counselor will send your transcripts and a counselor recommendation directly to colleges, and your recommending teachers will also submit their letters directly to colleges. In most cases, though, you must add them to your application in order for them to gain access as recommenders. Your submission process is separate from theirs, but double- and triple-check in with them to make sure they have everything they need from you!
SAT/ACT Scores	If you're reporting test scores on your application, you also must send official score reports to each college through ACTstudent.org or CollegeBoard.org — by the application deadline.
Supplemental short-answer essays	Supplemental essays on the Common App sometimes require a separate submissions button.

Understanding how the process works

The submission process itself is simple. In most cases (and for all schools on the Common Application), you follow these steps when making your submission:

1. **Press "Review and Submit" for the application you want to submit.**

   When you do, assuming that you have completed all required questions on the application, you'll get a PDF to review everything in print.

2. **Double-check the formatting for your essays and make sure everything looks the way you want it to look.**

   Seeing the essay you've worked so hard on in its final version where typically you won't be able to double space or indent (though I recommend leaving an extra line between each paragraph for a cleaner look) can be *slightly* demoralizing. Suddenly your page-long masterpiece looks like a few measly sentences in Arial font. Don't be swayed! The last thing you should do is go back in and add a few flowery adjectives because you're questioning yourself.

3. **After you approve the PDF of your application, you'll go to a Payments page, where you'll click "Return to Common App" to sign and submit your completed application.**

   You're not only signing your application, but also that the work you completed was your own and that you've answered honestly and to the best of your ability.

4. **If the application you're submitting requires supplemental short-answer essays and is on the Common Application, look for a separate "Review and Submit" button for the supplemental writing.**

   After you submit each page properly, a green checkmark appears.

   You aren't required to submit the application and supplemental short-answer essays at the same time, but I recommend waiting until you're ready and able to submit both aspects of your application in the same sitting to ensure your entire application is complete.

   You won't be asked to pay to submit your supplemental short-answer essays. After you complete the Payments page while submitting the application itself, you can put away your credit card — at least for this particular college.

Working with word count requirements

Word count on the personal statement on the Common Application is important, capped at a maximum of 650 words. If you've only been loosely aware of word count up, you're probably wondering, "Yeah, so around 675 or 700 words is okay, right?"

On the Common App as well as most other application platforms, *650 words means 650 words, ONLY* — though it's okay to be a bit under the word count. In other words, unlike a high school assignment, where word count requirements are usually more like guidelines, on the Common App, they're the rule. If your essay exceeds 650 words, you'll be alerted that you can't reach the "Submit" page.

Throughout the essay process, be aware of your word count. You don't want to paste in a gorgeously-written-but-50-words-over-the-limit essay and then discover you can't submit it because it's too long. If you've waited until the last minute (which I suggest *not* to do in the section, "Knowing When You're Really Done," later in this chapter), you may end up in a panic, realizing that the structure of your essay will topple like a block tower if you remove a single line.

If the Common Application isn't the only application you're working with, you may encounter some universities that require different word counts for your personal statement essay. For each application platform you're working on, I suggest you be aware of the essay prompt and word count requirement ahead of time so you're not scrambling at the last minute.

In case you do find that one of your applications has a word count requirement different than that of the Common Application, you can create a separate version of your personal statement essay in advance — for example, at 450 or 500 words. (As a bonus, some students even find that they like the "shorter" version of their personal statement better than the 650-word version, because they don't need quite so many words to get to the heart of their essay.) To see if that's the case for you, look at your two versions side by side, but be aware that I suggest that you don't submit a response shorter than 500 words for your Common App essay because more than likely you haven't showcased who you are.

As you revise and finalize your essays, edit for word count as well as quality. The Red Pen Exercise in Chapter 14 is a great way to easily and efficiently shave off extraneous words.

Working on short-answer questions

Sometimes, college supplements have a set of questions that require a few words, or sometimes a sentence or two, in order to respond (see Chapter 20 for more information). You may have ignored these questions for a while, figuring that you have time to figure out exactly what they are and how to approach them, only to realize that now those questions are all that stand between you and clicking Submit.

Short-answer questions aren't full-fledged *essays*, nor are they basic data questions like "City you were born in." As a general definition, I characterize anything less than 50 words as a short-answer question. Some examples of short-answer questions include these two from Stanford:

>> What newspapers, magazines, and/or websites do you enjoy? (50 words or less)

>> What five words best describe you?

Although you may be tempted to answer such questions directly into the application and possibly at the last second, I recommend you answer all these questions in Word or Google Docs so that you can see the entire picture before you submit.

You may not need to have anyone review your responses to short-answer questions, at least not nearly as closely as you have someone review your longer essays (unless, for example, you're not sure whether your response to a short-answer prompt comes across as funny or simply immature). Even so, you should carefully review your short-answer questions, and consider how they complement your longer responses. Remember, these questions help paint a clearer overall portrait of you as a candidate that you're sharing with the admissions committee.

You can often add some depth to short-answer questions giving a detail or explanation to complement your answer. Say the short-answer question you're dealing with is "What is your favorite book?" but your response can be up to 35 words. Instead of simply answering with "Jhumpa Lahiri's *In Other Words*," you can convey *why* it's your favorite by adding a line explaining how this memoir sparked a conversation with your father about the excitement and frustration of mastering a new language.

Submitting your application: The when

You've spent hours writing and revising your essay and ensuring you have all the essential information filled out on your application. After all that time, you'll want the submission process to be well-paced and celebratory, not anxiety-ridden and full of setbacks. In this section, I discuss what you need to know in order to complete submitting your application.

Though you should have a running list of colleges you're applying to with their exact deadlines, keep these broad deadlines in mind as you make your final submissions:

>> With few exceptions, November 1 or 15 (depending on the school) is the final deadline for Early Action/Early Decision (EA/ED) applications. I suggest you target October 15 or earlier for submitting EA/ED applications.

>> January 1 or 15 is the final deadline for most Regular Decision applications. I suggest you aim to submit by December 15. Then you'll have a clean slate going into the holidays and new year.

Your teachers' and counselor's deadline for submitting letters of recommendation is the same as your deadline. So, when you're checking everything over before submission, touch base with your recommenders, too, with a gentle reminder of your upcoming deadline. If you're sending SAT or ACT scores, you must also order official score reports by the application deadline. In other words, another benefit of finishing your essays far in advance is to give you a few extra weeks to deal with the logistical components of your applications.

Creating a Submission Plan

You think you're done, but you're not quite sure. When is it time to stop combing through your applications and complete the daunting step of putting them into someone else's hands? If you're wondering, "So can I submit?" Sometimes, the answer is, "Yes, right now!" Or after a final table read of your application, essays, and supplemental short-answer essays with the whole family (often a good idea). Other times, though, I suggest you *wait*, even when everything inside of you says that you're done.

Keep the following in mind as you prepare your submission:

>> **Before you actually submit everything, consider whether or not you're waiting on any senior year credentials that may enhance your application.** If you waited a few more weeks, would you be able to include anything on your application that isn't already there?

Perhaps you're just at the cusp of finding out if you'll be team captain of your badminton team this year, or you just took the SAT but haven't gotten your scores back yet. If you have the luxury of weeks (or months!) of wiggle room before your deadline, don't rush to submit before you've had the opportunity to add the new credential coming your way.

>> **Prepare your parents (or whomever is going to supply a credit card) for each application fee.** When you set a personal submission deadline, make sure they're aware of the total cost. If they're hoping to read your applications before you submit, make sure that happens well *before* your intended submission date. Don't wait until the night before the deadline and expect them to review everything.

However, if you're *not* weeks away from being able to update your test scores, GPA, or your resume page with a fancy-schmancy new title, and you can't imagine the quality of your essays (or the application itself) possibly getting any better, then that probably means it's time to pressing that magic submit button.

Of course, after you submit your application, you can't undo that process, and the essay you've marinated on for months will be in the hands of admissions readers. Go over everything once more. Revise after reading Chapters 14 and 15. Set your essays aside for a period of time before rereading them. If they read clearly and well, you're probably ready to go. If you're still not sure or feel too impartial to be a fair judge of your own work, put your writing in a drawer for about a week. (Go. Right now! Print out your pieces and put them in a literal drawer.) Now, take out your phone or planner and mark "Finalize essays" on your calendar, one week from today.

In a week, retrieve your printed copies and read them one last time. Sometimes, with fresh eyes, you'll suddenly notice a single word or turn of phrase — even a contraction that feels out of place or awkward — and wonder, how did I let *that* one slide? In other words, by giving yourself a bit of distance from your writing right before the end, you can see things more clearly. And if you read your essays and sigh with pride — or at least tell yourself you can't think of any small changes to try to make them better — you'll know that you're officially done.

THE PERILS OF TECHNOLOGY

Every year I set a (somewhat) arbitrary deadline for every single one of my students to have their applications submitted. For EA or ED candidates, that deadline is usually October 15, which is more than two weeks before November deadlines.

Nevertheless, every year, one student falls behind schedule and calls me a night or two before the *real* deadline, in tears. "I'm 48 hours ahead of the deadline, but the Common Application keeps *crashing*. I can't get in, and I'm probably going to be sitting here pressing 'refresh' all night long."

I bite my tongue to keep from reiterating that this is the *exact reason* why we set a deadline of at least two weeks ahead of what I call the "submission scaries."

The truth is that technology is unreliable, and sometimes, so are some students (I say with love and affection), so you can expect for the website traffic in the several days leading up to most college deadlines to be untenable. You may as well pretend that the application has already closed, because it will be impossible or unbearably slow for huge stretches of time to log on.

In 2020, the University of California application and several other universities had such dramatic online problems just before the deadline that they ended up extending the submission window by a few days. However, it was also a pandemic year, and no one had their act together. In short: don't rely on such miracles!

Finishing Your Submission

After you determine your personal statement and supplemental essays are complete and you verify word count (refer to the section, "Working with word count requirements" earlier in this chapter for more information), you're ready to submit. To help you execute well on this pivotal step, the following sections include all that you need to consider for a successful submission.

Pasting your essays into the application

You're confident in your essay and supplemental short answer essays and don't want to change another word. Then, it's time to transfer your final drafts into the application to eliminate even the slightest possibility of needless errors.

REMEMBER

Keep in mind these reminders when pasting your essay into the application:

>> **Check and recheck again to make sure your essay has the correct details, including the right school.** You'd be surprised at the number of times students include wrong (and embarrassing) information in their essay. Consider this snafu for your NYU essay: "I couldn't be more confident that the University of Michigan is the place for me!" (Believe me. That stuff happens.) Proof the essay and have a family member or friend read it to double-check you don't sabotage your chances of being accepted with an error that easily could have been caught.

>> **Clean the draft of all notes, comments, and tracking changes before you copy and paste.** You want to ensure you're working with a completely *clean* draft.

>> **If you change anything to the essay at the last minute before submitting it, make sure the you make the change for a very good reason.** After you decide your essay is ready to go, stay the course and *don't* impulsively edit your work after you transfer it to the application.

Submitting your essay: What you need

Before you make your final submission, make sure you have the final details taken care of. Here's the short list of what you need:

>> **A credit card:** You can find out the amount of each application fee in advance. Some colleges don't charge an application fee at all and others charge up to $85.

>> **Your transcript and Social Security Number:** You need them in order to double-check information in your application. Catching a potential mistake now is much easier to correct, whether that's a grade you entered incorrectly or something else, than having to report later that you made a mistake on your application.

>> **Your camera and likely a proud parent or mentor who may want to be a part of this final step with you.** Take a pic and share with your friends after you've submitted everything.

REMEMBER

You submit the supplemental short answer essays on the Common Application separately from the application itself, which means there are two separate submission processes. After you click "Submit" on the application, pay, and sign, you're not completely done until you also click "Submit" for the supplemental short answer essays. I've had many mystified students come to me, confused that their application reads "Incomplete," because they weren't aware of the second submission page.

Finishing the process: Signing, submitting, and celebrating

After you hit submit, congratulations. You did it. Now, request your favorite meal for dinner on submission night, because completing and submitting any number of applications is a big deal!

The next thing you'll want to do (after you celebrate) is watch for emails. You're probably immune to college email by now. More than likely, your inbox is flooded with marketing from various universities on a daily basis. After you're officially a prospective applicant, you won't want to miss a single message from a school you've applied to, because anything you hear in the next couple of months usually requires action from you — something they're still waiting to receive, for example, or updates on your status. If you're invited to create an account or portal with a school you applied to, make sure to do so, as this is where application updates will be posted. So pay attention, because not responding to an important notice from one of your top choices can mean the difference between getting accepted or not.

5

Analyzing Questions from Real Applications

Address specific types of college essay questions, such as those about other people, the college you're applying to, or an issue relevant to you.

Understand the role of supplemental essays in the overall picture of your application.

Take a closer look at specific prompts for supplemental essays and "fast facts."

Project into the future to answer questions related to who you'll be on campus and why a particular college is right for you.

Make every word count in your college essays and short responses, especially those that are less than 300 words.

Chapter **17**

Composing Essays Starring You

In addition to your personal statement essay (the 500-to 650-word response that you'll send to every college or university that accepts writing) the schools you're applying to may have their own additional essays, which the Common Application refers to as *writing supplements*. (Other applications sometimes label these prompts as *additional questions*.) No matter what the college or university you're applying to calls them, these supplements are another way to showcase your strengths, interests, and growth.

Many students don't find the additional questions nearly as all-consuming as drafting their personal statement. After you have a singular piece of writing that feels like a snapshot of who you are, writing supplements may feel like a matter of simply figuring out what else about you is interesting and beneficial to share.

This chapter — and the other Part 5 chapters — helps you begin to examine the opportunities within various types of supplemental essay questions and provides tips so you can take maximum advantage of the opportunity they provide for self-revelation.

Understanding the Supplemental Essays

Supplemental essays, by their very nature, are more specific than the broader "tell us about yourself" personal statement prompts. The reason is that each institution has its own culture and values (including in what it seeks in a class of freshmen). If a particular school has chosen to require or offer supplemental essays, the reason is to allow the admissions counselors to take a more specific look at how you'll mesh with the campus culture and its values. Supplemental essay questions often, but not always, fall into several themes:

>> Your academic goals

>> What you have to offer a community

>> Why you've chosen to apply

The following sections explore these and other themes.

Dealing with "Why us" questions

When the romantic partner of your rosiest and most far-fetched fantasies finally calls, you may be tempted to ask, "Why me?" just so you can hear how wonderfully attractive you are. The application version of the romantic "Why me?" is "Why us?" and resembles the following:

>> What aspects of this school influenced your decision to apply?

>> What experiences in your life prompted you to apply here?

>> Why are you a good match with our institution?

>> Discuss your reasons for applying to our school.

>> What characteristics of our school do you find most appealing?

You may imagine that the institution you're applying to has a collective ego and that this sort of question requires you to stroke that ego a little. Well, you're probably right! And yet, remember one extremely important point: *This essay is still about you.* Don't be fooled into rattling off a list of your dream college's attributes and statistics, because your dream college knows that it's a great school and probably agrees with you that you'd be lucky to be admitted. You don't need to waste your valuable word count writing a research paper on a specific college or university in order to aimlessly tell it about itself.

REMEMBER

So what question should you be answering? That's simple. Explain how you, as a prospective student, are a good match for the school and what attributes about the school are particularly compelling — not to the general public — but for *your own* strengths and interests. You can mention a program of study (including a specific course or professor) or something about the college community that has grabbed your attention. in fact, you probably should have several concrete factors (academic, social, cultural, geographic, or other) that have attracted your attention, and you must be able to explain why these factors are important to you.

Here are some other tips to keep you focused:

>> **Be as specific as possible.** In any sort of writing, specifics are better than generalities, but details are absolutely crucial in a "Why us?" response. A canned, vague statement such as "I want to learn and your school will help me do so" tells the admissions committee almost nothing (wouldn't you learn at just about any four-year school?). Remember, admissions committees want to admit students who will stay at their college through graduation. If you give the impression that you stabbed a pin randomly into a college list in order to make a selection, they may assume that you haven't taken the time to understand what the college can offer you (or even worse, that you're applying under duress, say because someone advised you to keep this school on your list).

>> **If you've actually visited the campus, refer to that experience, citing buildings and activities by name.** If you sat in on a class, explain why the professor or students impressed you. Once again, *be specific.*

>> **If relatives or friends attended the university you're applying to or the university representative visited your high school for an information session, you may cite their comments.** Explain what impressed you.

>> **Mention your own educational or career plans in relation to the college.** (*I'd like to study Egyptian pyramids with Professor Tomb of your archeology department and then excavate in conjunction with the Ministry of Antiquities,* for example.) At the risk of annoying you let me say it again: Be specific!

Time for some examples. Refer to Figure 17-1, a short-answer response for an application to Santa Clara University. The student who wrote this response had visited the college and interacted with current students, as the essay makes quite evident.

I have been familiar with Santa Clara my whole life. Growing up in the Bay Area, I have attended basketball games on campus as well as visited the museum, getting a taste of what it may be like to attend. I have chosen to apply Early Decision because SCU has the amazing academic experience, community, and connections that I seek in my college experience.

In my college search, I have been influenced by two things: community and quality of education. I want to apply to Santa Clara University because I was blown away by the way Santa Clara sets its students up for success and the amazing education opportunities. When doing research and speaking to local students and alum, I found that the school exemplifies what I desire in a college experience. I'm looking for a positive and uplifting community because, based on my experiences working with the Associated Student Body (ASB), I know how much this kind of atmosphere strengthens the student experience. I have watched several peers from local high schools go on to attend SCU and share how much they love it, especially for the warm and supportive nature of the community. SCU represents my ideal college.

FIGURE 17-1:
A short answer to the "Why us" question from a student who visited the university.

© John Wiley & Sons, Inc.

Now run your eyeballs over Figure 17-2. The writer wasn't able to visit the school personally, but she did attend an information session held at her high school and speak with alumni and current students. Her answer focuses on the college's academic offerings and her perception of its quality of life.

Community is one of the most important aspects of a college to me. In the information session and my interview, I could see clearly how community plays a key role at Occidental, which makes me feel confident that I would be able to create a loving community there. Additionally Oxy's focus on research allows me to pursue my interests with a level of depth that I have not seen at other schools.

I've always considered myself an academic who loves history, and recently began exploring fashion, something I'm also enthusiastic about, through a historical lens. The American Studies major at Occidental offers fashion history courses, which is something I have yet to find at another school. Additionally, the potential to pursue an interdisciplinary major that combines literature, politics, and history would offer me the space to explore my many intersecting passions. The use of critical theory in all of Occidental's courses offers a new perspective to examine my world and my experiences. Occidental is my top choice due to its unique academic opportunities as well as its strong community.

FIGURE 17-2:
A short answer to the "Why us" question.

© John Wiley & Sons, Inc.

One last example: The writer who composed Figure 17-3 also relates to specific aspects of the curriculum at Brandeis that intrigue her as well as features of the community that resonate with her goals.

I believe that in order to understand the world, I must read and listen to others' stories, learn about science, technology and politics, and explore other cultures. In high school I have pursued interests from aviation to politics to journalism, and at Brandeis I hope to explore a variety of subjects before settling on a major. I want to be in an environment with other students who are as passionate about learning and asking questions as I am. The emphasis on critical thinking at Brandeis will allow my peers and me to have in-depth conversations and exchange ideas.

While I am not religious, I have become increasingly interested in my Jewish heritage and am excited to be on a college campus that will encourage me to more deeply understand my background. Having grown up in the Bay Area, I am excited for the opportunity to learn and study with peers at Brandeis who may have different perspectives on the world.

I look forward to participating in the Brandeis Core as I narrow my academic focus. The niche classes offered through Cool Classes for Curious Minds will enable me to expand my knowledge and develop my creativity within a rigorous academic environment. Furthermore, the experiential learning opportunities outside the classroom such as The Immigrant Experience in Waltham: A Service-based Practicum, will help me to integrate academic and real-world learning. I hope to write for *The Judge* and meet friends at Chum's as a Brandeis student in the fall.

FIGURE 17-3: A short answer to the "Why us" question by a student who was applying with her major Undeclared.

© John Wiley & Sons, Inc.

Complimenting without flattery

When writing the "Why us" response for your dream school, the one you've been over the moon about for quite some time, you *do* want to make sure you convey your enthusiasm to the admissions committee, lest anyone think there is any-where else you'd rather enroll. However, if the admissions counselors are good at their jobs (and you should assume that they are), they also have a finely honed flattery detector.

REMEMBER

If you admire a particular aspect of an institution, you may say so, especially in answer to the "Why did you choose our school?" question. But don't heap mean-ingless praise in the hopes of impressing the reader. You're not standing in front of a celebrity with your mouth hanging open; you have time to collect your thoughts. Here are some examples of the difference between meaningless praise and something more legitimate:

Meaningless praise: The long, star-studded history of your institution impresses me. So many incredible people attended this university!

Legitimate compliment: When I look at the roster of alumni, I see many accom-plished writers such as Felonia Handwringer, Jackson Flounder, and Philip Poeticall. The writing program that nurtured their talent has several aspects that attract me, including small seminars, peer-to-peer criticism, and intensive grammar review.

Why version two is better: Version two is much more specific. The fact that the essay writer knows about Handwringer, Flounder, and Poeticall indicates that they have some knowledge of the school. The details about the writing program show that the essayist values these characteristics and also indicates genuine interest in the school's curriculum.

Meaningless praise: Words cannot express how totally honored I will feel if I am accepted.

Legitimate compliment:

Why the preceding line is blank: You can't fix that statement, so you should just delete it. Stay away from speculating about whether or not you'll be admitted. Just comment on the aspects of the university that appeal to you and explain (with specifics) how your talents and goals mesh with the university's programs.

Relating a Personal Experience

In your supplemental essays, avoid sweeping generalizations — especially because the word count for these essays is often far shorter than your personal statement. In order to avoid speaking generally (or telling when you should be *showing* your meaning), ground your essays in experience. Here I show you how to do just that.

Somewhere within your applications — each a doorway to a school you love — may be a question like one of the following:

>> It's cool to love learning. What excites your intellectual curiosity? (Tufts)

>> Describe one of your quirks and why it is part of who you are. (University of Virginia)

>> Who does Sally sell her seashells to? How much wood can a woodchuck really chuck if a woodchuck could chuck wood? Pick a favorite tongue twister (in originally in English or translated from another language) and consider a resolution to its conundrum using the method of your choice. Math, philosophy, linguistics . . . it's all up to you. (University of Chicago)

>> What is the truest thing that you know? How did you come to this conclusion? (Villanova University)

>> Pick one of your unique identities and describe its significance. (University of Colorado at Boulder)

To answer most of these questions, you'll probably want to draw upon two elements that, if you've already written your personal statement, you're expertly familiar with: (1) a story and (2) the reason you told the story. (Okay, the word "story" might imply something lengthy and verbose — and some supplements are as short as 50 words, so if the word "anecdote" suits you better, feel free to think of yourself as trying to come up with anecdotes and details.)

REMEMBER

Essentially, a good college admission essay is an interpretative piece of writing with a personal point of view. A good response to an admissions essay question often contains elements of a story, if — and only if — you include an evaluation of the events for the reader.

Your first task is to scan your memory bank for possible topics. The personal inventory in Chapter 3, as well as the guidelines in Chapter 2, can help. After narrowing the field, start collecting details and ideas, perhaps with some of the techniques from Chapter 5. Then it's time to write.

Now for some specific tips.

Choosing relevant material

You're not writing a complete autobiography; you're writing an essay. Ask yourself what unique aspect of your background you can showcase to answer the question.

Suppose that you're writing about the truest thing that you know (one of Villanova's supplemental prompts). You may have read this prompt and thought you don't *need* a story to answer it. You can just identify a truth that you believe in (watching to avoid clichés) and explain, right?

Not so fast. I recommend you brainstorm in a way that may seem counterintuitive: Create a list of your most meaningful experiences (maybe you already have a few ideas on the backburner; refer to Chapter 3 where I discuss completing your personal inventory). Then, try to connect one of those significant experiences to a larger truth or belief that is important to you.

Check out this example that answers the prompt through the use of a narrative experience:

> "Cross the line if you have ever felt hopeless." I attempted to swallow the lump in my throat and stepped forward, even though I was certain I would be alone. When I saw that Tamar, Matt, and Raimy were walking with me, and that Tamar was shooting me a supportive half-smile, I felt more seen and understood than I had at any other moment in my three years in high school. After several more rounds of "Cross the Line," I knew that our class of peers had permanently deepened our connection. We couldn't pretend not to see each other anymore.

This afternoon at our junior retreat helped me identify what has since become my most important truth: that every individual seeks, above all else, to be understood. This truth has shaped the way that I relate to my peers, the children I volunteer with at Fun Club, and even my two younger brothers. I look forward to listening and striving for understanding among a new group of peers in my future college environment.

Because this essay is grounded in experience — the anecdote about crossing the line — the reader feels much more connected to the student and their truth. The opening is vivid, and yet it only includes a few carefully chosen details (the lump in the writer's throat, Tamar's smile). As you choose details for your own supplements, remember that the narrative portion of your essay is *not* the whole thing. Leave room — at least half — for interpretation. (The section "Interpreting the story for the reader" later in this chapter explains this critically important part of your essay.)

Compare the previous example to this short supplemental essay about a personal truth *without* a story:

> The truest thing that I know is that every person is seeking recognition and appreciation. I have realized that no matter how different two individuals are, or how different their motivations might appear to be, we all simply want to be understood for who we are by the people around us. I believe that when people are loved for who they are, they are far more capable of reaching their potential and being successful. Whereas when someone is denied affection or feels misunderstood by the world around them, they are more likely to act out and especially to sabotage the success of others.

This response doesn't show. *How* does the writer know this to be true, or how did they develop this belief? Why is this specific truth important to this student? In other words, this response needs evidence — that's where the stories and details from your life come in. This response comes off as more of a philosophical rambling than a response that tells me more about the writer.

Ranging over a long period of time

The example I include in the preceding section occurs in a limited amount of time. But what if you want to explain an event — actually, a series of events — that took place over a few weeks, months, or even longer? How do you focus the essay in such a case?

Easy. Think of the whole period of time as a video. Choose one or two (okay, maybe three, but not more) frozen moments from the video that you think the reader should see — moments that represent important points in the arc of the whole experience. Go into greater detail about those selected moments.

Taking the story inward

A key part of the story you're recounting is internal. The incident you chose out of all the millions of events in your life matters to you. Maybe the incident changed you in some way, or perhaps your actions illustrate an aspect of your personality or character.

In either case you need to lead the reader into your personal reality. You can do so by simply telling the reader about what was going on. However, three techniques borrowed from fiction (but in the essay applied strictly to the facts and used *very* sparingly) create a path to the inside. Those techniques are thoughts, dialogue, and action.

Thoughts

What was going through your head at the crucial moment? Okay, I know that you didn't have some sort of psychic recorder running, but chances are you remember enough of your thought process to recreate it for the reader. In the fictional retreat example earlier in this section, the writer may have been assessing whether or not to step forward, and so the opening anecdote may also have included the following:

> The line seemed miles away, instead of a few steps. I wasn't sure I could summon the will to move my feet. The retreat felt like a safe space, but what if my classmates judged me for what I was about to reveal?

Don't overdo this technique. Thoughts are the equivalent of the slow-motion photography used in sports broadcasts. On sports shows, slo-mo is for the winning hit, the disputed call, or the season-ending injury — not for a routine double play. In your story, thoughts should be for moments of similar significance.

WARNING

Don't attempt to duplicate anyone's thoughts. You can't know what someone else was thinking, and if you attempt a guess, you've entered the realm of fiction and left essay-land. The admissions committee will have reason to doubt your grasp of the difference between fantasy and reality and may even question the rest of the information you supplied in your application.

Dialogue

Words reveal quite a bit about the person who says or writes them. (That's why you're composing an essay, right?) So consider adding some — not too much — dialogue to your essay to illuminate character or emotion.

In an essay of limited scope and length, you generally need only a few lines of dialogue — far less than you would for a scene in a novel or a short story. But placed at the right spot, dialogue displays character and enlivens the essay.

Notice what the dialogue in the retreat supplement reveals: a very private experience that the writer would be acknowledging by stepping forward. By opening with a line of dialogue ("Cross the line if . . ."), your admissions reader can also infer the entire context of the setting (many twenty- and thirty-somethings have participated in a similar type of exercise). Although this essay could have started in many different ways, the single line of dialogue reads much more effectively than a long-winded summary about how last year this student went to a retreat where eventually the leaders explained that they were going to play Cross the Line and then there was this one question . . .

Actions

How does the old proverb go? Actions speak louder than words. But remember to include more than the big, obvious actions when you recount an event. (As another proverb says, little things mean a lot.) Back to the example from earlier in this section:

> I attempted to swallow the lump in my throat and stepped forward, even though I was certain I would be alone.

A lump in one's throat is a small detail, but a significant one. The writer's fear comes across clearly in that tiny sentence. Of course, in an essay you should include only a very small number of action details. As long as you don't overuse this technique, you can get a lot of mileage out of it.

TIP

Not only your own actions, but also other people's reaction to you, may reveal your personality and character.

Interpreting the story for the reader

Okay, you've taken the readers into your reality for a few moments. But you also need to make them understand why the trip was necessary. A great part of the essay — up to half, perhaps — should be an evaluation of that reality. You may attach some sentences of explanation to the beginning or the end of the essay. (Chapter 10 explains introductions, and Chapter 12 tackles conclusions.)

Figure 17-4, an essay written by a student who worked on a political campaign, has plenty of detail about the events of those hectic months. (To protect the student's privacy, I changed the names and a couple of small details, but the basic writing is his and the general situation is true.) The essay traces the writer's growing realization that he cared deeply about the election and about his friend's reaction. Notice how much space the interpretation takes in relation to the events described.

It feels strange when I recount some of my experiences working on Arthur Black's senatorial election campaign, since, for as long as I can remember, I have been best friends with his son, Jon. Seeing things as both an insider and an outsider has always allowed me to know the candidate as more than just another politician, a name on some ballot. At the same time, though, it has left me with a distance letting, for example, my parents' dinner guests to criticize him without reservation in front of me. I no longer remember whether I had first encountered the candidate as a father, joking around with Jon and me as we passed through the living room, or if I had seen him first as a political figure, posing beside the mayor in the New York Times. So, as a result of the two contexts in which I knew him, I took on a dual role in working on his campaign.

When Jon would ask me whether I could give up a few hours to hand out literature down in Union Square, I would be doing my friend a favor to accept. If the campaign office managers sent me down to City Hall to record a press conference, I was working on a serious election. At first, despite my minimal knowledge of Arthur Black's political stance or experience, I figured that Jon's dad was a worthy cause. And so I had agreed to volunteer as an intern on the Friends of Black campaign and report each morning to a small closet-office, where my job consisted of mindlessly entering data into a computer or delivering packages. But, before I knew it, I became interested and more involved. I became an enthusiastic member of the Black team.

Once, outside a candidates' debate, Jon's older sister Jean, the volunteer coordinator, suggested that I be the one to publicize over the megaphone. I had the privilege of shouting to the whole block, "What color is that car? Is it Smith (his opponent)? No, my friends, it's black!" I was Jon's loyal, funny friend, there to help out.

There were, however, instances that forced me to abandon my particular view of Arthur Black as Jon's father and view him purely as a political figure. I was put in the position of defending and advocating my candidate, pointing out his years of experience, his attention to the average consumer, and his plans to re-build public schooling. And, although I knew in both my heart and mind that I was supporting the correct candidate, it amused me to see the shift that had taken place in my perspective over the past few years, a shift from strictly emotional to more rational judgment, without which, I am certain, I would have devoted far less of my time and energy to the campaign.

As the race intensified, I began to hear very disparate accounts of the election, first from Jon and then from local news correspondents. To each, I had a different reaction: a tacit sympathy for my friend and a relatively objective view of a candidate's political strategies. The week of the election, wearing the Black paraphernalia, the t-shirt, the stickers, and such, I was simultaneously advocating a candidate and offering support to Jon. Election Day, watching the poll results waver, I wondered, as a citizen, who would be my next state senator, and asked myself how I would console my best friend if his father were to lose. Perhaps one of the biggest challenges of being a good friend would be picking him up when things were looking down, and at that point they were; we were faced with a question I couldn't yet answer: "What if he loses?"

FIGURE 17-4: An essay example that interprets a story.

FIGURE 17-4:
(Continued)

I supposed, when Arthur Black lost the election, that all the volunteers were equally upset. Still, remarks that he was just another politician struck a chord that resonated against my image of the decent man and loving father I had known growing up, and I never understood how he could bear such slander. Often, discussing the issue with my father, who suggested, "That's politics," I realized that, for me, that wasn't politics. Politics meant where all our years of hard work would end up and how my friend would take the results. Politics concerned much more than just an agenda or a resume, but I accepted that voters would, and probably should, see things through different eyes; it was just a shame we didn't succeed in showing them how deserving and qualified a candidate he was, and, to them, Arthur Black became perhaps a name on some ballot after all. But whether it was, in the end, the campaign platform or the loyalty that I had to my friend that drove me to get involved, I'll always be proud of having worked on that campaign and having felt that human side of politics, to have supported a real person.

Explaining Academic Experiences and Your Intended Major (or Lack Thereof)

Educational institutions, not surprisingly, are interested in your academic experience — not just the numbers and letters on your transcript, but also the way you relate to school and learning. Examples of essay questions about your identity as a student and your intellectual or professional goals include

» Think about an academic subject that inspires you. Describe how you have furthered that interest inside and/or outside of the classroom. (University of California)

» How did you discover your intellectual and academic interests, and how will you explore them at the University of Pennsylvania? Please respond considering the specific undergraduate school you have selected. (University of Pennsylvania)

» What are your intellectual curiosities and why do you think Occidental is the right place for you to pursue them? (Occidental College)

» What interests you about your intended major? (California Lutheran University)

» Please tell us what influenced you to select your major. If you're undecided about your major, what attracted you to Emerson's programs? (Emerson College)

>> Describe your academic and career plans and any special interest (for example, undergraduate research, academic interests, leadership opportunities, etc.) that you are eager to pursue as an undergraduate at Indiana University. Also, if you encountered any unusual circumstances, challenges, or obstacles in pursuit of your education, share those experiences and how you overcame them. (Indiana University)

TIP

Faced with one of the preceding questions, you have some thinking to do. To describe an academic experience, consider focusing on a particular activity or assignment and ground your response in real experiences rather than making vague statements. Another way to answer the academic experience questions is to write an essay that surveys a year or more in one subject or field, explaining the progression toward deciding to pursue this field in your higher education.

Figure 17-5 is an excerpt from an essay written by a fine young mathematician. The time period discussed in the essay begins in third grade and continues through senior year in high school. The writer ends the essay with a dose of interpretation, explaining that her mathematical studies relate to other academic experiences, such as writing and art history. She closes with a punch line that delivers her main idea: "Whatever I do in life, I will always be thinking of an equation to go with it."

Writing an essay with an undecided major

But what if you *don't* have any idea of your major? These sorts of questions can be very intimidating for my "Undecided" friends, so let me offer you a pep talk. One of my role models, writer Elizabeth Gilbert, speaks about people as being either jackhammers or hummingbirds. Some students are jackhammers. They know what they love and hammer away as hard as they can. They're focused on a specific track from a relatively young age.

However, most people are hummingbirds. They have myriad curiosities, and that's okay. Exploring your interests is how you will, eventually, discover where it is you want to invest your energy in the future. So how do you write an essay about your intellectual curiosities or academic interests when you're applying to college with your major undeclared? Well, you do the same as your jackhammer peers and explain what it is that interests you — *with more than one example,* because you're an explorer! Your job is to explain to colleges how your exploratory nature is a good thing: ideally by showcasing that you have multiple interests, rather than none at all! Figure 17-3 offers a strong example of a supplemental essay written by a student applying to college without declaring a major.

"You know, your choreographic work is very mathematical," my friend said to me recently. Though my passion for dance is almost as intense as my passion for math, it was not until I heard this comment that I realized how closely related they are. This connection makes perfect sense as many things in my life are closely related to math.

My love of math started in third grade. At school there was, in addition to a science lab, a math lab. While other kids played softball, my friends and I sat on the floor of the math lab playing with tangrams (small, colored, polygonal blocks). We didn't need softball; math lab was playtime. The ordinary pieces could all fit together infinite ways to make anything from a big, multicolored square to a complex symmetrical snowflake. I still have a Polaroid of my third grade tangram masterpiece of the snowflake variety. Math became only more interesting to me throughout elementary school. My parents soon caught on, and during long car rides they used to give me strings of numbers to add, subtract, multiply, and divide to keep me from getting bored and asking if we were there yet. In fourth, fifth, and sixth grades I participated in the elementary school math Olympiads, and my after-school hours were sometimes devoted to discussing a problem or idea with my teacher.

In junior high, math was put on the back burner with my discovery of nail polish and hair dryers, but not for long. When I got to my new school in tenth grade, my interest was rapidly revived by Mr. W., my geometry teacher. He taught with an unsurpassable amount of enthusiasm and love for the subject, and the inspiration he evoked in me spread to my other classes too. My essay writing improved dramatically when I learned the techniques of geometrical proofs, and my ability to visualize molecular models in chemistry also got much better when I learned rudimentary trigonometry. When the math curricula from my old and new schools did not line up, Mr. W. was the one who supported my decision to take the tenth grade math course, Algebra II and Trig, in addition to ninth grade Geometry. This arrangement was normally against school policy, and taking two honors math courses was a load, but one I was quite happy to bear. In fact, it reconfirmed my love of math.

In my pre-calculus class during my junior year, all sorts of new doorways opened up. There is so much more out there than I ever dreamed of, and I am thoroughly excited to study as much of it as possible; I am doing an independent study in math this year, in addition to taking calculus. Studying art history in my junior year gave me a whole new outlet for my love of math. Renaissance art, one of my favorite genres, is firmly based on geometry. Its philosophy, as well as its aesthetic appearance, is highly organized and deals with several versions of the dichotomy of earth and heaven, including body and soul, and, to my delight, square and circle. My favorite music is quite mathematical; I love Bach and Mozart, and the idea of repeating modified themes is infinitely pleasing to me. My fascination with the mathematical permeates my other studies.

Many of my interests trace back to my love of math, not just as a subject, but as a way of thinking. To do math, one has to have a sense of organization as well as the ability to figure out something from a set of conditions. Whatever I do in life, I will always be thinking of an equation to go with it.

FIGURE 17-5:
An example of an essay on an academic interest.

Responding to the question of who you will be on campus

When met with a prompt like "How do you see yourself pursuing your interests at University X?" or "Please describe how you will contribute to our community", it's important to remember that the university is trying to get a picture of how you see yourself participating in your college life: academically, socially, and otherwise. Even though projecting into the future can feel intimidating, ensuring that you're well-informed about the opportunities available at the college *and* reflecting on your existing interests will help you craft a strong response.

WARNING

Be careful about questions related to your goals or hopes for your future college community. You can easily get carried away with them. After all, wouldn't the college want to hear that you're going to get involved in student government, play lacrosse, volunteer for about 17 different committees, and . . . you get the idea.

Give examples of how you'll engage in your campus community, and make sure your examples are believable. If the first thing you mention is that you want to write for your college newspaper, follow that statement with your experience or pursuit of journalism in high school because the best predictor of the future is the past. Establishing a connection between your future goals and what you're doing now shows you mean what you say.

That doesn't mean you can't take on something new in college (such as writing for the newspaper), but you may give a bit of context as to how you developed this interest or if some factor kept you from being able to participate (such as your high school didn't offer a journalism class or school newspaper).

Answering Questions on Diversity and Inclusion

In recent years, some colleges have been modifying the more general questions on how you plan to get involved on a college campus to focus more on issues of identity, inclusion, and engagement with diverse communities. Many students find these questions intimidating. They're worried about saying something wrong, which is understandable. That's why gaining a true understanding about what the colleges are really getting at when they ask about these themes is important.

Here are a few examples that I help you explore further:

>> At the University of Colorado, Boulder, no two Buffs are alike. We value difference and support equity and inclusion of all students and their many intersecting identities. Pick one of your unique identities and describe its significance.

>> The University of Oregon values difference, and we take pride in our diverse community. Please explain how you will share your experiences, values and interests with our community. In what ways can you imagine offering your support to others?

Alternatively, the University of Oregon also gives this option:

>> Describe an experience with discrimination, whether it was fighting against discrimination or recognizing your contribution to discriminating against a person or group. What did you learn from the experience? In what ways will you bring those lessons to the University of Oregon?

You may not even know where to start with questions like this. That's why I'm here. Let me give you a few general strategies when tackling these types of questions:

>> **Be honest and authentic.** Don't be embarrassed or shy away from the fact that perhaps the community you've grown up within *isn't* terribly diverse. A college that asks this type of question may be looking for how you feel about going from such a community to one that contains people from all backgrounds, not only culturally and racially, but also socially, politically, intellectually, and otherwise. If you're applying to schools because you *value* diversity, even if your experience has been somewhat limited, you can focus on explaining why diversity at the college level is important to you.

>> **Use your real experiences.** More than likely you've gained an understanding about broad concepts like "community" or "identity" from all kinds of environments. Maybe you learned an important lesson about how to relate to others from being a member of a youth group or a sports team. If you can answer the question as to how that experience has prepared you to relate to those who might see the world from a different perspective, then you're in good shape.

As you can see from Figure 17-6, some students choose to explore an aspect of their identity that is family-based. This student wrote about her role as an older sibling and how it has prepared her to advocate for others in the college environment (a great response, which shows that you don't have to focus exclusively on cultural identity).

After my father's passing, I helped to fill in the role of a parent for my younger sister. My experience as an older sibling in a single-parent household is an important part of my identity and has shaped the way I interact with others. The skills I have learned while supporting my sister academically and emotionally allow me to support and understand those around me.

I have always provided my sister with the academic support she needs because she has many learning disabilities. I have learned to work with her to set up systems to make her school life easier. Oftentimes, it is challenging to my sister to self-advocate for the accommodations in her 504 Plan; thus it becomes my mom and my responsibility to make sure my sister is getting the work the way she needs. When she comes home with a lengthy reading assignment, we try to find an auditory version online or we will read it to her ourselves. Advocating for my sister has taught me how to help my peers. I offer support to my friends when they are struggling in class and with their writing. In college, if a friend were having trouble managing their workload, I'd be happy to help.

I have also supported my sister emotionally, as she has trouble with social anxiety. I have learned through my own struggles with anxiety how to effectively help my sister and provide the emotional support she needs. Together we work on confronting fears; in social situations, I am there to support and encourage her when she has trouble connecting and talking to others. Because I have experienced firsthand the impact of understanding someone with emotional issues, I will be aware of peers in my future college community who may be struggling privately, and will extend understanding whenever I can.

Having to take care of my sister from such a young age has become an important part of my identity. I am a natural caretaker and feel I advocate and support those around me. My identity as an older sister has shaped my life, and I am proud of what I have to offer because of it.

FIGURE 17-6: An example of an essay responding to Boulder's prompt, "Pick one of your unique identities and describe its significance."

Notice the other aspect of Oregon's second question earlier in this section: "In what ways can you imagine offering your support to others?" That question gets at the crux as to what these questions are about. They're about whether or not you have the self-awareness, maturity, and openness to relate to all kinds of people on your college campus. More pointedly, how open will you be to connecting and learning from roommates, classmates, and colleagues whose backgrounds differ from yours? If you answer this question honestly (with evidence — consider using the questions in Chapter 3 about your relationships for examples of how you relate to other people) you won't go wrong.

Approaching Fun and Creative Questions

You may have a question (or several) that deviate from the serious tone or academic buzzwords of other supplemental essay prompts. These questions read like a breath of fresh air, but you're not sure how seriously you're supposed to take them. In general when you're answering questions like these, the rules still apply: Make sure you're addressing the actual prompt and providing specific details, and even though you can certainly be lighthearted or humorous, make sure you run that sort of content by a trusted reader.

Here are a couple of examples:

>> Write a letter to your future roommate. (Stanford University)

(*Hint:* What would someone sharing a bedroom with you need to know — there's the opportunity for self-awareness.)

>> Find X. (University of Chicago)

>> If you could change one thing about where you live, what would it be and why? (University of North Carolina)

Sometimes, however, you can put your own spin on the more befuddling fun prompts, using them as an opportunity to offer something about you that no one would know to ask. Figure 17-7 shows a student's take on the preceding prompt from the University of Chicago, a school known for its puzzling and brain-bending supplemental essay prompts.

She wanted to approach the prompt creatively, but ended up drowning in frustration until I asked her what she *wanted* to tell the university. She answered she wanted to share how she overcame the stigma of being bossy. I advised her to think a few days and to see if she could connect the story she wanted to tell to the prompt. Sure enough, days later, her mother left a note on her bed signed "Xxx" (and I didn't even have to pay her to do that). Mission accomplished. Although this particular essay's connection to "Find X" isn't clear until the last lines, that's fine — the University of Chicago chose a prompt intended to keep you guessing; and as a writer you're permitted to surprise your readers in return.

I've been called "bossy" for as long as I can remember. In first grade, I came home nearly every day with a 'stomachache'. My mom will tell you the real reason I came home was because none of the girls wanted to play princesses with me at recess, calling me 'bossy.' I suppose the feeling came from a broken heart, but as a child I innocently assumed the tightness in my belly simply must be a result of what I had for lunch. My mom explained that I was decisive, not controlling; I just knew exactly how I wanted the game to play out.

This issue has been a recurring theme throughout my life. My siblings have repeatedly reminded me that I am not their mother, but their sister. "You're not the boss of me - you can't tell me what to do," my siblings remind me. I used to act with a children's theatre group, but when I was eight, I came home from rehearsal and told my mom that I was tired of being told what to do - I wanted to direct. The first rule of the stage is to never tell another actor how to act (something I admittedly did quite a lot). I was obviously not destined to be an actress.

My mother sent me an article about a list of things women in positions of leadership were called "bossy," "petty," "mean," "self-interested," "combative," "condescending," "stubborn," "uncaring," "not approachable," "brusque," and "impossible." These were only the polite descriptors. Men, on the other hand, were praised for their leadership — "strong," "decisive," "a leader," "hard-working," "committed," and "confident."

As I read the article, I felt as if it was written for me directly. I had been called all of these things, and so had women before me — women like Hillary Clinton, Madeleine Albright, Angela Merkel, and Marissa Mayer. These women are powerful leaders, leaders whom I admired, and still do. These women are not petty or mean. We are simply women in a man's world, being scrutinized because we are not men.

I felt empowered. I was on the same path as my heroes. I realized that this trait of mine could, and should be, applied as a strength - to areas where bossiness was admirable because it was now reclassified as "having the skills required of a leader." And these leadership skills were desirable, not something to be ashamed of. I no longer cowered - or came home with an upset stomach - when people scrutinized me for being a leader. I have, of course, learned that people are best led through nudging rather than brute force. I learned how to use my innate ability to manage and organize to my advantage. I no longer felt as if I had to subjugate these skills beneath my more feminine qualities.

It felt as if my whole world had shifted, and everything was illuminated with a new perspective. I pushed myself to try new things - I began to stage-manage the musicals and the plays, and to manage my school's photography section of the yearbook. I embraced positions of leadership and did not allow myself to be dragged down by society's fear of a woman leader.

Three days ago, my mom left a pair of socks that said "I'm not bossy. I'm the boss" on my bed with a note that read "Found these and thought of you. Keep being 'bossy.' Xxx Mom."

FIGURE 17-7:
An example of a response to the University of Chicago's supplement, "Find X."

Daydreaming Your Way into College

How many times has an Authority Figure told you to "stop daydreaming" and get with the program? Surprise, surprise: Certain essays legalize daydreaming, requiring you to imagine yourself in an alternate reality. Questions in this vein resemble the following:

>> If you could have the job of any individual, living or dead, what would you choose and why?

>> If you could be anyone else for a day — a living, historical, or fictional figure — who would it be? Explain your reasons.

>> Imagine that you could work for a year with unlimited resources. What would you like to accomplish?

>> If you could create a new family or community tradition, what would it be?

The first three sample questions give you a chance to "walk in another person's shoes." I won't deal with those questions here, but in Chapter 18, I explain in detail how to write about other people. The last two questions — working for a year with unlimited resources and creating traditions — directly address your values. An essay responding to this sort of question may be structured in any one of several ways:

>> **Recount an imaginary event — as if it were something that had actually happened.** For example, what you would do in a limited period of time with unlimited money or how you would celebrate the tradition. Use present tense (*As the final brick in the Homes for the Homeless House is cemented into place, I see the smiles of the future tenants. . . .*) or past (*With a joyous peal of bells, Help Each Other Day drew to a close. . . .*). After taking the reader into a "you are there" reality, explain at length *why* the event is important — to you or to the larger community.

Whenever you recount an event, real or imaginary, leave room — at least half of the essay — for interpretation or evaluation.

TIP

>> **Create a mosaic.** In this case, a mosaic is a series of snapshots of moments from the course of the time period specified in the question. Suppose you declared your desire to spend a year negotiating peace in one of the world's trouble spots. You might briefly describe a conference early in January, the progress of a community project halfway through the year, and the renewed hope of participants as your year draws to a close. Be as specific as you can about your plans, and be sure to clarify when you depart from reality into your fantasy achievements.

>> **Include a survey approach.** This may suit the "year with unlimited funding" question. Discuss all the reasons why action is necessary, exactly what you would do to improve the situation, and the possible results. Be sure to provide detail for the most important aspects of the project. For example, don't simply say that you'd work on your community's homeless problem. Explain where and how you'd build housing.

>> **Begin with a narrative.** The "description and interpretation" technique may be applied to fantasy as well as reality. Imagine that you're creating a "Help Each Other Day" town tradition. Describe the town square before and after the day's cleanup. Be sure to evaluate the impact of your new tradition on the town and on yourself.

Chapter 8 provides a detailed explanation of these various ways to structure your essay. Regardless of how you organize the essay, remember to do the following:

>> **Write about something you know well.** If you're fairly clueless about the topic, more than likely you won't be able to fool anyone with your essay, even though you're claiming the topic is close to your heart. Not a good message!

>> **Avoid journalistic reporting.** You're writing an admission essay, not a term paper. Skip footnotes and lengthy factual explanations. Be specific, but remember that the focus is on you and your relationship to the topic.

Chapter **18**

Describing Significant Strangers and Friends: Essays about Other People

've always wanted to answer one particular college application question. Unfortunately, no one asked that question when I was writing my admission essays (not long enough ago to qualify for a slab of rock and a chisel, but close). Here goes:

If you could have dinner with any figure, living or dead, who would it be and why?

My answer? The 19th-century British writer Mary Shelley. This woman doesn't get enough credit. At the age of 19, she wrote one of the best novels of all time and essentially created the genre of science fiction when she published *Frankenstein*. In addition, she knew a thing or two about resilience: Shelley was the daughter of the feminist philosopher Mary Wollstonecraft, who died a few days after giving birth to her, and the wife of poet Percy Shelley, who was reputedly unfaithful and then died in a boating accident at 29. Poor Mary Shelley. I guess it doesn't sound like the giddiest dinner party of all time, but still I'd take it because I've looked up to her genius for most of my life.

You may not get the "ideal dinner companion" question either, but chances are at least one of your applications will ask about the people who have influenced you in a supplemental essay prompt, or that you may write about an important relationship in your personal statement. In this chapter I tell you all the secrets of essay questions about others — which, like all admission essays, are really about the star of the show, you.

Defining Others' Influence: You Are Who You Know

A famous motivational speaker once claimed that people are each the average of the five people they spend the most time with (feel free to stop and ruminate on that for a moment!), and social psychologists have been debating the merit of this idea ever since. Regardless of whether you agree, many applications, including the widely accepted Common Application, inquire in one way or another about a person who has had a significant influence on your life. Some want you to stay within the bounds of reality:

>> Reflect on something that someone has done for you that has made you happy or thankful in a surprising way. How has this gratitude affected or motivated you? (Common Application Essay Prompt 4)

>> Describe someone who you see as a community builder. What actions has that person taken? How has their work made a difference in your life? (University of North Carolina, Chapel Hill)

>> Describe a situation in which you had to work with a person who is different from yourself. (Read more about such questions in Chapter 17.)

Other questions allow you to step into the realm of fantasy:

>> Which person (alive or dead) would you like to interview and why?

>> If you could work for a year with a nonpolitical person who is not personally known to you, whom would you select? Why?

>> If you could be anyone else for a day — a living, historical, or fictional figure — who would it be? Explain your reasons.

REMEMBER

Before answering any of the "person who influenced you" questions, spend a few minutes thinking about the significant others in your life. The questions in Chapter 3 about your family and other influences are a good place to start; in the case of historical or literary figures, you may do some light research. When you have several possible subjects, answer these questions about each one. (If the question addresses a real person, stick to the facts. If the question allows you to daydream, send your imagination into the arena.) Here are a few more questions:

>> When and how did you first become aware of this person?

>> What qualities or accomplishments do you associate with them?

>> What would your life be like *without* the presence of this person? This last exercise in *subtraction* should give you a good definition of what this person has *added* to your life.

>> List several significant occasions with this person — times when you interacted in a special way. How did you feel during these interactions? What did you learn?

>> List some normal activities that you shared with this person. How did you feel during these interactions? What did you learn?

REMEMBER

By the time you've finished "auditioning" several possible subjects, someone should emerge as a nifty topic. As you make the final selection, follow one key principle: The essay isn't really about the individual who influenced you; it's about *you* in relation to this person.

You're looking for a subject that gives you ample room for discussion of *your* character, development, or values. Chapter 17 explains that you shouldn't be fooled into believing that you're writing an essay about why your dream college is a wonderful place. That's a given. Instead, you should write about why your dream school is a wonderful place for you.

The same rule applies to writing about an influential person. If you're writing about a person, rather than focusing on that person's biography, the actual question you're answering is, why has this person been influential to *you?* What meaning do *you* take from the relationship (if you're writing about someone you actually know), and what qualities of theirs do you identify with or hope to emulate?

After choosing your subject, the hard part is over. Now all you have to do is write the essay. The next section of this chapter shows you how to tackle real people who are or have been a presence in your life. The section, "Relating Strangers' Lives to Your Own," later in this chapter also guides you through essays about current or historical figures — people you know from the media or from textbooks but have never personally met. The final section of this chapter, "Entering the Fictional Universe," tells you how to write about literary and other imaginary characters.

Writing about Friends and Relatives

During the spring of 2020, my daughter, who was four at the time, was engaged in virtual learning. (In preschool, that mostly looked like some good morning songs and a story or two, but it kept her occupied for close to an hour and reminded her that her friends were also at home, just like her.) One day, I logged her into the virtual classroom early so that she could have a chat with a friend she especially missed. Remaining within earshot, I heard my daughter remark, "I know you're feeling sad." When her friend responded in the affirmative, my daughter offered, "You can just do your best!" I'm not doing justice to the cuteness of a preschooler attending to her friend's psychological welfare, but I think of that moment whenever I ponder the role of familial influence — because each of the phrases she used so naturally she had heard first from yours truly.

As a teenager, you may open your mouth sometimes and hear not only wisdom you've gleaned from the big figures in your life, but also your peers. In writing about a person who has influenced you, your task is to define and reflect on the influence of that figure in your life. The following sections walk you through the process of figuring out how you relate to those around you, including where you draw inspiration and where you may differ from those in your circle.

Choosing the "big figure" in your life

Which relationships have most impacted you? Parents are an obvious choice, but siblings, teachers, coaches, friends, and neighbors are all possibilities. As you take inventory of those figures in your life, keep in mind that the person you choose may have had a positive *or* a negative influence. If you go with a negative, be sure to emphasize the growth or resilience you learned to practice from this relationship. For example, several of my past students have written about a family member's struggle with addiction. If you're considering writing such an essay, make sure you explain the impact of the family member's decisions. You may also describe the strength you had to cultivate in order to grow up in an unpredictable (or predictably difficult) environment. You may reflect on how you've attempted to come to terms with your loved one's mistakes and how those experience impacted the sort of life you hope to create for yourself.

If you write about someone who has made your life more difficult, take care to maintain perspective (see Chapter 14 for a more thorough explanation of why perspective matters in college essay writing). For example, a student who grew up surrounded by addiction may highlight the theme of practicing resiliency, with or without strong role models. This point of emphasizing personal strength would come across quite differently if the student's difficulties only involved overly strict curfew-setters or a little brother who habitually read their diary.

Focusing on your ties to a group

Sometimes supplemental essays may ask about your relationship to a group, not a single person. Such an essay may be a response to these types of prompts:

>> Describe a community that is important to you. How has that community prepared you to engage with, change, or even build the Wake Forest community? (Wake Forest University)

>> Describe the world you come from and how you, as a product of it, might contribute to the UW community. (University of Washington, Seattle)

Try not to be intimidated by prompts like the UW one. The best way to approach this type of question is to consider not your *entire* world, which undoubtedly includes a wide array of communities (your school community, your family, your neighborhood, your religious or ethnic community, any teams, clubs, or committees you have been a part of, and more) but one particular aspect of your world where you can identify the impact *and* explain how that impact prepares you to be a member of a college community. After selecting a community to write about, make sure to consider your own role and how the experience taught you about what you have to offer others in addition to explaining what you've learned from other community members.

Check out Figure 18-1, a student essay describing the impact of the cross country community on the writer's life. She uses details not only about her first practice (which serves as the opening anecdote), but also shows how the *ethos* (the general spirit) of the team shaped her personally. She supplemented the general description with a couple of specifics about her fellow runners:

First practice students are lounging on the grass (not stretching or posturing).

Runners are described as ranging in skill (from state qualifiers to casual friend-seekers).

Runners cheer for each other at every practice and never run alone.

Both the opening images and the later explanation of how the team became further united after a loss combine to form a complete picture. The essay would be much less effective if it had lacked either of the two elements.

I showed up to my first high school cross country practice fifteen minutes early, anticipating a grueling yet fulfilling workout amongst competitive runners. Instead, I found students sprawled across the grass, eating Peeps and rice cakes. Over the next ninety minutes, I met members of the robotics team, state qualifiers, and people who just wanted to find friends.

Within the cross country community, I found a group of peers who valued sportsmanship over speed, and taught me to always run with a partner and cheer for each runner as they crossed the finish line. Though initially disappointed that our team was not as serious as I had anticipated, cross country soon became my escape from stress, in part because there wasn't pressure to be the best or to outdo my team. As time went on, I realized the spirit of the cross country community was the direct result of the seniors' efforts to unite the team – a realization which deepened when one of our graduating seniors, a friend who had been a force of positivity, took his own life. With this loss, I wondered: would cross country mean as much to the incoming freshmen if they didn't have this sense of belonging and family?

I helped my teammates come up with a plan: we began to share stories with new recruits about what cross country meant to us and planted a memorial garden in our school's quad. Previously, we had only spent time together at practices, but slowly, we began to carpool, socialize after school and organize celebrations for birthdays and the last day of finals. At practices, I started running with freshmen, giving them advice about the races and asking them about their transition to high school. After crossing the finish line, I would cheer for the incoming runners and others joined me.

Last spring, our team captains appointed a fellow runner and me co-captains by presenting us with the infamous Flop, a flip-flop signed by all previous captains. As we begin to navigate our final season, I look forward to leading my teammates and continuing the community spirit.

FIGURE 18-1:
An essay that discusses the significant role a group has played in the writer's life.

© John Wiley & Sons, Inc.

Selecting the scene

You also have to define the *how* and *when* of the essay. You can't accomplish your goal — to show the influence of a person or community on your life and character — with a bunch of general statements such as the following:

> Mrs. Gabble inspired me to become a better person.
>
> Chick's friendship meant a lot to me.
>
> I never understood heroism until I met Aunt Molly.
>
> No matter what, I can rely on my mother.

All these statements may be true, but they ask your reader to trust your judgment and accept what you say *without any evidence.* Lacking specific examples, the reader has no basis on which to envision or understand the dynamic of your relationship. A much better strategy is to present a little scene, the sort that might appear in a short story or a novel. (However, everything in *your* scene must be true.)

To zero in on the best scene, play a mental video of memories. Watch yourself interacting with the person or community you're writing about. Choose moments in which the influence of this relationship(s) was readily apparent. When you write the essay, remember to include all the ingredients that make your scene come alive — action, dialogue, and description. (Check out Chapter 17 for tips on writing a vivid scene.) Also remember to leave room for interpretation. The next section of this chapter shows you how to do so.

TIP

If one scene won't do the job, you may want to create a collage of moments during which the influence of your subject is evident. See Figure 18-2 where the student effectively uses a collage structure to show how she relates to her community and surroundings. The moments that this student selected reveal her grappling with her own identity, but also how being thrust into a new community helped her achieve a new level of understanding and self-acceptance.

Another strategy to help you set the scene for your influential figure is to focus on an object related to the person who is the subject of the essay. Figure 18-3 is a student essay about a saxophone once used by the author's grandfather. The author describes the instrument in detail, but he's really writing about his grandfather and father and their feelings about family. Needless to say, the author's great love for his family also shines through.

I am Chinese American.

My mother always said that we were a "bad" Chinese family because we do not speak Cantonese and ask for forks at Chinese restaurants. Nevertheless, I thought we were an average Chinese American family. However, after working one summer in Chinatown, San Francisco I was proven wrong.

I try my best.

"I can order," I insist to Emmy. I approach the glass case, stick out two fingers, and timidly say *cha siu bao*. The lady responds, "Two for $5" in English, but they look too small. As I start to pay, Emmy, my coworker who grew up in Chinatown, stops me, says one *cha siu bao* and takes two one-dollar bills from my wallet. The bakery lady reaches in the back, grabs one larger, normal-sized bao and I realize my efforts to blend in were dismissed as *too* American.

I make mistakes.

On the first day of the job, I am responsible for walking with 30 elementary school children from the center to swim class. In the chaos of herding children through traffic and construction zones, I make it back to the center with 29 kids. While my mother would have organized a search party for me, the parents and the lost child nonchalantly accept my apologies. At school, I am the composed Yearbook Editor, self-assured and decisive. I had woven myself seamlessly in two high-intensity counseling settings; yet somehow in Chinatown, I became vulnerable almost immediately.

I embrace who I am.

After I discovered I am not "American" like the rest of my white friends or "Chinese" enough to order my own bao, I realized I will never be one or the other, no matter how hard I tried. Instead I learned how to accept my American accent when I try to speak Cantonese and my craving for Chinese rice porridge over chicken noodle soup when I am sick. My summers working in Chinatown taught me to embrace both my American and Chinese identities because I would not be myself without both.

FIGURE 18-2: An essay that uses a collage structure.

© John Wiley & Sons, Inc.

Where it was once shiny, it is now tarnished. In the past, it made music. Now it simply makes noise. It was once exercised daily by a professional, but now it is practiced on by an amateur. Formerly, it was used to entertain and make people happy. Now it serves as a means to remember.

My father tells me that he was a great man, a caring husband, and a wonderful musician. I never really knew him, however, as he was disabled by Parkinson's Disease when I was very young. Grandpa's life, as I understand it, revolved around his job. As the co-president of a musical entertainment company, he had many responsibilities. This meant that he was never home on weekends. From Thursday night to early Monday morning, there was always a wedding, a society gala, or a business party to play. The rest of the week was spent at the office, meeting with prospective clients, auditioning musicians, and making contacts with party planners at hotels and country clubs. With a wife, a widowed mother, and two children to support, my grandfather had to meet many economic demands. Unfortunately, his success in the music field limited his ability to be, in the conventional sense, a family man.

When he is not at work or spending time with his family, my father can often be found exercising his fingers at the piano that sits in our living room. Music and family have been and will be forever joined in his mind. As a result, my sister and I were encouraged to play an instrument from an early age. Neither of us enjoyed the piano, the instrument of choice. Practicing was a chore that prevented us from enjoying other activities. We developed an utter distaste for the piano. However, our parents urged us to continue. Much to my father's dismay, my sister quit. Having grown tired of the piano, I would have followed my older sibling had it not been for a wonderful gift.

When my grandfather passed away, I was given his Selmer Marc VI tenor saxophone. I was told many stories about his musical career and the amazing things he did with this horn. Despite the death of his dad and his career in medicine, my father has continued to perform on club dates. With this sax, he hoped that I would one day accompany him on a "gig."

Although overwhelmed by the gift and excited about the prospects of joining my father on a club date, I was never eager to practice or perform. Originally I thought my lack of interest was the result of my early experience with the piano. I simply viewed music and practicing as punishment. With considerable introspection, I now believe my reluctance stemmed from something else.

Every time I looked at the horn, I saw the tarnished brass on the bell and the trunk. My grandpa spent so much time playing that the sweat from his hands penetrated the once glistening finish. The unsettling images of my father as a boy competing with this instrument for his father's attention disturbed me. Because my father has always praised my grandfather, I was unable to allow myself to feel anything but affection for him; conflicting thoughts focused on music, and, more specifically, my grandfather's saxophone.

Perhaps it is maturation that now allows me to play every day. With persistence and focus, I will learn all the songs in his repertoire. When summer arrives, I will once again accompany my father on club dates, but my former apathy will be replaced with enthusiasm.

Music is still an important part of my family. It once served as a means to build a relationship between my father and grandfather. Now it will help to sustain and strengthen the strong bond between my father and me. I am beginning to realize just how complex relationships can be. My grandfather played his hand as best he could. My father, with a different score and a different drummer, plays on. I hopefully synthesize what went before, learn as much as I can, and compose a new score.

FIGURE 18-3:
An essay that focuses on an object as a way of discussing a significant person.

© John Wiley & Sons, Inc.

Interpreting the influence

Why do you want your reader to know about this influence on your life? When the admissions counselor finishes reading your essay, they should have an answer to that question. You can make sure the reader gets the point in any one of several ways:

>> In the introduction or conclusion, state the main idea in a couple of sentences. For a good illustration of this technique, sneak a peek at the essay in Figure 18-1 earlier in this chapter, which brings everything together in the last paragraph.

>> If you've written a scene, let the point come across in dialogue. But *don't* stray into fiction. Quote only what people actually said — at least as best as you can approximate it.

>> Weave the interpretive material throughout, in narrative and/or dialogue. The reader has to work a little harder to figure out what you're trying to say, but if you do a good job, the extra effort is worthwhile.

CONSIDERING A COLLAGE STRUCTURE

One of my favorite collages appears in *String Too Short to Be Saved* (published by David R. Godine), an autobiography by poet Donald Hall about his boyhood summers on his grandparents' farm. In one chapter Hall describes a family friend, Washington Woodward, with several sharp verbal snapshots, including the following:

- Removing rocks from fields (his hobby)

- Eating only one type of food until his supply was exhausted and then moving on to another (ten days of canned peas followed by a week of tuna fish, for example)

- Collecting and straightening used nails

These and other such scenes feature young Donald's interactions with Woodward, as well as the boy's reactions *to* Woodward. The piece clearly reveals the author's admiration for Woodward's strength and perseverance, but it also shows the terrible waste of Woodward's efforts. No one scene could accomplish these two tasks.

Relating Strangers' Lives to Your Own

Unless you hang out with people whose names regularly appear in tabloids or on Reddit, a question on your college application may require you to write about a stranger — someone whose job you'd like to have or a person whose accomplishments reflect your values. Here are a few examples of such questions:

>> Yale's residential colleges regularly host conversations with guests representing a wide range of experiences and accomplishments. What person, past or present, would you invite to speak? What question would you ask? (Yale University)

>> If you could trade lives with someone (fictional or real) for a day, who would it be and why? (Scripps College)

Writing about a stranger, a figure you don't know but that you admire for some reason or other, may actually be easier for you than writing about someone you know. A measure of emotion is subtracted when the subject is a stranger, and you don't have to feel guilty for including a critical comment. (Nor do you have to worry about hurting the feelings of anyone involved in your day-to-day life.)

TIP

Before you choose the subject of your essay, consider the goal of the question. For Yale's question, you may select a figure that will illustrate your future plans or current passion — someone whose individual wisdom will be useful to you and your university peers as you prepare for the professional world. You may also consider someone who is a Thought Leader — maybe you aren't choosing this person simply for their career prowess, but because their perspective, encouragement, and overall philosophy can help shape you into a more grounded adult.

Here are a few other guidelines for an essay written about someone you don't know:

>> **Choose someone or something that you're already pretty familiar with as the topic of your essay.** If you're just vaguely familiar with the figure or job you're writing about, the resulting essay will be, well, vague. For example, I'm curious about the life of Bill Gates, but I know very little about him, beyond the Netflix documentary "Inside Bill's Brain" that I watched more than a year ago. My lame, general discussion of Gates would never make the grade. But ask me about any of the major 19th century novelists and I can go on for days!

>> **Don't hesitate to discuss both the advantages and disadvantages of the life of the subject you've selected.** This is especially true if you're writing about a celebrity, which isn't forbidden, by the way, but should be approached with appreciation for both the achievements and limitations of that person's life and wisdom.

>> **Be honest, even though you're writing an essay that is essentially a fantasy.** If your essay is about the President of the United States, don't ignore the reality of Congress, the Constitution, party donors, and other factors that are part of the President's reality.

>> **Don't go overboard on factual background information.** Assume that the reader is educated (because the reader of your essay *is* educated). Do a little research if you want — checking, for example, birth dates or other statistics. But the essay shouldn't sound like a school report. The admissions office won't appreciate an "I looked this stuff up and I'm going to use it if it kills me" attitude.

>> **Remember the admissions committee will expect to learn about your values from this (and every) essay.** The *why* portion of the question is crucial to the essay's success. Don't skimp on the details. Take a look at these examples:

- **Too general statement:** I would like to interview Greta Thunberg, the Swedish environmental activist, because her job is interesting.

- **More specific statement:** I would like to interview Greta Thunberg, the environmental activist who has also publicly acknowledged her diagnosis of Asperger's. Though I cannot imagine speaking at the UN as a teenager or refusing to travel by plane out of concern for carbon emissions, I am interested in people who are willing to make personal sacrifices and bold decisions instead of simply ignoring the climate crisis. I would ask her about the pressure she must experience as the youngest leader of the environmentalist movement, and her experience as someone who is neurodivergent.

Entering the Fictional Universe

When I'm immersed in a good book, I often feel that I've stepped between the covers and entered an alternate reality. A great film also pulls me out of myself. I may not be on the screen or between the covers of the novel, but if the artwork is vivid enough, I can certainly imagine the characters' lives. That's exactly what some college applications ask you to do, in questions such as these:

>> To what fictional character do you most relate, and why? (Ohio State University's Honors College)

>> Which well-known person or fictional character would be your ideal roommate? (University of Southern California)

>> Pick one woman — an historical figure, fictitious, or modern individual — to converse with for an hour and explain your choice. Why does this person intrigue you? What would you talk about? What questions would you ask them? (Barnard College)

The techniques in the previous section of this chapter may apply to the this type of essay as well. These additional points can help you tackle this sort of essay:

>> If you're writing about a character who is likely to be widely known to a university audience — Shakespeare's Hamlet or Yoda from the *Star Wars* films — don't include a long list of identifying factors. Do cite the elements of the character that appeal to you. Check out these examples:

> **Unnecessary summary:** Hamlet is the Prince of Denmark, returned from his university studies to find his father dead and his mother remarried. He knows that he must kill his father's murderer, but he can't act on this belief.

> **Relevant information:** The title character of Shakespeare's Hamlet intrigues me. For much of the play he ponders the issue of revenge, struggling with the morality of killing the murderer of his father. When he cannot act, he delves into his own personality and questions the meaning of his own existence. I like the fact that Hamlet is a thinker; he takes nothing lightly and perceives the complexity of human motivation.

> See the difference? The first example gives background, but the second interprets the character.

>> If you're writing about an obscure creative work (rather than a household name like Hamlet), anchor the reader by providing a few sentences of context and character description. Then go on to discuss the aspects of the character that appeal to you.

>> Always use present tense when writing about literature or other creative works. Hence, "Hamlet dies," not "Hamlet died."

Chapter **19**

Focusing on More Essay Question Types

An admission essay is supposed to reveal facets of your character, but some aspects of your character are bound to be more well-developed than others. The creative questions I discuss in this chapter are often the ones that students struggle with most or fail to know what to do with. *Supplemental essays*, in particular, help colleges and universities with the following:

» **Spot the fakers.** A clumsily written supplement, specifically if you don't appear to possess much insight or background knowledge on your topic, is a strong indication that the college you're applying to isn't high on your priority list (as in, "Oh, there's one more supplement? Let me draft that before the deadline on Friday . . ."). Even worse, being ill-prepared to respond to a supplemental prompt can suggest that you aren't aligned with the school. After all, the admissions committee has defined these questions as important for future students to engage with.

» **Gauge your intellectual vitality and further understand what makes you tick.** The more creative supplemental prompts invite you to either grapple with an intellectual concept or tell a story about something important to you.

When you do either, your response is bound to be self-revelatory. If you find yourself stuck in the "Who the heck is this question even for" mentality, remember that your thoughtfulness and ability to develop your reasoning are both the means and the end of writing a good supplemental response.

Especially if you have a wide variety of supplemental prompts to respond to, the tips in this chapter can help you achieve maximum success.

Responding to "Is There Anything Else You Want to Tell Us?"

Many students know about this type of question, but may not be sure where to find it or what exactly the prompt wants. Not to worry. Here I explain both points.

First, where can you find this question? In the Common Application's Writing section, you can locate the option to add additional information below your personal statement, which is where you can post a response to this question that will be shared with every school you're applying to.

Sometimes, colleges or universities ask this question outright in the supplemental areas (though it's almost always optional). So, should you include a response to this sort of prompt at all? What does "anything else" or "additional information" even refer to?

This prompt ties into the concept of *holistic review*, which gives colleges every opportunity to thoroughly and fairly understand your qualifications in all areas, rather than simply seeing you as the numerical value of your GPA. Hence, you want to be as transparent as possible and give the colleges the information they need to better understand and know you, particularly if there is more to your background than meets the eye because of adversity or other factors. (Chapter 1 discusses holistic review in greater detail.)

Refer to Figure 19-1 for an example of this type of essay that was written by a student whose A grades were hard-won because he spent much of the year on airplanes traveling to participate in weekend-long fencing tournaments. Because he was constantly catching up from jet lag, communicating with his teachers to ensure he received all assignments and managing to complete his coursework while answering to Olympic-level coaches, he wanted to ensure that the colleges he applied to understood the context of his (still strong) grades.

> Although I am a high-level athlete in a uniquely extreme sport, I find that the real extreme sport I participate in is homework.
>
> I spend much of my time on planes, or trapped in airports because of a delayed flight, or in random cities across the world awaiting my next tournament. This means that I have to be extremely adaptive when it comes to managing my learning. Often, I must teach myself a lesson or complete an assignment when my internal clock tells me it is the middle of the night. On rare occasions, I muster up the confidence to request an extension. As an internationally competitive fencer, I need to be able to learn and stay committed to school anywhere, at any time, or I will start slipping.
>
> Working with my teachers and deans closely has allowed me to distribute my time in a way conducive to my growth as a student and a person. I was able to miss classes in order to compete, but at the same time I have pushed myself to my academic limits while on the other side of the world. And despite this being the most demanding year of my life so far, I've had more successes than I could have ever imagined. From getting my best grades of my high school career to being ranked top 5 in the nation at fencing, I continue to strive towards improvement with the help of everyone around me — along with my ability to work in strange or foreign places.

FIGURE 19-1: An example of an "Anything Else You Want to Tell Us?" essay.

© John Wiley & Sons, Inc.

REMEMBER

The focus of such an essay is to shed light on factors that have impacted your academics — *not* to make excuses or complain. For example, if you got a low grade in chemistry and, despite your best reflection, can't think of anything to say except that you "had a bad teacher," don't write that (unless there was a major, concrete problem, in which case you can report the basic facts while doing your best to focus on your own efforts to circumvent the problem or self-advocate).

Here are some examples of reasons why you may choose to respond to this prompt:

>> You have a learning difference or have faced adversity in your education.

>> You experienced a setback in your personal life that impacted your grades for a given period of time.

>> You're involved in a major commitment of (say, 15 hours per week or more) and therefore have had to develop essential skills just to remain on top of your schoolwork

>> Your grade for a particular class (or possibly your performance on standardized testing) has suffered for reasons you can concretely explain.

On the other hand, say you're someone for whom high grades and test scores have never come easily. Some students have apprehension about sharing a learning difference diagnosis. However, in most cases, sharing can only help you showcase what you've discovered about the *way* you learn and explain any barriers that you have overcome. Figure 19-2 is an essay written by a student with a history of struggling with dyslexia. Notice how he writes from a growth perspective.

Being diagnosed with dyslexia at a young age, I was often frustrated with how much more challenging academics were for me. As an elementary school student, I switched schools several times because my teachers weren't sure how to help or create a pace I could keep up with. I was too confused to even be frustrated. All I wished was to be able to effortlessly read or solve math problems like my peers.

To cope with my struggles as a reader, in fourth grade I decided to read books for an hour every day, without fail, especially graphic novels, which combined language with images. What seemed like a hurdle I would never conquer soon became one of my biggest passions. My cousin Yusuf introduced me to the *Redwall* series, and I was hooked. I moved on from graphic novels to many other genres, continuing to read for an hour every day.

Just recently, I helped start a book club with a friend of mine. Reading *Vox* by Christina Dalcher alongside friends allowed me to get over my fear of reading aloud, and I was able to further improve my reading habits.

Living with dyslexia has helped me to become much stronger mentally. When I work for my father's construction company, I now help him read the layouts for the structures he is building, which have large amounts of text, technical specs, and measurements. This all takes time and careful attention, and my experiences with dyslexia and working have taught me the importance of attention to detail. I have always known that with hard work, my diagnosis would become manageable, and I'm proud to say it has now become an asset.

FIGURE 19-2:
A sample
"Anything Else
You Want to Tell
Us?" essay.

© *John Wiley & Sons, Inc.*

You may wonder why talking about challenges in your academic history would be helpful. Think about it: If you were a college administrator, wouldn't you want someone on your campus who, for example, knew whether they were an auditory, tactile, or visual learner and had worked to develop distinct study methods or coping skills they could use to be successful? Being able to advocate for yourself and problem-solve in high school is essentially reasonable assurance that you'll do the same when you arrive at college. If you've figured out what resources or methods serve you best when it comes to your schoolwork (even if that has taken you many years to do), that journey is highly important. More obviously, if you experienced a period of low grades but wish to convey to the admissions counselors reviewing your transcript that you have since troubleshooted your way to a more successful approach to your studies, you now have the opportunity to make that case.

WARNING

On the other hand, if there isn't more to your transcript than meets the eye, I don't advise that you plug in a random creative essay in response to this question, simply to avoid leaving it blank. What this space is for is something fairly specific. This prompt is essentially asking: Is there a contextual factor the admissions counselors need to know about when reviewing your application? Or, have you faced hardships that the admissions counselors should understand while evaluating your candidacy?

Answering Literature and Writing Questions

I love questions that tap into literature or creative writing. These essays tend to fall into several categories: the "favorite book" or "reading list" topic, or the creative writing sample. The English-oriented questions roam around a bit, depending upon the application. Some schools place them in the short answer section, and others make them full-length essay topics. You can apply the helpful hints in this section to either situation. Chapter 20 provides additional detail on squeezing everything you need to say into a brief response.

Discussing books

The "book" questions are an attempt to identify what you read and what you think about after you've read it. Questions in this vein include

>> Explain how a work of fiction you've read has helped you understand the world's complexity. (Wake Forest University)

>> Which book, character, song, or piece of work (fiction or nonfiction) represents you, and why? (Emory University)

>> List the titles of books, essays, poetry, short stories, or plays you read outside of academic courses that you enjoyed most during secondary/high school. (Columbia University)

As your answers reveal something about *your* values and desires, so too do supplemental prompts say something about the school you're applying to. These sorts of questions reveal at least somewhat of a loyalty to the liberal arts — these institutions are interested in accepting students who read for pleasure and who are familiar with the experience of being moved by art. That said, you're free to (and should) pick works that genuinely interest you, even if they aren't in the most highbrow genre. You'll write better that way, and I love to see a student make an interesting case for a book or even a song that I wouldn't normally consider analytically.

Don't even *think* about choosing a book that you haven't read. Admissions counselors are sometimes former teachers and *definitely* former students. They know when someone is blowing smoke into their eyes. If they suspect that you've taken a shortcut or chosen a random title in hopes of impressing them, they've learned something important about you — something that will undoubtedly hurt your chances for admission. Better to go with a title you know and love, regardless of the level, than to pretend that you've read a scholarly work.

After you decide on a topic, keep these points in mind:

>> If you're writing about a nonfiction book or article, briefly mention the important points or at least the points you related to. Don't waste space recounting lots of facts. You're not taking notes for a test; you're discussing the book in relation to your own life, values, and ideas.

>> Don't retell the plot of any literary work. Simply refer to the events, providing enough information so that the reader may understand your point. If the book is a well-known classic, don't bother giving background information. Explain a bit more about obscure works.

>> In writing about literature, use present tense. Romeo *loves* (not *loved*) Juliet, because whenever the play is read or enacted, the drama unfolds anew.

>> Don't go off on a scholarly tangent. "Book" questions aren't English literature tests. The university is interested in your writing skills, true, but more interested in how you relate to the work. If you're discussing *Of Mice and Men*, for example, don't go off on the symbolism of the dog's death in relation to a particular school of literary criticism. Instead, concentrate on your connection to the novel. Consider this example:

>>> **Too scholarly and impersonal:** The dog dies because he is no longer productive. The lives of the ranch hands, Steinbeck implies, are similarly expendable. As critic I. Noitall commented, "The 'I-Thou' nexus of communication . . . blah blah blah blah.'"

>>> **Better, personal version:** I was particularly moved by the death of the dog. What sort of society tosses "useless" members away? I ask myself these questions as I chat with my great-grandmother. At 90 she can no longer work, but her wisdom and her love for my family is a treasure. In the world of Steinbeck's novel, she would be considered expendable, just as the dog is.

>> Do be specific about the effect of the book on your worldview or actions, as in this example:

>>> **Too general:** After I read Steinbeck's novel *Of Mice and Men,* I became interested in social justice.

Better, specific version: After I read Steinbeck's novel, I volunteered at our town's homeless shelter. Each "client" who came in became a possible Lennie or George to me.

Writing creatively

Of course, all writing is creative. But some writing is *officially* deemed "creative," including these classic questions:

>> You have just finished your 300-page autobiography. Please submit page 217. (University of Pennsylvania)

>> "Do you feel lucky? Well, do ya, punk?" – Eleanor Roosevelt. Misattribute a famous quote and explore the implications of doing so. (University of Chicago)

>> You are required to spend the next year in either the past or the future. To what year would you travel and why? (University of Richmond)

For these topics, take your spirit out of its tight shoes and let your mind run barefoot in the meadow. (See? Just thinking about this sort of writing ignites my imagination.) Have some fun! The colleges that place these questions on their applications want to see your creative side.

TIP

Creativity all bottled up? The first thing you need to do is relax. The imaginative part of your brain shuts down when you tense up. So go for a walk, wash the dishes, or turn to some other mindless, physical activity. Personally, when I'm trying to break through writer's block or settle on a new idea, I let my thoughts marinate idly for several days — while I'm driving, on a walk, or before going to bed at night. When a student tells me that they have no idea how to approach a given prompt, I usually help them break through this limited thinking by helping them brainstorm not just one, but three possible approaches. Options are liberating! After a student has several approaches to choose from, they can spend a couple of days figuring out the best one. Refer to Chapter 13 for other tips on overcoming writer's block.

A few — very few — guidelines do apply to creative questions:

>> **Just because you're being creative doesn't mean you should ignore the question.** If they've asked for a slice of your autobiography, don't write, "This page is blank" (as one student planned to do) because it represented his view of the meaninglessness of all individual lives. If a college or university asks for an autobiography, give them an autobiography, not a stationery sample.

>> **Show the finished product to someone you trust.** (Chapter 6 explains what kind of help is legal and what you must avoid.) Ask the reader to summarize the impressions or ideas your creative piece conveys. If the reader's comments match your intention, fine. If not, consider adjusting your work. For example, suppose your piece entitled "A sparrow falls" is, you believe, a serious statement about the nature of life and death. If the trusted reader laughs and comments that he's never seen a better parody of artistic snobbery, you may want to rewrite.

Bottom line: You can be as creative as you wish, within a few, sensible limits. Go for it!

Discussing Current or Historical Events

Issue-based questions reflect a desire for students who can think critically about their communities and the world. Fortunately, most of the prospective applicants I meet with are impressively aware of national and global issues (thanks, 24-hour news cycle, social media, and smartphones), so try not to be intimidated by the prospect of writing about one of them. In this section I take you through two different types — the current event "issue" essay and the less common historical event essay.

Writing an essay about a current event

One of your supplemental essay prompts may ask you to comment on a topic that feels "way too big for my personal commentary," as one student put it. (Then again you're growing up in the times of Malala Yousafzai and Greta Thunberg!) No need to panic — when asked about current events on college applications, the expectation isn't that you will outline a brilliant solution to a major national or global problem.

Your job, usually in a few hundred words, is simply to offer a perspective that shows critical and moral thinking and an ability to engage with nuanced issues. Maybe the issue you write about will actually be the impetus for your future career, or maybe it has simply led to many a heated debate at your family's dinner table. Either way, a university that asks a question like those below wants to know what issues are important to you.

Here are some recent examples of questions related to current events:

>> Briefly describe a curre_____ ___ social movement that is affecting a city, town, or place that is _____ ___cribe its significance to the

community as well as its future implications for that community. (Occidental College)

>> What is the most significant challenge that society faces today? (Stanford University)

>> What is an urgent global challenge, social justice topic, or racial injustice issue about which you are passionate? What solutions or outcomes do you hope to see? (University of Richmond)

>> Where are you on your journey of engaging with or fighting for social justice? (Tufts University)

For a great example of an issue essay, check out Figure 19-3. This student includes all of the major touchpoints of a good issue-based essay:

>> An explanation of her perspective on the issue and why it matters

>> How the issue has impacted her own life

>> Her vision for how she'll grow into an adult advocate for this cause

As I write, the sky is burnt orange; we are in our longest wildfire season on record. I fear it is only a matter of time before our reckless behavior and misuse of land lead to a fire in the dense, green hills of my hometown.

October of 2017 was when California wildfires became an inevitable signal of autumn, along with shorter days and falling leaves. For the first time, I realized that my community is at risk. Since then I have often asked myself: Why do we not realize the gravity of danger until we are confronted with it?

Recently my family and I sat at the dinner table, as fires raged at a popular campground only an hour away from our house. We reviewed our evacuation plan and what belongings we would grab if we had five minutes, fifteen minutes, an hour. So far, we have not had to leave, but for the first time I began to wonder what would happen if I lost my home.

Climate change is a worldwide issue, but it didn't feel like an imminent threat until friends from Santa Rosa to Santa Cruz began to lose their homes. I know that my town is at risk for fires; we have been lucky thus far, but we must take action now to prevent fire from destroying the historic community I love so dearly. In college, I hope to take courses on environmental policy and find ways to turn this knowledge into action. I hope to advocate for policies that will protect the forests that I have spent my life hiking through from the spark of a lightning bolt. For now, I continue to repeat my mantra that this threat is real and we need to act.

FIGURE 19-3:
An example of an issue essay.

Not every issue essay may require all these factors, so be sure to read each prompt you're responding to closely.

The best responses to these prompts have two ingredients (which I examine in greater detail in this section):

>> An illustration of your understanding of the issue

>> A discussion of your personal involvement or connection to the issue

The two elements don't need to be equal in length, but they must both be present.

Illustrating the issue

In order to illustrate the issue you've chosen to write about, remember that you aren't summarizing or offering a report of factual information. You can assume that your reader has a basic understanding of current events. Instead, because this essay is ultimately about conveying your perspective, you should attempt to illustrate the issue through your own eyes, focusing on an aspect of the issue that has made an impression on you personally. Notice how in Figure 19-3, the author illustrates (or shows, not tells) an understanding of the issue of climate change through specific details (the burnt orange sky).

If you're not writing about an issue you've witnessed firsthand, then you can still aim to illustrate the issue by offering, for example, a detail or fact that resonated with you, and explain the context of when you learned this information. Did you begin to dig deeper into your topic in preparation for a class debate, for example? Or watch a documentary that left you spinning with questions? Perhaps you remember a conversation with older relatives who shared their observations? Those contextual details can help you set the stage before you further explain why this issue matters to you — and what you hope to do about it.

Discussing its connection to you

When you choose a topic for the "issue" question, you'll probably find it easiest to write about something that connects personally to you. Remember that a purely intellectual topic risks sounding like a school report or, at worst, like a lecture from someone who hasn't explored how they can contribute to the cause. On the other hand, your involvement doesn't have to be direct — for many high schoolers, activism or making a personal connection to an issue looks more like asking questions, striving to become informed, and making small steps that are plausible within your own life, like starting a family compost (or one at school!) if your issue is climate change.

Suppose that you've been deeply affected by television coverage of school shootings. Because of what you've seen, you've formulated a strong opinion on the subject of gun control and have a lot to say. Go for it! Anything that arouses your passion can turn into a fine essay, even if all your experiences with the issue occur via the media. If you can venture a way you can advocate for this cause as a young professional, even better.

TIP

Don't fret that other students are likely to write about the same topic as you. Colleges and universities know that they're inviting thousands of responses on the same few topics when they present this prompt. But what's the actual topic of this and every other admissions essay that you write? That's right – the essay ultimately should reveal something about you, your identity, and values. You may not tell your reader anything that they don't already know about world affairs, but that's not the task at hand. The task is to explain your perspective on what matters and why. Your ability to engage with difficult and nuanced issues also reveals what an asset you would be to conversations (in your dorm, classroom, and elsewhere) at the college level.

Delving into the past

Much less common than the issue essay are questions asking you to evaluate past events. Some of these questions concern people ("Which historical figure would you like to meet?" and other such questions). For help with that sort of essay, turn to Chapter 18. Other essay questions resemble this one:

What historical event do you wish you could have witnessed? Why?

TIP

Before selecting a historical event to write about, consider your family history. Do any events from the past connect to your forbearers? I once read a fine admission essay about the Great Hunger, a period in Irish history also called the Potato Famine. The student's ancestor had left Ireland alone, at the age of 14, to seek his fortune in the United States when the family's potato crop failed. The essay writer did a great job relating those 19th century events to his own family. Of course, you may write about a moment that is simply the subject of curiosity for you. In that case, you may give context as to when and how you learned about this historical event and *why* exactly you find it so compelling or puzzling.

When you write a "historical event" essay, remember these points:

>> **In discussing a historical event, be accurate.** If you have only a little knowledge about an aspect of history (World War I had something to do with trenches and gas, but you're not sure what, for example), you won't be able to write effectively on the subject without a deep dive into your favorite search

engine, which isn't the point of these prompts. Choose the historical prompt and topic only if you're reasonably secure about your understanding of the material.

>> **Don't overload the reader with dates and obscure facts.** You may include *some* specifics, but be sure that the details support the general points you want to make.

>> **Decide on one main idea, the point you want the essay to make.** That point should relate to your own life and beliefs or to society today. Imagine that you're writing about the struggle for women's suffrage. Why do you care about the vote? What form does that struggle take for a citizen of the 21st century? Your essay should connect the past to the present.

Chapter **20**

Getting the Most out of Short Answers

A
s you start to comb through your applications more thoroughly, you may notice a few blank boxes await your attention. Some applications include a series of short-answer questions where you may only have room for a sentence or two (I refer to these as *fast facts*). Other supplements may allow you a couple short paragraphs, but there simply isn't enough room for a thorough and detailed essay, which is confusing because as I state several times throughout this book, the name of the game in college essay writing is *detail*.

To get the most out of these questions, you need to get the most information *into* the space or word limit provided. If you only have 50 words, you can't ramble on philosophically about your favorite extracurricular activity or meander through a long explanation of your favorite books, television, movies, and music. You have to make your point fast and leave a memorable impression.

In this chapter I show you how to squeeze the maximum benefit from the lines allowed you in short-answer sections. I also provide helpful hints and examples of the most common brief responses.

Saying a Lot in Little Spaces

Compared to the full-length essays, short answers appear simple at first glance. After you've sweated over a 650-word personal statement, you see a single blank row and think, "Piece of cake." But when you start to choose words for those lines, you realize even the answers to these questions create a distinct impression of who you are.

REMEMBER

To create an effective short answer, keep one word in mind. Which word? *One!* Here's what I mean:

>> **Make sure each short answer makes *one* important point.** If you're writing about your most meaningful activity, for example, you can't explain everything you learned from your stint as president of the Coding Society, describing the three new programming languages you mastered, your triumphant bake sale to raise funds for new computers, and the club trip to Microsoft. If you really want to say all that, turn the Coding Society topic into a full-length essay and use it elsewhere. If you choose that topic for the short-answer section, limit yourself to an explanation of your new understanding of programming languages or to one of the other relevant ideas.

>> **Don't waste space repeating information or observations from the full-length essay.** Your short-answer responses are submitted to colleges alongside your supplemental essays and personal statement, giving you an opportunity to say something completely distinct from what you wrote. Make sure to take advantage of each opportunity.

>> **If you can, let your short answer open the door to *one* additional idea.** Besides the details you give on your main point, include a few words suggesting something more. Again, I refer to the Coding Society:

> I never understood logic until I figured out a mapping program with my fellow debuggers. (main idea of the short answer = cooperative work; additional suggestion = you mastered logical thinking)

Let the power of *one* be your guide through the short answers, and you won't go wrong.

For example, look at a short-answer question, the University of Maryland's "My favorite thing about last Monday was . . ."

The response to this prompt must be less than 160 characters (just 20 characters more than a tweet, my students tell me) so, again, you can relax in the knowledge that this *isn't* an essay; it's one in a series of finish-this-sentence fast facts.

But what is the University of Maryland getting at with this kind of prompt? Can I mention the truly excellent hamburger I ate last Monday, you might wonder, or is the university expecting something prestigious? What if I can't even remember last Monday?

If you're paying close attention, you might notice the description at the top of this section of the application: *At the University of Maryland, we encourage our students to go beyond the classroom to engage in opportunities that further both their academic and personal growth.* What does that have to do with asking about last Monday? Well, first of all, opportunities are everywhere. In reflecting on the events of the last week, you might find yourself recalling some small victory or opportunity (academic or otherwise) you chose not to pass up or that you handled in a way that makes you proud to recall. Sure, you could choose to write about your hamburger, but if you do, that puts a bit of pressure on your other finish-that-thought questions to go a bit deeper — you don't want all your answers in this section to be frivolous. Instead, show that you're a conscious participant in the world around you.

Other memorable responses to this prompt might include a mini-victory in sports or another extracurricular activity, a compliment you received that shows the school how others see you and that you remembered the remark (you're engaged with your surroundings!), or a simple moment of pleasure you took in a personal interest. No need to claim that you were a guest on Oprah's podcast or rescued a kitten from a tree a mere few days ago, or to try to come up with something unbelievably witty. Try and pinpoint a small moment that shows your involvement or a moment that you savored in your everyday life.

ONE COLLEGE'S SUPPLEMENTAL QUESTIONS AND FAST FACTS

I take a closer look at the supplementary section of the private college in Southern California: Chapman University. Although you may or may not actually apply to this school, I want to share these prompts because Chapman allows you to cover a lot of ground in its supplementary area. Not only does the Chapman admissions committee review your complete Common Application (including your extracurricular page, personal statement, and "Anything Else You'd Like to Tell Us" essay), but the committee also requires three supplemental essays and a series of fast facts.

Here are all the prompts to give you an idea how they create the overall portrait of you:

- **"Why us" supplemental essay prompt:** "Out of the thousands of universities and colleges, why are you interested in attending Chapman?" All applicants are required

(continued)

(continued)

to answer this in 200 or fewer words. (See Chapter 17 for further details on how to write a great "Why us?" essay.)

- **Academic supplemental essay prompts:** "Please tell us about your interest in the major you selected." This prompt is for students who have declared a specific major on their application. The response must be 200 or fewer words.

  "Chapman University encourages academic exploration through our dynamic liberal arts curriculum. It's okay to be unsure of what you might want to major in; however, please tell us about the academic areas that interest you." This prompt is an alternative to the preceding prompt for all students entering as undecided majors (required length: 200 or fewer words). Chapter 17 can help undecided applicants. (**Hint:** Present yourself as an explorer — someone with many interests, rather than zero.)

- **Identity and engagement supplemental essay prompts:** The applicant has two options:

  Option 1: "Every Chapman student holds multiple identities that create the diverse fabric of our community. Our committee would like to hear about the intersectionality of your identities and how those have played a crucial role in your life." This prompt is unusual, but I like it because like Option 2, the key to this question is to reflect on your understanding of diversity and consider how you are or can be an advocate for yourself or others. Applicants need to respond in 200 or fewer words. (Check out Chapter 17 on how to respond to supplemental essay prompts on diversity and inclusion.)

  Option 2: "Part of the Chapman student experience is to grow or transform your own perspectives. What impact would you like to have at Chapman and what legacy would you like to leave on our community?" To truly understand this question, consider the communities of which you are already a member. Then you can bridge into how you'll interact with peers at Chapman. What experience do you have (be specific!) that prepares you to engage with a diverse college community? Applicants need to respond in 200 or fewer words.

I hope you can see a pattern on the supplemental essays: why you've chosen to apply to the school, what you bring to a diverse campus community, and how your academic interests demand rigorous attention. These supplemental essays can help the admission people understand who you are as a student and community member. Furthermore, they allow you to make your best case that, in this case, Chapman is the place where you can be your best self. Go ahead and paint that portrait for them.

Meanwhile, here are Chapman's fast facts, each of which you're required to answer in less than 200 characters, or approximately 30 words:

- Please list three words to describe yourself.

- What song should we be listening to while reading your application?

- What is your dream job?

- What is your favorite subject?

- What is the top thing on your bucket list?

- Name one dish you would cook for our admission team.

- What makes you happy?

- If Chapman's admission team came to visit your hometown, what site would you take them to?

- What can you give a 30-minute presentation on without any preparation?

- If you could teach a college course that best describes you, what would it be called?

- What is something you have always wanted to learn but never had the chance to?

On the other hand, the fast facts are more lighthearted. They're a chance to help the admissions team get to know your personality, and they also fall under the category of "Can help, but unlikely to hurt" your admissions chances. What does that mean? Well, if you have something really memorable to say in the fast facts area, you have an added attraction to endear yourself to your reader and further a good impression. If you put some degree of thought into your answers to fast facts, you're unlikely to make a negative impression. Just be thoughtful and honest — and let your genuine responses do the rest.

Answering the Most Common Short-Answer Questions

Perhaps more than any other section of the application, the short-answer questions produce a sudden desire to flee the country rather than spend even one more minute writing quick facts about yourself for people you've never met. Depending upon where you apply, you may encounter only a handful — or dozens — of different short-answer questions. Fortunately, most fall into a couple of categories. In this section I give you hints for the most common short-answer questions.

Playing favorites

In general, college and universities don't care about the show you're most likely to binge on Netflix when you're supposed to be studying for a math test or your favorite color. But institutions often do ask you to write briefly about other kinds of favorites, in questions such as these:

>> Briefly elaborate on one of your extracurricular activities, a job you held, or responsibilities you have for your family.

>> Which academic class in high school did you most enjoy?

>> Describe one summer activity during your high school career.

>> What activity from your high school career would you most like to continue during your college years?

Your transcript and extracurricular activity sections of the application have already listed *all* your clubs, honors, courses, jobs, and service projects. The preceding questions give you a chance to shine a spotlight on one element. But which one? Don't feel obligated to choose the activity that looks the shiniest on your resume. Instead, go for the experience that truly has significance for you. In other words, answer the question honestly.

TIP

After deciding on a topic, select one point to highlight in your answer. Ask yourself why this particular activity/class/teacher impressed you so much. What did you learn? How did you change as a person or as a student as a result of your participation? Identify the message you want to convey. (For example, *I learned how to deal with people who are different from myself. I never before understood the horror of income tax.*) Search your memory bank for a moment when that message is obvious or look for examples illustrating the main idea of your answer.

REMEMBER

Although you're working with a tight word limit, *specific* is always preferable to vague. Also, because including every detail isn't an option, look for representative moments or examples rather than a general summary.

Check out Figure 20-1, a "favorite activity" short answer that focuses on the author's volunteer work at a local hospital. The author's main idea is the satisfaction he gets from distracting children from their pain and illness. Notice the specifics, including:

Board games such as Chutes and Ladders, Monopoly, and Candyland

Teaching reading and math

As a volunteer in the Emergency Room, my greatest challenge is to divert the child's attention away from his/her illness or wound. After triage and initial treatment, the patient and I engage in activities including playing board games, reading, and simply conversing.

On the cancer ward, my responsibilities are more complex. The majority of these children are terminally ill. Removed form their homes, schools, and friends, these patients realize that they are not leading normal lives. In order to insure that their education is not compromised, the hospital provides classes. I teach reading and math to elementary-aged children. When the lessons are over, we play games including Twister, Monopoly, Chutes and Ladders, and Candyland. On occasion I have entertained them with my saxophone.

From my exposure as an EMT and as a volunteer in a dialysis unit, it is apparent that I am lucky to be healthy. Dedicating myself to helping these less fortunate children feel better about themselves brings me tremendous satisfaction.

FIGURE 20-1: An example of a favorite activity short-answer essay.

Playing the saxophone

Name of the hospital (changed here for privacy)

Connection to high school community service projects in peer tutoring and teaching 7th graders

Mention of other work as an EMT and in the dialysis unit

Another "favorite activity" answer is Figure 20-2, in which the author describes a leadership experience that, though rewarding, included challenging moments for the writer. Once again, pay attention to the number of specific details such as the following:

Sample questions students were asked to discuss

The initial resistance to opening up

Student reactions: laughing, giving mean looks, shaming

How the writer handled this resistance

Positive assessment of the experience

Breaking Down the Walls is a several-day event intended to bring students closer together through workshops and dialogue. When I found out the event would be coming to my high school, I applied to be a trained leader and host the activities. On the first day, everyone had the opportunity to share their story and struggles in small groups. We encountered questions like "What about school makes it hard for you to come?" to "Do you know someone that died from a homicide?" At first, students hesitated to answer personal questions with strangers, but they slowly began to appreciate this opportunity to witness that others also face abuse, trauma, and mental health struggles.

The hardest part was supporting resistant students while creating a safe environment. I identified people shaming others, giving mean looks, or laughing. To promote a positive atmosphere, I approached those students with supportive reactions like, "I need to help this student feel safe so they don't make others feel unsafe." Though it was difficult to separate my peers from their friends, for those who wanted real change, I was their defendant and supporter.

Overall, I learned students feel more comfortable when they recognize that their problems are universal. As a senior, I continue to seek opportunities to relate authentically to my peers. I will continue to seek these community-strengthening opportunities as a college student.

FIGURE 20-2:
Another example of a favorite activity short-answer essay.

One more example: Read Figure 20-3, a "favorite class" description I adapted from a student's essay. The description zeroes in on the teaching methods in an art history class. She includes lots of specifics:

Names of paintings and artists

The use of stories

The topic of a paper she wrote

Enthusiasm about art history

It was the beginning of February, spring was a long way off, and I was fifteen and in a teenage slump. In the past art history classes had been something for me to try to stay awake through. I was mildly interested sometimes, but most of the time I had to struggle to keep my eyes open when the lights went out for the slides. But Dr. Elgar's ninth grade art history class was magical. Because of her teaching, two dimensional slide projections became four dimensional stories with real people in them. Her style was matter-of-fact but contained intense enthusiasm and love for the subject. It was as if she had just come in from having lunch with Carravaggio. I was no longer counting the minutes until the end of class but instead trying to get the seat closest to the front so I could find all the hidden symbolism in David's "The Death of Marat." At the end of her classes I felt invigorated and eager to learn more, and I even found myself reading more than the assigned material. For my final project in the course I wrote a comparative paper about Degas' "The Dance Class," and Homer's "Bathers" that I actually enjoyed writing. I do not remember all the stories Dr. Elgar told, but I do remember how to study and appreciate art history.

FIGURE 20-3:
An example of a favorite class short-answer essay.

WRITING ABOUT FAVORITE BOOKS AND FILMS

Psst! Read any good books lately? Been to the movies? Great, you've got college application material, specifically, these variations of the "favorite or most significant activity" short answer:

- Write about 200 words discussing a book you've read.

- What is your favorite film? Why?

Information in Chapter 19 helps you with both questions. Remember that the admissions counselors judge what you choose to write about as well as how you explain your interest in that particular work. Don't aim over your head, selecting something you think will make you appear more intellectual than you actually are. (And don't *ever* write about something you haven't read or seen.) Ideally you should go for a book or film that has aftereffects — the kind of art work that bears thinking about. If it's instantly forgettable, with no levels of meaning to explore or information to digest, it's not a good choice.

Moving on: The transfer question

A variation of the "Why us?" question is aimed at applicants who already attend a university or graduate school and want to transfer to another. This sort of "Why us?" question may call for a full-length essay or a shorter response. I include information on writing such a response in this chapter because most students in this position feel like it simply isn't possible to convey in just 650 words the cumulative experience of realizing that their current school isn't the right fit. (Chapter 17 deals with this question for students not transferring.) However, I recommend you keep the transfer essay fairly direct, sticking to the two main factors influencing your decision:

>> **Discuss what is lacking in your current college experience.** Don't trash the place where you're enrolled (this is key); simply state what you need that your current college can't provide — a larger student body, more activities, smaller classes, whatever.

» **Explain how the college you want to transfer to can fill the gaps in your educational experience.** For example, if you've expressed a desire for a career in international diplomacy, mention the Foreign Affairs major of the school you're applying to.

The main reason for being straightforward is that this is a bit like when a future employer asks you why you left your last job. Sticking to the facts (instead of waxing on about how horrible that job was) allows you to be respectful and courteous and lets your listener fill in the details on their own. By focusing confidently on the future, you show that you're confident that your next position (college, in this case) will be much better suited to you and that you've grown all the wiser from your past experiences.

WARNING

Do your homework and be sure that the school you want to transfer to actually offers what you say you want. In other words, don't tell a college with an average class size of 300 that you're seeking intimate seminar-style learning with plenty of professorial attention. You'll look like a fool and, more importantly, you'll end up dissatisfied even if they do admit you.

» **Discuss the primary attractions of the new school.** Include as many specific details as possible and why these features are important to you.

Figure 20-4 is a full-length transfer essay adapted from one written by a student dissatisfied with his freshman year at a major university, its name changed for privacy.

Figure 20-5 shows you how this response may be shortened for a school that places this question in the short-answer section. In both versions, the author states what's good about his current school, which I've called Central State, and what is lacking. He identifies factors that will be different in his hoped-for new school, Northern State.

No, I am not homesick. I have friends. The work is not overwhelming. Nor has it interfered with my involvement in extracurricular activities. My first semester has been a time of transition as it is for most college freshmen. Making decisions regarding course selection, seeking advice from advisors, and utilizing time efficiently have all been part of the process, accomplished at a distance from the familiar support structures and cues of both home and high school. As a result, I have developed a greater sense of myself and my abilities, both academic and social. The experience has been satisfying. However, with all due introspection and now retrospection, I feel a change is necessary.

Sociologist Lev Vygotsky believed that peers play a major role in an individual's development and learning. The students and friends with whom I grew up were extraordinarily bright, competitive, and creative. In high school, discussions and opinions on almost any subject were spontaneous and interesting. At Central State, the small class size and the seminar formats have presented a great setting in which to learn. The highly motivated professors, who encourage participation, have been the highlight of my experience thus far. However, the level of student interaction has not been gratifying. Conversations concerning classroom topics and related materials have been limited. I have not been sufficiently challenged or stimulated by my peers.

During my first semester, I have come to realize the influence a community has on my learning and growth. At Central State, the campus is active from around eleven in the morning until three in the afternoon, Monday through Friday. One Saturday in October, while walking to the dining hall, I realized that I was one of five people on campus. With the majority of undergraduates living in on-campus dorms, the campus of Northern State fosters a unique intimacy. The campus is lively throughout the day. Such activity creates a comfortable environment that promotes interaction and the formation of strong bonds between members of the community. Having experienced a year of college and dorm life, I am more aware of what is best for me. As a transfer student, I would appreciate this style of living even more.

Based on conversations with current students, it is my understanding that members of the Northern State community make it a unique place to live and learn. Many renowned professors choose to teach at the undergraduate level. Having the chance to interact with an instructor such as Avery Marks, whose passion and mastery of botany are unrivaled, would be quite an experience. The most defining aspect of Northern State's faculty, however, is the manner in which they approach their role in influencing a student's life. Professors, instructors, and advisors guide the student so that he/she can make independent decisions.

Furthermore, the structure and aspects of Northern State's residential colleges foster the formation of relationships. For the remainder of my undergraduate years I want to return "home" to a very close group of friends for nightly dinners and conversations concerning daily activities. The strong bonds that are formed within a diverse group of people who make up these individual communities create an optimal atmosphere in which to grow, socially and intellectually.

All aspects of Northern State seem to enhance learning. Guidance from faculty members and challenges from peers within Northern's close-knit community create a setting in which I can pursue current interests and discover new one while simultaneously discovering my future direction. This is the purpose of the undergraduate experience.

FIGURE 20-4:
A full-length essay in response to a "Why transfer" question.

No, I am not homesick. I have friends. The work is not overwhelming. Nor has it interfered with my involvement in extracurricular activities. I have developed a greater sense of myself and my abilities, both academic and social. However, with all due introspection and now retrospection, I feel a change is necessary.

The students and friends with whom I grew up were extraordinarily bright, competitive, and creative. In high school, discussions on almost any subject were spontaneous and interesting. At Central State, the small class size and the seminar formats have presented a great setting in which to learn. However, I have not been sufficiently challenged or stimulated by my peers. At Central State, the campus is active from around eleven in the morning until three in the afternoon, Monday through Friday. One Saturday in October, I realized that I was one of five people on campus. With the majority of undergraduates living in on-campus dorms, the campus of Northern State fosters a unique intimacy. The campus is lively throughout the day.

Having the chance to interact with an instructor such as Avery Marks, whose passion and mastery of botany are unrivaled, would be quite an experience. The most defining aspect of Northern State's faculty, however, is that professors, instructors, and advisors guide the student so that he/she can make independent decisions. Furthermore, the structure and aspects of Northern State's residential colleges foster the formation of relationships.

FIGURE 20-5:
A shortened version of Figure 20-4 to fulfill the short-answer "Why transfer" question.

© *John Wiley & Sons, Inc.*

6

The Part of Tens

Break down college essay misconceptions you may be wondering about.

Review (and hopefully appreciate) ten personal essays that can serve as inspiration for college essay writing.

Examine the essential musts of college essays (feel free to think of these as your "Too Long, Didn't Read" or TLDR summary).

Examine tips and tricks to help you answer supplemental essays, get the admission committee's attention, and keep it.

Chapter **21**

Ten False Beliefs about College Essays

Especially in the midst of fall mayhem, frantic seniors tend to trade ideas about admission essays — and the rumor mill moves *fast*. The only problem is that lots of what "everyone knows" to be true about the essay is pure fallacy. In this chapter I present and then puncture ten rumors about the college admission essay.

Drafting at the Last Minute Is No Biggie

If your English teacher can easily spot the difference between an essay you began weeks ago as opposed to one you hastily assembled the night before a deadline, how much more obvious must the difference be with an essay that requires deep self-reflection about your life experiences and identity? "Well, I work best under pressure," you may be thinking. Fine. Save that mentality for a math test. College essay writing simply isn't the time to test that theory.

Limiting the Focus to Your Achievements Is Wise

Some students assume that they should use their essay as an opportunity to recap all their most impressive accomplishments. Usually, that simply isn't the case. The application has a place to list your tangible achievements — on your Extracurricular and Honors/Awards sections. After all, an essay that boils down to "I've always been really good at this thing, and I've been recognized in the following ways . . ." simply isn't interesting.

TIP

Instead, take the opportunity to share something about yourself that the admissions readers can't see elsewhere. That doesn't mean you shouldn't ever write about your extracurricular activities or achievements, but if you do go that route, you must find a fresh and unique angle to show their meaning to you — or you simply won't be writing a personal essay at all. Turn to Chapters 2 and 3 for ideas on how to mine your life for essay material.

Requesting Help from Lots of People Strengthens Your Writing

Many applicants, nails bitten raw and anxiety risen to stratospheric heights, look for help with their admission essays. But don't go overboard on the help aspect. Chapter 6 explains you how to tell the difference between legitimate assistance and "Do not pass go; proceed directly to jail" over involvement.

TIP

Choose one helper — a teacher, college advisor, or parent — who you trust and who will honor *you* as the writer of your own stories. Don't enlist multiple readers in the beginning or middle of your writing process, which is where you might get conflicting and confusing input. If you choose to share your work with secondary readers after your essays have been revised several times and are ready for outsider input, you'll then be prepared to determine what feedback is helpful and constructive to you and finalize your pieces accordingly.

Figuring Out Your Story Is No Big Deal

"You can write about anything as long as you write well." Not necessarily. True, zillions of topics are possible winners, depending upon how you handle them (and, yes, how well you write). But the admissions committee wants to see something of significance to *you*.

If your essay leaves them scratching their heads, asking, "Why did this applicant tell me all this stuff?" you're in trouble. And if *you* can't figure out why you told them all that stuff, you're in bigger trouble. Bottom line: Spend more than a couple of nanoseconds selecting a topic that reveals an important aspect of your experience or personality.

Focusing on a Certain Topic Guarantees Admission

This rumor is more persistent than the "Tupac is still alive" theory and just as silly: that colleges have such strong preferences for certain topics that you can turn the tide in your favor simply by writing what they want to hear. Nope! No shortcuts here.

REMEMBER

You have to discover and develop your own topic and write it well. Accomplish that task, and you've taken your best shot. Then you'll either get in or you won't. The application process has no guarantees at all, ever, for anyone — least of all when you go with a gimmicky approach.

Writing without Restraint Always Works

There is certainly merit in writing without a filter (at least in your early drafts). It's also true that if you handle a topic properly, nothing is an automatic rejection. However, warning flags may go up if the admissions committee reads about *unresolved* problems that are likely to cause trouble for you — and for the college — as you move on to the next level of study. If you haven't managed to finish even one homework assignment all year, if you have a persistent desire to cut class, or even if you're stuck in an unhealthy romantic relationship, seek help from a guidance counselor or trusted adult. And until you've got the situation under control, write about something else on your applications.

If you're wondering whether topics banned from Thanksgiving dinner, like politics or religion, are acceptable, the answer is that you should tread a bit more carefully than when writing about other experiences. Showing political awareness is more than okay, but you also don't want to alienate your reader. Make sure that the relevance of whatever you're discussing to your *own life and identity* is clear.

Talking about Ordinary Lives Is a No-No

Spreading faster than a celebrity breakup rumor is the rumor that near-death experiences and starvation-level poverty are prerequisites for the college essay. A regular, happy life with non-toxic parents and an average trip through high school also make the grade, at least in terms of essay material.

The secret is that most applicants, generally young adults or late teens, haven't had very many newsworthy experiences. But if you write about your own life honestly and thoughtfully, with the details only you can provide, you'll stand out from the crowd.

Using Scholarly Language Is Impressive

When the admissions committee members read the essay, they want to meet *a real person*, not some souped-up version of a dictionary/encyclopedia merger. Nor do they want to see your latest research paper (unless of course they specifically request it) or a book report. So don't plug in every word from your *Scarlet Letter* vocabulary quiz or twist normal verbal expression into some tortured pattern that appears intellectual. If you do this, you risk sounding haughty, unnatural, or (and this would be especially unfortunate) like an adult did your writing for you. Your best bet is to sound like you.

Writing One Essay Is Enough

You can — and should, in the interest of maintaining sanity — adapt one essay for several different applications. Chapter 1 tells you how to do so. But if you try to squeeze an essay about a current issue into a slot the college has earmarked for a description of your views on art, you may be in trouble. I say "may" because censorship/funding of the arts is always in the news, and an essay about that current issue works well for the artistic-viewpoint question. However, if you wrote about carbon tariffs, you can't make that essay relate to art.

Bottom line: Don't force an essay where it doesn't belong just to avoid drafting something new. Adapt where logic decrees you may do so, but write something new when nothing else will do. If you're genuinely interested in the school you're writing the essay for, the effort will be more than worth it.

Believing No One Reads Your Essays

I wish I knew why this rumor persisted. My best guess is it spread out of wishful thinking, because if it were true, that would certainly take the pressure off writing well. The truth is, colleges don't ask for essays they aren't willing to read. In fact, the essay is often the *first* thing your admissions readers turn to — even before they review your transcript, extracurricular pages, or recommendation letters.

REMEMBER

However, your readers may not spend more than a few minutes on each of your responses, especially if your writing is poor. In order to make a strong impression in that amount of time, every word counts, so take your time and amply revise. Chapter 14 discusses revising in greater detail.

Chapter **22**

Ten Great Essays to Inspire You

This chapter is a list of some of my favorite essays, a mixed bunch in terms of style, subject matter, and length. If you need a spark plug to get your essay-writing engine going, browse through a few of these gems. None were written as college admission essays, but all display masterful writing from a personal point of view — the goal of your admission essays.

Because they're all excellent, these essays are anthologized in many collections and you can easily find them online. In no particular order, here are ten great essays, along with some thoughts as to what you might take away from each writer's skill set.

"Us and Them" by David Sedaris

I'd like to count myself as David Sedaris' biggest fan, and I'm pretty sure that you would be, too, if you knew his work (and perhaps you do). Sedaris ends up on a late night talk show because the host can't get enough of his book, and as someone who has stood in a crowd of hundreds of people listening to him give a book reading, I can affirm that he has officially achieved celebrity status. Anything you read by him is a master class in observational humor, so if you're even thinking of trying to be funny in one or more of your essays, he's worth checking out.

What are other college essay takeaways from Sedaris, particularly from the "Us and Them" essay? This piece offers clear proof that writing about someone else is really showing something important about yourself (in this case, the Sedaris family's obsession with the Tomkeys' television-free lifestyle is a clear indicator of their own relationship to the TV). He's also a master of *detail*, which, though I explain again and again its importance throughout this book, you may have to see in action to truly understand. Consider the following sentence: "My mother made friends with one of the neighbors, but one seemed enough for her." How much more intriguing (and, yes, humorous) to add "but one seemed enough" than to simply say that his mother made a friend in the neighborhood.

"I Am Not Pocahontas" by Elissa Washuta

Many applicants will grapple with the issue of identity at some point in the college essay writing process. Using nuance, details, and personal anecdotes, all of which are key to producing strong essays, Washuta writes exceptionally well about her complicated relationship to the question "How much Indian are you?" and to her Native American identity in general. She explores how film and media characterize Native American characters, and she explains how this impacts not only the (predominantly white) people she grew up around, but also herself.

TIP

Washuta doesn't attempt to tie anything up with a neat pink bow by the end of her essay — and I don't recommend you force a false conclusion onto your own essays about complicated topics, either. (Chapter 12 offers suggestions for how to end your essay on the right note.) Instead, look to Washuta's example to understand the importance of the messy truth.

"Total Eclipse" by Annie Dillard

Are you thinking of writing about an experience in nature, whether from the approach of an adventure story or a coming-of-age moment (or both)? If so, consider looking at this essay. Dillard writes stunningly about her own experience with a natural phenomenon as a viewer of a solar eclipse. But of course the essay isn't *just* about an eclipse — it's about what the eclipse forces Dillard to reckon with (which, as it turns out, is everything). Interestingly, she mentions several times that the eclipse happened two years ago before she began to write "Total Eclipse," as if she were still struggling to put into words what it meant to her, and you can decide for yourself the impact that this retrospective view has on the narrative. She describes the experience of the eclipse using Gothic horror details, and her analogies are both surprising and memorable (the sun becoming "an old wedding band in the sky" and her husband, in the strange gray light of the eclipse, looking like "a dead artist's version of life"). Chapter 9 offers a thorough discussion on how to incorporate memorable details into your own writing.

"A Talk to Teachers" by James Baldwin

Even though James Baldwin wrote this essay in 1963, much of what he has to say about the inherent tension in the education system — specifically, his observation that Black children are taught to obey a system "operated for someone else's benefit" — is still relevant today. Baldwin first gives a broad description of what he sees as the United States' most pressing social challenges, and only after he has done so with precision and insight does he tie in the role of teachers in supporting children in a way that is constructive, rather than destructive, as they come into consciousness of the world around them.

"Professions for Women" by Virginia Woolf

If you don't yet already know and understand the phrases "Angel of the House" and "A Room of One's Own," read this essay. Woolf was not only a master of metaphor, but she was acutely perceptive of pervasive social issues. She uses herself as an example of the obstacles facing women entering the workforce (as was becoming more common in the 1930s), and to render the conclusion that what working women face may not be simply external resistance, but internal and psychological battles. Chapter 9 explains how you might incorporate your own metaphor into an admission essay.

"On Keeping a Notebook" by Joan Didion

Author Joan Didion provides plenty of examples of what writers write in their notebooks and then interprets the significance of the items she jotted down, illustrating how authors come to understand the meaning of what they write often *after they have written things down.* (Didion would definitely believe in the freewriting method I describe in Chapter 5.)

Her notebook examples aren't long-winded explanations, but rather quick snapshots. Taken as a whole, they reveal the purpose of a writer's notebook. To understand how to create a vivid image in a few lines and why true writers jot things down constantly, rather than only when they're inspired, read this.

"The Search for Marvin Gardens" by John McPhee

This essay has a strange but extremely effective structure. McPhee bases this piece on the fact that the properties in the original Monopoly game were named after places in Atlantic City, New Jersey. Here he cuts back and forth between two stories — two players zooming through a series of Monopoly games and descriptions of the actual places that are bought or landed on during the games. The title comes from the one spot that McPhee can't locate in Atlantic City. McPhee's structure may stir your creativity; also notice the sparse but vivid details he chooses to create word pictures of each street.

"Mother Tongue" by Amy Tan

Novelist Amy Tan reflects upon the nature of language in this essay. Her mother immigrated to the United States from China, and her English always reflected the grammar and usage of her first language, Chinese. Tan relates several incidents in which people respond differently to the same message delivered in her mother's imperfect English and in Tan's own college-educated speech. Tan's weaving together of anecdotes and interpretation may serve as a model for your admission essay structure. See the reflective questions in Chapter 3 if you're interested in finding out how to generate memories of your own family.

"On Lying in Bed" by G.K. Chesterton

This essay starts "Lying in bed would be an altogether perfect and supreme experience if only one had a coloured pencil long enough to draw on the ceiling." Dynamite beginning, don't you think? As you may have guessed from the spelling of "coloured," Chesterton was British. Written in the early 20th century, the essay points out the lying in bed is one of life's pleasures. According to Chesterton, the simple things in life should take precedence over other goals usually deemed more important. Agree with him or argue until your tongue dries up. Either way, Chesterton draws you into the subject from the first line.

"Generation Why?" by Zadie Smith

If you want to see a clearly thought-out argument about a popular topic — social media — read this one. Smith is probably one of the most readable essayists on this list and manages to be easily comprehensible at the same time as she is an expert at tying in the two elements of writing I most want you to understand: personal anecdotes and deep reflection.

Chapter **23**

Ten Absolute Musts for College Essays

The college essay is a variable creature. One writer's effort may be totally different in form and content from another applicant's work, even though both essays achieve their purpose — an acceptance letter from the college. However, a few hard and fast rules do apply to the college essay. Which rules? Read on.

Saying Something They Wouldn't Otherwise Know

Your personal statement (and even your supplements) are meant to reveal something *personal* about you. Sounds obvious, right? That doesn't mean you can't write about a meaningful extracurricular activity, but it does mean you should write about it with much more depth than what already covered on the extracurricular section of the application — your statistics, position, time spent, and other achievements. Chapter 5 offers helpful tips to steer you in the direction of more personal and specific essay ideas.

Keeping It Real

Your readers — the admissions committee members — want to meet *you* — not what you imagine a prime candidate for admission to be. The essay should sound like a real person, not someone who swallowed a vocabulary book or embellishes more than an intoxicated uncle talking about his youth. Present your best self, but be authentic.

Answering the Question

If a supplementary essay asks you to write about a person who influenced your choice of career, don't submit an essay describing every stain on your childhood baseball mitt. True, lots of application questions are so intentionally broad that the approach and direction of your response is up to you. But that one little word — "almost" — is crucial. Read the question before, during, and after you write the essay, and be sure that you answer it. Chapter 24 provides some tips to answering supplemental essays.

Being Specific

Don't confuse being specific with being totally and completely original. The quest to choose an essay topic that no one else has already written about is likely in vain, and that's no failure on your part. So if you're one of those students worrying whether your essay topic has been done before, you can relax and instead focus on what's important: that the *details* of your experience are always unique.

REMEMBER

If you write with specifics, you'll emerge as a distinct, one-of-a-kind person with your own unique lens. Plus, your essay will be more interesting to read. Chapter 9 focuses on how you can be as specific as possible.

Showing, Not Telling

I have a rule for students' college essays: Watch your adjectives. Most of the time, the presence of adjectives is an indication that you're telling something you should be showing instead. For example, never say, "I'm dedicated." instead, go for a detail like, "I'm the first one to show up and the last one to leave." Similarly, instead of "I was excited," show this emotion by writing, "My legs jittered uncontrollably all through math class." In an essay about music, you don't have to say "I love music!" Rather, make that point by offering details that *show* your enthusiasm. In other words, make sure to replace any lazy telling statements with a more thorough effort to show your meaning. Refer to Chapter 9 for more on how you can show your story.

Getting Personal

The essay is about *you*, no matter what the topic. A detached, scholarly assessment of the Green New Deal may attract a publisher or impress the instructor of your Contemporary History course. But an impersonal college essay won't achieve its primary goal — to present *you* to the admissions committee.

Avoiding Clichés

This advice goes hand-in-hand with the information I present in the sections, "Being Specific" and "Showing, not Telling," earlier in this chapter. If you use an appropriate amount of detail in your essay, there's no way that you're going to skim the surface with a simpering cliché.

REMEMBER

Steering clear of cliches and general platitudes (more in Chapter 7) is one of the most important things you can keep in mind when writing your college essays. The growth and theme in your essay must go deeper and be more personal than a line from an illustrated children's book.

Holding Their Interest

Even if your essay rises to the entertainment level of the instructions on an income tax booklet, the admissions counselors will read it. They have to, because reading admission essays is part of the job. But they won't read your essay happily unless it's interesting. To attract and keep their attention, you don't need shocking events or strange sentences. You need good writing.

Meeting the Deadline

If the application is due on November 15 (or January 1 or whenever), that deadline is a brick wall that you can't smash through. Not only must you submit your application and essays by this date, but you must also completely fill out the application and forward your standardized test scores (if you're using them) by the deadline. Your recommenders (including your counselor) must have also submitted their letters by the deadline, too. Start early in order to get it all in on time. Refer to Chapter 16 for guidelines about the submission process and why you should have applications submitted at *least* a week before each deadline.

Revising Your Drafts

Students often struggle to formulate a single coherent sentence about their experiences when I sit down with them for an initial brainstorming session. They aren't inarticulate; they're just trying to put words to experiences and insights that they may never have reflected on before.

If you've worked on your personal statement in a single sitting (or even several) and think you've gone as deep with your topic as you probably can, I'd place a pretty hefty bet against you that you haven't. Reflecting on your life's experiences and what they have taught you takes *time,* and so does coherently expressing yourself to a reader who doesn't know you. So revise early and often! (Part 4 provides more insights into revising your drafts.)

Chapter **24**

Ten Tips for Writing Supplemental Essays

Many students struggle with how to approach supplemental essays. Are they just for fun? Are they as important as your personal statement? And what about the especially short ones, the ones that hardly seem to count as essays? The short answer: Yes, they're important.

In this chapter, I present ten central strategies for you to keep in mind in understanding the role of supplements to your overall application.

Saying Something Distinct from Your Personal Statement

The job of your personal statement is to say something distinct from what appears on your transcript or resume. The job of your supplemental essays is to say something distinct, too — knowing that the readers of your supplemental essays (also known as the admissions committee) will have already read your personal statement.

REMEMBER

Mild overlap is okay (perhaps your personal statement mentions your intention to pursue a nursing degree, and your supplemental essay touches on the university's nursing program and why it's a match for you . . . no problem!) but there is no need to repeat the same story over again. Depending on the prompt, you can use your supplemental essays as a chance to showcase another side of you or to lean into your goals for your college experience.

Starting Early

Your personal statement is arguably your *most* important admission college essay (being the longest as well as the essay you send to a variety of schools). Even though supplemental essays are more unique for individual schools, you should take them just as seriously.

REMEMBER

Don't treat the supplements like a last-minute add-on. Like any essay, you'll likely want to work through multiple drafts, talk through your ideas with someone you trust to offer sound advice, and, in the case of a question like "Why us?", make sure you're informed enough to answer the question. (You can read more about "Why us?" questions in Chapter 17.)

Being Direct

Supplemental essays are notorious for their low word count. If you only have 200 or 300 words to answer a question (see Chapters 17 and 19 for example of supplemental essay prompts), your final draft needs to bypass extraneous information or a winding introduction and get immediately to the point. Of course, as with any college essay, being specific and detailed matter, too — in your first draft you may write 500 words (or more!) to lay out all of the content you'd like to include before cutting the response down to the essentials. By the time you get to a trim finished product, each line must be purposeful and relevant to the question.

Grounding Your Response in Past Experience

"I know I would be successful at a liberal arts school." "I plan to participate in undergraduate research." "I am drawn to the opportunity to join the campus ministry." Although pinpointing factors that appeal to you about a given campus is often a must in a supplemental essay, if you want to make any sweeping claims about what would be best for you or what opportunities you would take advantage of, you need to also explain to your reader *why* and *how* you know that these factors are a good fit.

Without some context from your high school life (maybe you're in a Christian youth group now, which is why college ministry feels like the next logical step), you run the risk of sounding like you're bluffing or simply plucking things from the school's website.

Answering the Right Questions

Some students search online for supplemental essay prompts early in the summer after junior year, which is great, except that the Common Application relaunches every summer on August 1 and, on occasion, colleges do change their supplemental essay prompts. The last thing I want you to do is to answer a question you found online and write multiple feverish drafts only to log into the Common App sometime in the fall and find that (whoops!) your response is no longer useful.

REMEMBER

Even though you should give yourself plenty of time to write your supplements and indeed start on them early, be sure to double-check the Common App (or whatever application you're using; refer to Chapter 1 for more information) after August 1 to ensure that you have in your possession the exact and updated questions required on your application.

Paraphrasing the Prompt

Depending on the university, some supplemental essay prompts contain befuddling quotes or prestigious academic language, or they're simply confusing to understand. To avoid getting bogged down in semantics, use a strategy you may have picked up in your high school classes: put the question into simpler wording (and watch for familiar question types, such as those I discuss in Chapters 17, 19, and 20).

REMEMBER

The goal of any supplemental essay question is to get to know more about you — so ask yourself what it is about you that the university is trying to figure out, without assuming that a complicated question requires a complicated answer.

Looking for Patterns

This tip is aimed at helping you streamline your writing process — a necessity if you're applying to a high number of universities. You'll probably have some overlap amongst your supplemental essay prompts (even though each supplement goes to only one school). For example, the anecdote you wrote about your role on a leadership committee may in fact be useful in a couple of different responses, if the heart of each prompt is to talk about an experience that helped you grow or even what you bring to a college community. (See the section, "Grounding Your Response in Past Experience," earlier in this chapter to better understand why a story about your high school community can help answer what you bring to a college campus.)

Meshing with the College or University

Many supplemental essay prompts ask about your intentions as a college student. Whether the question is why you've chosen to apply, what your goals are for your academic experience, or what you bring to a campus community (Chapter 17 offers more specifics for answering these questions), you want to showcase that you have a clear understanding of not only why the college you're applying to is an excellent one, but why it's an excellent one for *you*. Blending your own strengths and interests with what would be available to you at a given school is the key to making a good case that you belong there.

Researching Specific Programs (and Knowing What's Available)

If you're lucky enough to have a precise degree in mind, count yourself among the fortunate. However, you may have a reason why you're opting to apply to a school or two that doesn't offer the exact degree you have in mind — so you'll want to double-check the specific undergraduate program listings anytime you're answering a question about your academic interests or your interest in a given college or university. (The last thing you want to do is state that you hope to get a degree in biochemistry to a school that doesn't offer a biochemistry degree.)

Being an Explorer

The average college student is likely to change their major at least once. Although that may or may not be you, it's okay to acknowledge in your supplements that you have multiple interests that you hope to explore in the college environment — especially if you can explain why the college you're applying to is an optimal setting for your exploration. (Maybe the school has interdisciplinary programs or an intriguing option to earn a minor in one of your secondary interests.) Painting yourself as someone with a few possible paths is more than okay — some colleges even ask you to write about an academic subject of interest to you *other than* your intended major!

Appendix A

Well-Written College Essays

I usually steer students away from reading too many sample essays when they're still new to the college admission essay process — with the caveat that by the time you get to a finished product, you've cut away all the fluff and every single sentence says something distinct and meaningful. A finished product can therefore feel quite dense, and hopefully pretty polished, too — but that usually doesn't happen without giving yourself permission to write messy drafts, rambling freewrites, tentative outlines and whatever else it might take for you to figure out what it is you are trying to say! (For a more thorough understanding of the writing process, see Chapter 4.)

So, if you're still in the early stages of writing, you might read just a few of these essays and then set this appendix aside to reference again later. After you're in need of more inspiration (perhaps as you're moving toward your final drafts or have a submission date in mind) you can always peruse additional samples. Here you find a variety of sample personal statements and supplemental responses with some thoughts as to what makes each one successful and what you can take away from the writer's content and style.

Sample Personal Statement Essays

Your personal statement, as you may know, is the central essay for the Common Application (or whichever application portal you're using; refer to Chapter 1 for more about the Common App or the different application portals) that you want sent to all colleges you apply to. The goal of a personal statement is to share something that can't be seen elsewhere on your application and to share more of the story of how you came to be the person that you are. The essays in this section give you a sense of how varied your options are, in terms of subject matter, tone, structure, and more!

Personal statement 1

An essay about funky socks — what's not to like about that? The personal statement in Figure A-1 does an excellent job starting with a *very* specific detail of the student's identity (being attracted to colorful socks) and ends up making connections to her family and first-generation identity. That choice is available to you, too, if you find that you gravitate toward Common App's Prompt 1 — the prompt that invites you to share a "background, identity, interest, or talent" that your application would be incomplete without.

This essay is a great example of how to take a characteristic about yourself and use it as a motif or metaphor. Such an essay accomplishes two things:

>> A memorable image (a teenager with Van Gogh socks peeking out from her shoes)

>> As the essay progresses, a deeper understanding of the student's identity, as she ponders whether or not her "sick socks" would have come to be without her parents' immigration story.

Personal statement 2

The essay in Figure A-2 uses a well-chosen opening anecdote approach — something you can read about more in Chapter 10. When you read it, notice how the writer seamlessly moves from a narrative moment (with dialogue and action) into self-reflection, which guides the rest of the essay.

Usually, the last thing I think about before nodding off to sleep is socks. I pick a pair in my head and then plan what I'll wear the next day around the selected pair.

Most of my socks have some of the most celebrated paintings of all time on them and I can't help but wonder, is this an insult to the artist? Imagine, you have invested yourself into the greatest piece of your life and some teenager is wearing them with Birkenstocks. I know Frida would have detested me but something tells me Van Gogh would have been 100% okay with it.

I also wonder if I could have gotten away with my sick socks in my parents' hometown back in México. I was born in the San Francisco Bay Area and grew up learning and appreciating individualism. People think my socks are awesome here, which they totally are, but when I visited México I realized that awesome socks are not held to the same standard as they are here. I would have not developed an obsession for awesome socks living there, which is incomprehensible to me.

My parents left México because their big dreams didn't fit into their small town; America is the land of success, legacy, and equality, and this beckoned them. It was a place where they could be different and still fit in. However, because we're Mexican, we're too different; to be American we must hyphenate: Mexican-American. Rather than holding my parents back, this subtle racism fueled their rapid assimilation. My sister and I are completely integrated into American society. My mother always beams as she says, "Mis dos hijas have accomplished what takes three generations in one." My parents desired total integration but their cultural ties were too strong to be severed. I grew up speaking Spanglish, eating bacon wrapped hot dogs (Guadalajara style), and sitting through the festive and loud Spanish mass at seven on Saturday nights.

However, by refusing to cut this cultural tie, my sister and I, first generation Chicanas, were handed a heavy burden; "You're the representative of the Mexican race, mija," my mother told me at a young age. "It is up to you to change the way we are viewed here." The weight of this burden separated me from most kids my age. I hated this and only wanted to be like everyone else.

Then I got into socks. Around the end of my middle school years, a pair of Van Gogh's Sunflowers socks caught my eye. I had never seen anyone wear socks like that, and quietly wondered if I'd dare wear them in public. I ultimately bought them and two other pairs. As my drawers accumulated more and more socks, I began to venture into wearing my socks in public. When my jeans would ride up, my socks would peek out, revealing my deviation from the standard. Eventually, people began to notice and even looked forward to getting peeks of my rebellious ankles.

However, I still hadn't mastered individualism. My years of discomfort with my burden resulted in shame for my skin tone, my features, and even my parents. It wasn't until my AP Biology class, in which I was reminded daily that I was the only Mexican, that I became — ironically — comfortable with this aspect of myself. During the reproduction unit, I realized that the chances of my existence are about one in 400 quadrillion. I'm sure it's even less likely that my Mexican parents would have had American children. Chances say that there isn't anyone else exactly like me. So ruin that by trying to be like everybody else? I'd practiced being comfortable with individuality with my socks; it was time to apply it to my "burden." This comfort with being Mexican grew into an appreciation and more recently, a deep love for my skin tone, my Spanish, my parents' origins story, my "burden" and the duality of my Chicana identity.

Socks keep me up at night because they're an affirmation of myself as an individual. One cannot have Amelia without awesome socks, just as one cannot have Amelia without being Mexican.

"So you're the student prodigy," said a deep voice from behind me. I turned, still holding my laparoscopic instruments in my hands. The man had been standing there awhile, his eyes squinted as I practiced laparoscopic sutures on a training machine. I eyed his ID badge, which read "Dr. Siedhoff, M.D." My palms started to sweat. "Your work is impressive for only a college student," he said. I had never been more flattered.

In fact, I had been struggling with the suture. As I was trying to loop a miniscule needle attached to a long black thread through a seemingly microscopic piece of plastic, I had questioned myself incessantly. I had no idea if I could complete the stitch and tie the knot that came at the end. However, with the help of Dr. Siedhoff, I soon realized that I had the potential to make it in the medical field. While I wanted to dance around and celebrate like a toddler, I was able to contain my excitement like the surgeon I was training to be.

I had been eager to get my hands on a suture ever since I first saw my mentor, Dr. Kate O'Hanlan, working in the operating room a year before. I was enchanted by her skills and unfazed by her subsequent invitation to hold a human uterus, but what had the most impact on me was what happened after the patient was closed and in recovery.

We walked out from the operating room side by side, through the hallways of the hospital and out to the waiting room where the patient's family sat. "Everything went very smoothly, and she will be up and walking in no time," Dr. O'Hanlan said gently.

I transferred my gaze to the family. I had never seen so much excitement and happiness come from such a seemingly simple phrase. This experience reminded me that the way doctors communicate is as essential and delicate as the surgery itself.

I have always been drawn to surgery due to the high risk environment and the perfection and detail it requires. As a child, I exuded perfectionism through extravagant tea parties — every cup and saucer would be placed just right. Most importantly though, the tea would flow from the teapot with delicacy and grace, without spilling one invisible drop onto the wrinkle free tablecloth. Needless to say, a career in medicine would cater to my meticulous nature.

Recently, my father suffered from a stroke. For the week that he was in the hospital, I spent much of my time pacing up and down the halls of the hospital, turning random corners. At every opportunity, I would question his doctors and ask to see scans so I could truly understand what was happening. I stood behind the cardiologists that came to my father's hospital room and gaze at their monitors. They would have one hand on a keyboard and the other on a wand moving over my father's heart. The human attached to the medicine had never been more clear to me.

I am still only a high school student, and in my opinion, my ability to suture could still use some work. I now learn from my failures, whereas just a few years ago I would have been mortified by my mistakes. I have embraced my challenges and fears and am using them to develop my personality and shape my view of things outside the world of medicine. In English class debates, I have often taken the less popular standpoint — something my younger self never would have done. While I still have room to develop, I know full well that self-doubt is surpassable and empowering to overcome.

FIGURE A-2:
An example essay for Common App Prompt 5.

© John Wiley & Sons, Inc.

Chapter 2 takes a proceed-with-caution approach when it comes to writing your personal statement on an extracurricular or pre-professional activity — after all, you have the extracurricular and honors pages for including that information in your application. However, when it comes to this writer (and specifically her interest in pursuing medicine), the professional *is* personal. She didn't simply convey her ambition to become a surgeon; she traced her meticulous nature to early childhood tea parties and vulnerably explained how her father's recent stroke gave her a deeper appreciation for the humanity of each patient.

Personal statement 3

The essay in Figure A-3 is a response to the sometimes-befuddling prompt to write about a "challenge, setback, or failure." (Remember that the honest truth is far more interesting, compelling, and believable than being excessively self-congratulatory.)

The anecdote about the woman who had been hit by a car in front of CVS could have, very simply, been easily discarded as not-personal-statement-worthy. Sure, the moment was dramatic, but it was only five minutes of the student's life, which hardly sounds like a vital part of her background. This essay, however, is a good example of one that arose from careful questioning.

As I listened to the writer describe her frustration that she had to be the one to keep the woman conscious, rather than the adults, it became clear that she was talking about more than the five-minute interaction. The essay is a result of her insight that seeking control is a major theme in her life, and her understanding that this desire probably originated with her early struggles in the classroom. Several drafts later, and the writer had not just a dramatic anecdote, but several layers of meaning.

Personal statement 4

This student's work ethic is obvious from a look at her resume. But her willingness to consider more deeply the why behind her drive to be self-sufficient is what makes the essay in Figure A-4 unique — along with the interesting metaphor of "switching hands" to convey resiliency, just as she can switch hands as an ambidextrous tennis player.

When I see what's happening in the CVS parking lot, I take a quick, deep breath and say, "Max, hold my stuff."

As I squat next to the woman laying on the asphalt, surrounded by blood and several bystanders, someone calls out, "Are you a medical professional?"

Clearly, I am not; I am just a 16-year-old girl that just knows how to do more than just stand there. I move the injured woman onto her back, take off her bag, and hold her hand tightly.

"Do you have any pets?" I ask, as the woman meets my gaze with confusion. I am met with a few weak laughs from the bystanders. "I'm just trying to keep her conscious," I state defensively, while keeping pressure on her head wound. The old woman answers with a weak "no" and states that her name is Mary.

It isn't long before I find myself swapping hands with a burly firefighter, who offers a quick thanks. My eyes find Max, who looks quite pale and shaken up. As we walk back to my house with my bloody hands, he hounds me with questions: "What happened?" "Is she okay?" "Are you okay?"

I was okay - perhaps more so than I should have been, as this wasn't even my first time witnessing an accident (casualty of growing up in San Francisco). But the only thing on my mind was why I, and not the adults around me, did something to save Mary's life.

I'm always trying to be in control to make up for the time I wasn't. By that, I mean in elementary school before I knew I was dyslexic and sought help, I struggled a lot with school. I had so little control of my situation that I stopped talking for a month in kindergarten just because I couldn't sing the ABC's. At home I didn't have any control, either, as my brother would tease me mercilessly because I couldn't contain my anger.

Though I'm pretty much the furthest thing from the mute kindergartner I used to be, I still notice the pattern: I fell in love with competitive sports, but felt anxious when I wasn't in control of the outcome of the game. In relationships I'm always caring and there for my friends, but can get overinvested in their problems, even when their scope is beyond me. I have always loved the side of myself that is willing to take charge: in class when nobody answers the teacher, I'll always be the one to speak up and offer an idea. Some see me as just assertive or engaged, but as with every good thing, there is always a downside. I can't control the speed of how I process things or read, or even the fact that I make mistakes.

Control is still my biggest struggle. But everyday I am reminded that I can only control my own actions and responses. I am beginning to understand that sometimes I can literally or figuratively "save the day"; other times I might have to let go. Though I thought of nothing but Mary the day after our parking lot encounter, and even asked my mother to find out if Mary was at the hospital where she works, I had no control over whether she was okay or not. All I had were those five minutes, but I'm certainly glad I chose not to simply stand by.

FIGURE A-3:
A sample essay in response to Common App Prompt 2.

I fractured my right elbow when I was four. Since my family's tennis trophies lined our house and I took my earliest steps at tennis tournaments, I was inspired to get out on the court. I was eager to join my first tournament when I was five and already felt late to the game. When my pediatrician advised that I refrain from using my newly healed right arm for sport activities, I quickly grasped my kid-sized racket using my non-dominant hand. To this day I am able to play tennis with both hands and even switch them mid-game on the court, which has been a huge asset as a player. I use this mindset in all aspects of life by stretching my limits in the face of new challenges.

At twelve, I jumped into babysitting. My Friday and Saturday nights were spent playing Candyland or Sorry! before trying to get three kids under eight years old to go to sleep. Through the families I worked for, I met a contact who ran Peninsula Tennis Academy, a tennis coaching business. This was fitting for me and I was offered a job to help coach kids in my favorite sport, where my ambidextrous skills once again helped me work with any type of player. I've always aimed to grow my self-sufficiency and independence, even if switching hands is how I get the job done.

Simultaneously, I interviewed to work at Cafe Central where I would end up being their youngest employee hired at age sixteen. During long and chaotic days at the café, I took hundreds of orders with lines out the door while serving the food and attending to customers' needs. If something was not going right, like the visual display of pastries needed refilling or a customer's order needed to be changed in the kitchen, it was in my hands to make it right. To respond to customers in real time and be successful, I had to be creative and toss up my own ideas.

Recently, during the pandemic, my family struggled financially. Quarantine hurt my dad's small business (he books entertainment for events, which is not profitable during lockdown). He also booked himself as a performer because he is a musician. His passion for music has carried onto me because I love playing guitar, singing, and performing. I saw him take matters into his own hands and begin to perform his music digitally on different platforms through live streaming. The way my dad was able to adjust and switch gears inspired me even more to use that same drive and resilience. Although things were difficult during this time, I noticed our shared adaptability as my dad and continued to channel that mindset in school, tennis, and work. The unexpected obstacles became easier to face because of the resilience I gained from "switching hands" in my own life while observing my dad's example.

My older brother, Riley, was diagnosed with autism at age five as well as anxiety and depression disorders throughout his teen years, and finally schizophrenia at age 21. I have watched him endure severe mental pain, bullying, hospital visits, switching schools, programs in and out of state, and struggling in social situations. My parents' focus on him added to my self-drive as I always knew I was capable of doing things my brother could not. Riley instilled motivation in me to work hard at everything I do, because he fought each day to overcome his mental battles.

If I face setbacks in the classroom, on the court, or during a long work shift, I remind myself to appreciate this opportunity that may seem "normal" but some, like Riley, may never get. This year, Riley passed away from suicide. His mental illness was severe and he fought extremely hard to want to stay alive given his many mental challenges. I understand why he is not here with me, but his strength shines through me, as inspiration which motivates me towards greatness. I will continue to adapt, switch hands when needed, and appreciate the opportunities in front of me every day.

FIGURE A-4:
A sample essay in response to Common App Prompt 1.

This essay covers a lot of ground: Instead of focusing on one specific experience, it spans from age five to essentially when the student submitted the essay. Be sure to have a very clear idea of the connection between ideas if you decide to try this approach.

Sample Supplemental Essays

The following essays are shorter than the 650-word personal statement, and most are written just for one school (or system of schools). Unlike your personal statement, supplemental essays usually focus *not* on giving an impression of your character as a whole or a deep dive into your identity, but on a specific, narrower topic, like an extracurricular activity or why you have chosen to apply to a given school. Here you can read a variety of examples.

Supplemental essay 1 and 2

The examples in this section answer the University of California's personal insight question, "What have you done to make your school or community a better place?" Look at Figure A-5 to see how an extracurricular or leadership activity can reveal quite a bit about a student's values and sense of community.

Notice that an essay of this length (less than 350 words) needs to jump in with some specific details about the activity the student participated in — in other words, establishing the who, what, when, where, and why before reflecting on the significance of the activity in the student's life.

Figure A-6 is another example that answers the same University of California question. See how the student uses imagery and detail to paint a vivid picture of her responsibilities ("prying toddlers away from each other," "asking open-ended questions," and "drawing butterflies" paint a much clearer picture than what she could convey on a resume!).

Some rules are meant to be broken . . . especially rules about writing. This writer broke the rule that you should focus on one central topic for shorter essays, but she did so with such intention and voice that I was all in favor of her writing about two distinct volunteer opportunities in the same essay.

Last spring, I organized an event that I believe brought positive change and awareness to my high school campus. I was inspired to organize an event called "Rainbow Week" so after learning about a dwindling club at my school called Diversity Club, which was essentially a revised GSA (Gay-Straight Alliance). The plan I initiated for Rainbow Week was to have each day of the week correspond with a color from the rainbow and have something to do with pride. For example, Thursday was "Green Day (Not the band)," when we encouraged people to normalize all types of relationships by being more emotionally open to their peers through dialogue and open-ended questions. Every day of Rainbow Week had a great response from the student body and it seemed to be an eye-opening experience to some.

I wasn't alone in this endeavor. The remaining members of Diversity Club helped me promote our weeklong event while I took care of the logistics, like dates, availabilities, and perfecting the execution of our events. This is truly one of the few things I hold up high in my achievements for change, and I hope to do similar things in my college life.

Rainbow Week taught me a lot about human interactions and how people react to taboo topics or those which are undiscussed in their everyday life. One of the challenges I faced while organizing this event was pushback and resistance, which is exactly why hosting this event was so important! At first I attempted to set aside the pushback and do what I needed to do; yet I had to address the negativity at some point so that my peers felt safe. It can be difficult to explain the importance of Pride events, and the concept of "if you know, you know" certainly comes into play. Despite our few critics, I felt like my actions benefitted the closeted population at my school. In fact, I am confident that they did — I had several such individuals contact me via Snapchat explaining that they were happy that someone finally brought the subject of pride to the student body. As a senior and even in my college community, I'm hoping to bring a solid foundation of acceptance and understanding into my school's atmosphere — and to continue to revamp my dreams for Pride.

FIGURE A-5:
An example of a supplemental essay.

Supplemental essay 3

The writer wrote a supplemental essay to the Gonzaga University question, "Please share an experience you had outside of the classroom that has contributed to your personal growth." Alternatively, the essay in Figure A-7 could have served as the student's "Anything Else?" essay about an academic hardship — Chapter 19 explains this essay type in greater detail.

FIGURE A-6: An example supplemental essay.

© John Wiley & Sons, Inc.

This essay covers a lot of ground, in terms of addressing an academic setback (coming down with a devastating case of mononucleosis) *and* simultaneously showcasing how she refused to succumb to two months of complete idleness. By finding a way to engage with a creative goal — launching a photography website — the writer shows both grit and innovation. (I, for one, wonder if I would have anything to show for a two-month bout of mono beyond a thorough understanding of my favorite TV show binged on Netflix.) Still, the essay is believable — the writer acknowledges that teaching herself calculus in bed was utterly impractical and that the full website launch didn't happen until she was recovered and back at school. Your essays, like this one, should aim to be both detailed and honest.

In my junior year, a serious case of mononucleosis left me completely immobile and on bedrest for six weeks. I couldn't go to school, I couldn't move the lower half of my body, and I had no desire to eat. I could do nothing but lie in bed for hours on end, often times just staring at my ceiling because the constant movement of the television made me dizzy. Reading was simply unthinkable, and, as much as I wanted to focus on calculus, my brain couldn't process the complex integrals. But I had to do something. I couldn't just lie in bed for nearly two months moping about and wishing my life were even the slightest bit more interesting.

Before I became sick, I had thought about designing a website for my school's yearbook. I was tired of the incessant text messages and emails from my peers asking me to forward them the photographs I had taken of them; I wanted some place where I could upload the photos, and my peers could have access to them without a second thought on my part. So I grabbed the paper by my bedside, and drew. I drew a homepage, a mock-up of what the photography pages should look like, and I thought through a membership portal, so that only those who had purchased a book could view the photographs. Then I took a nap.

When I told my advisor what I had planned, she loved it. I didn't use technology to design the website until I got back to school, thankfully recovered, but by that time, the hardest parts were over. I had the Graphic User Interfaces needed and just had to put all the pieces together.

After the website launch, I no longer received messages asking me for photos. I suppose the motives were a tad selfish, but the results not only benefited me, but also my community. Parents, coaches, and students appreciate the work I continue to put into the website, and I draw a great amount of pride and joy in the finished product.

FIGURE A-7:
An example supplemental essay.

Supplemental essay 4

This writer responded to the University of California's question, "Describe how you express your creative side." As you can see in Figure A-8, she identifies a pretty typical creative target: music and dance.

In addition to a great "show, not tell" opening (see Chapter 2 for more about how to get your family members to recount their best stories of you) this student does a great job of ending her essay with a connection that shows how dance serves her in other environments than in her studio, such as when nerves threaten to over-take her before a school presentation. You can read more about how to craft a strong ending in Chapter 15, but keep in mind that it's always a good idea to ask yourself to consider the broader impact of what you're writing about, including how a given experience or interest has changed you as a person. (Another way to think of this is to simply ask yourself: "So what?")

My dad often recounts a story from when I was younger: the moment he knew I had a connection to music. We were in the car driving to school, Adele playing on the radio when he said, "Doesn't this song just make the hairs on the back of your neck stand up?" to which I replied, "You can feel that too?" When I was a kid, if music was playing, no matter the genre, I moved along with it, tapping my feet and drumming my fingers to the beat or getting up and dancing around.

By the time I reached middle school, I was pleading with my parents to enroll me in dance classes at a local studio. It was only a five minute walk from my house and I started to spend two afternoons a week there. I still remember my very first performance, a jazz dance to "The Boy From New York City" by the Ad Libs. I started dancing later than most, and while I was only a few years older than the others, I was significantly taller and stuck out like a sore thumb. It's the kind of thing I might be embarrassed about now, but at the time, I didn't have a care in the world. The only thing that mattered to me was being up on stage in that flashy red costume with the big skirt and polka dots.

I started dance as an outlet for my restless energy and the way that music moved me, As the years pass, its significance in my life only grows, with benefits that persist long beyond when I step foot off the marley floors. I tend to break into goosebumps whenever I have to get up in front of thirty other teenagers, the anticipation making my hands shake. I am grateful that my creative side has allowed me to stop trying to expel or suppress this nervous energy, instead teaching me that embracing it can be most rewarding.

FIGURE A-8: An example essay on a student's creative outlet.

Supplemental essay 5

In this essay the student answers the University of Chicago question, "How does the University of Chicago, as you know it now, satisfy your desire for a particular kind of learning, community, and future? Please address with some specificity your own wishes and how they relate to UChicago." Figure A-9 takes a personal approach in explaining the student's goals in relation to the opportunities available at the university to which she is applying.

The key to a good "Why us?" essay (which you can read more about in Chapter 17) is a strong ratio of "I" statements — which means that you have to be able to envision how *you* will take advantage of the opportunities at a given college, instead of simply telling the college about all its wonderful attributes. This student strikes the right balance of pinpointing specific factors about the University of Chicago that appeal to her (showing that she's informed about the school), then explaining why those factors would be beneficial or meaningful given her own academic and personal goals.

Supplemental essay 6

The student writes a supplemental essay that answers Occidental College's question, "Quirks, idiosyncrasies, peculiarities. They help differentiate us. What is one of yours?" Figure A-10 illustrates how you much of your character can come through in less than 150 words — assuming you carefully select your details!

This essay is pure fun, just like Occidental's prompt. And who wouldn't want to be around someone with enthusiasm for the little things? Gently, this writer suggests how her character "quirk" will be a strength at the college level, suggesting that for her, change is exciting, rather than daunting.

To be in a place like UChicago that has contributed so much history, whether through the Manhattan project or the work that merits 10% of Nobel Prizes, would be a dream come true. At the University of Chicago, I'll have opportunities to grow and flourish as a both a student and an individual: to not only grow as a mathematician, but also as a pioneer.

Intellectual stimulation stems from differing beliefs and the challenging of the current notions, both of which thrive at UChicago. The core curriculum at the University paves the way for students to be well versed in almost every aspect of society, while the smaller classes allow the community to be close-knit. These two factors create a united community, one in which students not only support each other, but also challenge one another.

Even though I hope to dedicate my time and brain power primarily to mathematics, I also want to be well-grounded in the arts. The Chicago Careers In program thus intrigues me, because though my brain works in a mathematical sense, I am a very hands-on, creative, and visual learner. I hope to use this program to balance my love for the core STEM classes, but also my other passions. I also hope to take advantage of the incredible study abroad programs UChicago offers, to further develop my ease and clarity of expression in Spanish. Spanish fluency is something I hope to retain for my whole life, and the study abroad programs provide me the opportunity to do just that, all the while keeping up with my studies.

UChicago is exactly the place for me to pursue my passions and loves, academically, socially and professionally.

FIGURE A-9: An example supplemental essay for a "Why us?" question.

I tend to get excited easily. My shirt with a doodle of a bulldog wearing a hat is enough to have me giggling all day. Filling up a stamp card makes my week. My habit of wearing funky socks is enough to plaster a secretive smile on my face.

I look for the mundane joys in life, for small deviations from the ordinary. Life can get overwhelming, but if I have my own little deviation, I know things will be okay. I like to keep busy; falling in a rut absolutely devastates me. Getting excited about small things prevents that.

It gets me to see the differences in each new day.

I'm excited for college; with so many new things, I don't think I'll ever be bored.

FIGURE A-10: An example supplemental essay.

Index

A

"A Talk to Teachers" (Baldwin), 299
academic experiences, writing about, 242–245, 267–268, 280
accuracy, importance of, 275–276
achievements, myth regarding, 292
ACT scores, 9, 220, 222–223
actions, within writing, 240
adaptation, 18, 201
additional information concept, 266–269
adjectives, 143–144
admissions committee/office, 10–11, 98–101, 186
admissions counselor, 98–99
adverbs, 143–144
adversity prompt, 78–79
ambiguity, leaving room for, 125
amethyst butterfly effect, 19
anecdote, 151, 152, 237
announcing, 157, 173
anxiety, 184–189, 209–210
anything else concept, 266–269
application fee, 224, 226
applications, 184–189, 220
ApplyTexas, 14
arrangement, essay
  bookends within, 172
  cause-and-effect, 120–121
  chronological, 112–113, 114–115, 123, 126, 127
  collage, 259, 261
  compare and contrast, 123
  defined, 111
  description-and-interpretation, 119–120, 126, 127, 251
  functions of, 122–123
  hybrid, 118–119
  interest pursuit within, 126–127
  interrupted chronological order, 113–115, 116, 123
  of meaning, 122–125
  selection of, 124–125
  survey, 115–119, 126, 127, 251

uncertainty within, 125
artist, personality of, 61
athletes, timeline for, 99
attention, capturing and keeping, 101–103, 145, 150–154, 305
attitude, change of, 184, 188
authenticity, 11, 82, 246, 304
autobiography, themes within, 25–29
avoidance
  of bigotry, 217
  of branding, 93
  of clichés, 106–107, 153, 157, 305
  within collaboration, 83–84
  of double descriptions, 214
  of essay purchasing on the Internet, 82–83
  of exaggeration, 105–106
  of hammer sentences, 197–198
  of journalistic reporting, 251
  of offensive language, 217
  of overediting, 209–210
  of prejudice, 217
  of profanity, 217
  of qualifiers, 215
  of repetition, 213–215
  of sexism, 217
  of slang, 217
  of thesaurus use, 103–104
  of untruth, 105–106

B

Baldwin, James, 299
Barnard College, supplemental essay question from, 264
battle lines, redrawing, 187
better list, 188
Beyoncé, 28
big figure, choosing, 256–257
bigotry, avoidance of, 217
binding admissions plan, 15, 100
boasting, revealing *versus*, 31

body (paragraph)
  breaks within, 160
  cliffhangers within, 161–162
  details within, 166
  drama within, 161–162
  length of, 164
  logic within, 160–161
  one-sentence, 162
  punctuating your points with, 160–162
  scope sentences within, 162–164, 164–166
  timing within, 159–160
  transitions within, 167–170
bookends, 113, 172
books, writing about, 269–271, 285
boredom, "so what?" concept and, 77–78
Boston College, application question of, 200
Boston University, application statistics for, 100
bragging, taboo against, 30–31
braindumping, 61, 72–76
brainstorming, 61, 62–68, 76, 237
branding, avoidance of, 93
break, paragraph, 160, 162
broad topic, 53
Bryn Mawr College, application question of, 200
butting-in comment, 86

C

California Lutheran University, supplemental essay question from, 242
campus community engagement, 245, 310
campus quad, 150
campus visit, writing about, 233
career, writing about, 42–43, 126–127, 233
cause-and-effect structure, 120–121
celebrities, writing about, 262
chain-of-logic conclusion, 178
challenges, theme of, 26, 38, 77–78
change, embracing, 187–188
Chapman University, supplemental essay questions from, 279–281
character interpretation, 264
Chesterton, G.K., 300
chronological order of details, 166

chronological order structure, 112–113, 114–115, 123, 126, 127
citations, pitfalls within, 158
cliché, 106–107, 145, 153, 157, 305
cliffhangers, drama within, 161–162
Coalition Application, 14
collaboration
  avoidances within, 83–84
  challenges of, 87–88
  within detail gathering, 85
  focus on, 40
  legitimacy and, 82
  listing technique and, 71–72
  myth regarding, 292
  of rough draft, 86–87
collage structure, 259, 261
college counselors, 82
college sports, 99
colors, within brainstorming, 64
Columbia University, supplemental essay question from, 269
comment, 84, 85–87, 216, 272
Common Application (Common App)
  agreement within, 83
  alternatives to, 13–14
  examples from, 315, 316, 318, 319
  familiarization of, 12–13
  overlap within essays, 196–197
  sample question from, 254
  submission process for, 220
  timeline for, 100
  word count requirements within, 221–222
  writing supplements for, 231
community, 40–42, 257–258, 310
compare and contrast structure, 123
complementing, flattery versus, 235–236
conclusion, 165, 172, 173–181
confidence, projecting, 201–203
connection, within essay sentences, 102
connotations, 104
context, theme of, 27
creativity, 265–266, 271–272
curiosity, theme of, 27
current event, writing about, 272–275
cutting, during revision, 146

D

daydreaming, writing about, 250–251
deadline, 306. *See also* timeline
denotations, 104
description, 143–144, 155–157, 214
description-and-interpretation structure, 119–120, 126, 127, 251
details
  choosing, 139–140
  chronological order within, 166
  within the conclusion, 179
  fog of, 190
  gathering of, 54, 70, 85, 140
  geographical order within, 166
  overediting of, 209–210
  purpose of, 166
  of scope sentence, 164–166
  specificity within, 130–136
  structure for, 166
dialogue, within writing, 239–240, 261
dictionary definitions, pitfalls within, 158
Didion, Joan, 299
difficult experiences, writing about, 27–29
Dillard, Annie, 298–299
directness, within supplemental essays, 308
discovery writing, structuring and outlining *versus,* 55
diversity, questions regarding, 245–247
Donne, John, 40
double descriptions, avoidance of, 214
drafting stage, 50
drama, within paragraphs, 161–162
dump the blocks, 60

E

Early Action (EA), 15, 99–100, 222
Early Decision (ED), 15, 99–100, 222
Edison, Thomas, 28
editing
  from brainstorming, 68
  cutting during, 146
  defined, 50
  detail within, 210
  expectations within, 216
  feedback, 84, 85–87, 216, 272
  guidelines for, 83–84
  overview of, 56
  process of, 146, 306
  Red Pen Exercise, 207–208
  rough draft, 55
  Track Changes use within, 92
  while writing, 190–191
  writing anew, 209
electronic submission process, 220
Emerson College, supplemental essay question from, 242
Emory University, supplemental essay question from, 269
engagement, campus community, 245, 280
essay sand traps, 1
exaggeration, avoidance using, 105–106
expectations, 216
explorer, 311
extended family, influence of, 36
extracurricular activities, prompts regarding, 282

F

failure, 27, 28, 185, 204
family, 34–37, 91, 255, 256–261
family history, writing about, 275
fantasy, writing within, 251, 254, 262–263
fast fact, 277, 281
favorite activity short-answer essay, prompts regarding, 282–285
fear of change, 187–188
fear of failure, 185
fee, application, 224, 226
feedback, 84, 85–87, 216, 272
fiction, writing within, 263–264
films, writing about, 285
first draft
  admissions committee/office and, 98–101
  attention capturing within, 150–154
  cause-and-effect structure, 120–121
  chronological order structure, 112–113, 114–115, 123, 126, 127
  description-and-interpretation structure, 119–120, 126, 127
  detail choices within, 139–140
  developing your voice within, 107–109
  editing during, 190–191
  expectations within, 146–147
  interrupted chronological order structure, 113–115, 116, 123
  metaphor use within, 144–145

first draft *(continued)*
   openings for, 155–157
   overview of, 86–87
   parts of speech use within, 141–144
   review process of, 55
   sensory details within, 137–139
   specifics within, 130–136
   stopping and starting within, 191
   strategies for, 100–101
   survey structure, 115–119, 126, 127
   timeline for, 99–100
   tone of, 154–155
   uncertainty within, 125
Five-Paragraph essay, structure of, 111
flashback, within interrupted chronological order, 113
flattery, complementing *versus*, 235–236
flowery language, 104–105
focal point, 65
format
   bookends within, 172
   cause-and-effect, 120–121
   chronological, 112–113, 114–115, 123, 126, 127
   collage, 259, 261
   compare and contrast, 123
   defined, 111
   description-and-interpretation, 119–120, 126, 127, 251
   functions of, 122–123
   hybrid, 118–119
   interest pursuit within, 126–127
   interrupted chronological order, 113–115, 116, 123
   of meaning, 122–125
   selection of, 124–125
   survey, 115–119, 126, 127, 251
   uncertainty within, 125
free spirit, personality of, 61
freewriting, 24–25, 33–34, 124, 146
friends, writing about, 256–261
full-circle conclusion, 177–178
future, 27, 42–43

G

gap year, 188
general essay, example of, 132
general prompts, 45
generality/generalizations, 130–136, 236, 263
"Generation Why?" (Smith), 301

geographical order of details, 166
Gilbert, Elizabeth, 243
global village, focus on, 41–42
Gonzaga University, supplemental essay question from, 321–322
grade point average (GPA), 100
grades, 100, 267–268
graduate program, writing for, 103
grammar checking, 105
grandparents, influence of, 36
gray areas, acknowledgment of, 125
group, ties to, writing about, 257–258
group experiences, focus on, 40
growth, personal, 29–30, 68

H

Hall, Donald, 261
hammer sentences, avoidance of, 197–198
historical event, writing about, 275–276
holistic review, 9–12, 101, 266
honesty, within supplemental essays, 246
humility, 188, 201
hummingbird, metaphor of, 243
humor, 108, 109, 155, 217
hybrid structure, 118–119

I

"I Am Not Pocahontas" (Washuta), 298
idea gathering, 52–53
identity, theme of, 26, 43–44, 280
ill-preparedness, spotting, 265
illustrating the issue concept, 274
imaginary event, recounting, 250
imagination, 85, 250–251
inclusion, questions regarding, 245–247
independent counselor, 83
Indian University, supplemental essay question from, 243
influence, 254–255, 256–261
Inglourious Basterds (film), 159
inner editor, tricking, 62
instructors, 39, 91, 101
Internet, 82–83, 91
interpretation, of influence and personal experience, 240–242, 261

interrupted chronological order structure, 113–115, 116, 123
intervals, memories within, 23
intrigue, capturing attention through, 151, 152–153
introduction, conclusion *versus*, 172
issue essay, 273–274

J

jackhammer, metaphor of, 243
journalistic reporting, avoidance of, 251

K

killing your darlings, 80

L

lead, essay, 150–158
learning, theme of, 27
learning disabilities, writing about, 267–268
learning styles, 39–40
left brain, 51, 52
length of essay, 146–147
letters of recommendation, 101
linked transitions, 167–168
listing, 61, 68–72, 76
literature questions, writing about, 269–272
logic, 160–161, 189
logican, personality of, 61
Louisiana State University, holistic review and, 9

M

main idea, function of, 197–199
major, writing about, 126–127, 233, 242–245
McPhee, John, 300
meaning, structuring, 122–125
meaningless praise, 235–236
memories, collecting, 23–24
mentor, role of, 91
metaphor, 66, 144–145
micromanagement, of parents, 88–89
mining your life, 22
monotony, 211–213
mosaic, creating, 115, 250
"Mother Tongue" (Tan), 300
movies, writing about, 285

My Perfect Resume website, 101
myths, of college essays, 291–295

N

narrative, beginning with, 251
no-category prompts, 45
noun, use of, 142–143

O

object, focus on, 259–260
observation, capturing attention through, 150–151
Occidental College, supplemental essay question from, 242, 272–273, 324–325
offensive language, avoidance of, 217
Ohio State University Honors College, supplemental essay question from, 263
"On Keeping a Notebook" (Didion), 299
"On Lying in Bed" (Chesterton), 300
one-sentence paragraph, 162
openings, examples of, 155–157
opinion, unnecessary, 214–215
optional essay, as working together, 196–197
origin story, within chronological structure, 112
outline, 85–86, 161
overediting, avoidance of, 209–210
overlap, 196–197, 308

P

paragraph
  breaks within, 160
  cliffhangers within, 161–162
  details within, 166
  drama within, 161–162
  length of, 164
  logic within, 160–161
  one-sentence, 162
  punctuating your points with, 160–162
  scope sentences within, 162–164, 164–166
  timing within, 159–160
  transitions within, 167–170
paralysis, coping with, 185–186
parents, 34–35, 88–90, 224
passion, theme of, 27
pasting, submission tips regarding, 226
pattern, 212–213, 310

perfectionism, 185–186
personal experience, 236–242, 246, 308–309
personal statement
  challenge of, 56–57
  distinctness within, 307–308
  examples of, 314–320
  features of, 101–102
  getting your point across within, 197–199
  overview of, 29–30
  purpose of, 303
personality, theme of, 27
perspective, 189, 204–205
phrase transitions, 169
pitch, getting your point across within, 197–199
pitfalls
  of bigotry, 217
  of branding, 93
  within citations, 158
  of clichés, 106–107, 153, 157, 305
  within collaboration, 83–84
  within dictionary definitions, 158
  of double descriptions, 214
  of essay purchasing on the Internet, 82–83
  of exaggeration, 105–106
  of hammer sentences, 197–198
  of journalistic reporting, 251
  of offensive language, 217
  of overediting, 209–210
  of prejudice, 217
  of profanity, 217
  of qualifiers, 215
  of quotations, 158
  of repetition, 213–215
  of sexism, 217
  of shock value, 157
  of slang, 217
  of thesaurus use, 103–104
  of untruth, 105–106
poetic descriptions, 144–145
politeness, to parents, 89–90
power, reclaiming, 186–187
praise, meaningless, example of, 235–236
prejudice, avoidance of, 217
present tense, 264
previews, 151, 153–154
pre-writing stage, 50, 52–54, 140

profanity, avoidance of, 217
professional future, focus on, 42–43
"Professions for Women" (Woolf), 299
prompt
  academic, 267–268, 280
  adversity, 78–79
  books, 269–271, 285
  campus visit, 233
  career, 42–43, 126–127, 233
  celebrities, 262
  challenge, 38
  from Common App, 13
  community, 41
  community contributions, 257–258
  confident statements to, 202–203
  creative, 248–249
  current event, 272–273
  daydreaming, 250–251
  difficult experiences, 27–29
  diversity, 245–247
  engagement, 280
  extended family, 36
  extracurricular activities, 282
  family, 36–37
  family history, 275
  fantasy, 251, 254, 262–263
  fiction, 263–264
  films, 285
  friends, 256–261
  fun, 248–249
  general, 45
  global village, 41–42
  grades, 267–268
  grandparent, 36
  group experiences, 40, 257–258
  historical event, 275–276
  identity, 44, 280
  inclusion, 245–247
  influence, 254
  intellectual or professional goals, 242–243
  learning disabilities, 267–268
  learning styles, 39–40
  literature, 269–272
  major, 126–127, 233, 242–245
  paraphrasing, 309
  parent, 34

personal experience, 236
personal quirks, 79
regarding favorites, 282
relationships, 256–261
school experience, 38–40
short-answer, 222–223
sibling, 35
strangers, 262
strength, 38
teacher, 39
tentative statements to, 202–203
thoughts, 239
ties to a group, 257–258
transfer, 285–288
"Why us?" concept, 18, 232–236, 279–280, 324
writing, 269–272
Purdue University, application question of, 200

Q

qualifiers, avoidance of, 215
question
  academic, 267–268, 280
  adversity, 78–79
  answering, 200–201, 304
  books, 269–271, 285
  campus visit, 233
  career, 42–43, 126–127, 233
  celebrities, 262
  challenge, 38
  from Common App, 13
  community, 41
  community contributions, 257–258
  confident statements to, 202–203
  creative, 248–249
  current event, 272–273
  daydreaming, 250–251
  difficult experiences, 27–29
  diversity, 245–247
  engagement, 280
  extended family, 36
  extracurricular activities, 282
  family, 36–37
  family history, 275
  fantasy, 251, 254, 262–263
  fiction, 263–264
  films, 285
  friends, 256–261
  fun, 248–249
  general, 45
  global village, 41–42
  grades, 267–268
  grandparent, 36
  group experiences, 40, 257–258
  historical event, 275–276
  identity, 44, 280
  inclusion, 245–247
  influence, 254
  intellectual or professional goals, 242–243
  learning disabilities, 267–268
  learning styles, 39–40
  literature, 269–272
  major, 126–127, 233, 242–245
  paraphrasing, 309
  parent, 34
  personal experience, 236
  personal quirks, 79
  regarding favorites, 282
  relationships, 256–261
  school experience, 38–40
  short-answer, 222–223
  sibling, 35
  strangers, 262
  strength, 38
  teacher, 39
  tentative statements to, 202–203
  thoughts, 239
  ties to a group, 257–258
  transfer, 285–288
  "Why us?" concept, 18, 232–236, 279–280, 324
  writing, 269–272
quotations, pitfalls within, 158

R

recommendation letters, 101, 220
recording, writing your essay by, 105
recruitment, timeline for, 99
Red Pen Exercise, 207–208, 211, 222
refocusing, 75
Regular Decision (RD), 100, 222
relationships, writing about, 256–261

relatives, 34–37, 91, 255, 256–261

relevant material, choosing, 237–238

repetition, avoidance of, 213–215

resources

  ACT, 220

  ApplyTexas, 14

  Coalition Application, 14

  Common Application, 12

  My Perfect Resume, 101

  SAT, 220

  University of California, 14

Restrictive Early Action, 15

resume, importance of, 101

revealing, boasting *versus*, 31

reviewing/revision stage

  from brainstorming, 68

  cutting during, 146

  defined, 50

  detail within, 210

  expectations within, 216

  feedback, 84, 85–87, 216, 272

  guidelines for, 83–84

  overview of, 56

  process of, 146, 306

  Red Pen Exercise, 207–208

  rough draft, 55

  Track Changes use within, 92

  while writing, 190–191

  writing anew, 209

right brain, 51, 52

rough draft

  admissions committee/office and, 98–101

  attention capturing within, 150–154

  cause-and-effect structure, 120–121

  chronological order structure, 112–113, 114–115, 123, 126, 127

  description-and-interpretation structure, 119–120, 126, 127

  detail choices within, 139–140

  developing your voice within, 107–109

  editing during, 190–191

  expectations within, 146–147

  interrupted chronological order structure, 113–115, 116, 123

  metaphor use within, 144–145

  openings for, 155–157

  overview of, 86–87

parts of speech use within, 141–144

review process of, 55

sensory details within, 137–139

specifics within, 130–136

stopping and starting within, 191

strategies for, 100–101

survey structure, 115–119, 126, 127

timeline for, 99–100

tone of, 154–155

uncertainty within, 125

Rowling, JK, 28

S

Santa Clara University, supplemental essays for, 233–235

SAT scores, 9, 220, 222–223

scare list, 188

scene, presenting and selecting, 258–260

scholarly language, use of, 294

school experience, writing about, 37–40

scope sentence, 162–166

Scripps College, supplemental essay question from, 262

"The Search for Marvin Gardens" (McPhee), 300

Sedaris, David, 297–298

self-awareness, 11

self-doubt, 188–189

self-editing, 51

self-reflection, 187

sensory details, 54, 119, 137–139

sentence

  connection within, 102

  hammer, 197–198

  length of, 211–212

  monotony within, 211–213

  scope, 162–166

  stinginess within, 215

  stylish, 211–213

  topic, 162–166

sequence of events, 113

serious tone, 154

sexism, avoidance of, 217

Shelley, Mary, 253–254

Shelley, Percy, 253

shock value, pitfalls within, 157

short answers

  common questions within, 222–223, 281–288

  overview of, 278–281

show-not-tell essay, 130–136, 304–305
siblings, influence of, 35
sight, sense of, 137
significant others, reflection regarding, 255
similes, use of, 144–145
single event, within chronological structure, 112
slang, avoidance of, 217
sleep, importance of, 134
smell, sense of, 137, 138
Smith, Zadie, 301
"so what?" factor, 77–78
Social Security Number, 227
sound, sense of, 137, 138
spare time, writing within, 17
specificity
  example of, 263
  importance of, 282, 304
  of moments, 53, 233
  within writing, 130–136
speculation, within details, 85
Spielberg, Steven, 28
Stanford University, 15, 222, 248, 272–273
statement, personal
  challenge of, 56–57
  distinctness within, 307–308
  examples of, 314–320
  features of, 101–102
  getting your point across within, 197–199
  overview of, 29–30
  purpose of, 303
stories, collecting, 23–24
The Story of Me, 26
strangers, writing about, 262–263
Streisand, Barbra, 44
strengths, 38, 201–205
structure
  bookends within, 172
  cause-and-effect, 120–121
  chronological, 112–113, 114–115, 123, 126, 127
  collage, 259, 261
  compare and contrast, 123
  defined, 111
  description-and-interpretation, 119–120, 126, 127, 251
  functions of, 122–123
  hybrid, 118–119
  interest pursuit within, 126–127
  interrupted chronological order, 113–115, 116, 123
  of meaning, 122–125
  selection of, 124–125
  survey, 115–119, 126, 127, 251
  uncertainty within, 125
structuring and outlining, discovery writing *versus*, 55
submission process, 219–225, 226–227
subtraction exercise, 255
supplemental essay
  of Barnard College, 264
  of California Lutheran University, 242
  of Chapman University, 279–281
  of Columbia University, 269
  defined, 12, 37
  directness within, 308
  of Emerson College, 242
  of Emory University, 269
  example questions for, 236
  examples of, 320–325
  of Gonzaga University, 321–322
  honesty within, 246
  of Indian University, 243
  interest pursuit within, 126–127
  mining your life within, 22
  of Occidental College, 242, 272–273, 324–325
  of Ohio State University Honors College, 263
  overlap within, 308
  overview of, 16, 232–236
  personal experience within, 236–242
  purpose of, 265–266
  recycling, 18
  relevant material within, 237–238
  of Santa Clara University, 233–235
  of Scripps College, 262
  submission process for, 220
  themes of, 232
  timeline for, 308
  tips for, 307–311
  of Tufts University, 236, 272–273
  of University of California, 242, 320, 323–324
  of University of Chicago, 28, 236, 248, 271, 324
  of University of North Carolina, 248
  of University of North Carolina, Chapel Hill, 254
  of University of Pennsylvania, 242, 271
  of University of Richmond, 271, 272–273
  of University of Southern California, 263

supplemental essay *(continued)*
  of University of Virginia, 236
  of University of Washington, Seattle, 257
  of Villanova University, 236
  as working together, 196–197
  of Yale University, 262
support system, expectations for, 216
survey structure, 115–119, 126, 127, 251

T

Tan, Amy, 300
Tarantino, Quentin, 159
taste, sense of, 137, 139
teachers, 39, 91, 101
teasing statement, 153
technology, challenges with, 225
tense and nervous syndrome, 214
test-optional schools, 9–12
theme
  academic, 267–268, 280
  adversity, 78–79
  within autobiography, 25–29
  to avoid, 79
  books, 269–271, 285
  campus visit, 233
  career, 42–43, 126–127, 233
  celebrities, 262
  challenge, 38
  from Common App, 13
  community, 41
  community contributions, 257–258
  confident statements to, 202–203
  creative, 248–249
  current event, 272–273
  daydreaming, 250–251
  defined, 25–29
  difficult experiences, 27–29
  diversity, 245–247
  engagement, 280
  extended family, 36
  extracurricular activities, 282
  family, 36–37
  family history, 275
  fantasy, 251, 254, 262–263
  fiction, 263–264

films, 285
friends, 256–261
fun, 248–249
general, 45
global village, 41–42
grades, 267–268
grandparent, 36
group experiences, 40, 257–258
historical event, 275–276
identity, 44, 280
inclusion, 245–247
influence, 254
intellectual or professional goals, 242–243
learning disabilities, 267–268
learning styles, 39–40
literature, 269–272
major, 126–127, 233, 242–245
paraphrasing, 309
parent, 34
personal experience, 236
personal quirks, 79
regarding favorites, 282
relationships, 256–261
school experience, 38–40
short-answer, 222–223
sibling, 35
significant, 26–27
strangers, 262
strength, 38
teacher, 39
tentative statements to, 202–203
thoughts, 239
ties to a group, 257–258
transfer, 285–288
"Why us?" concept, 18, 232–236, 279–280, 324
writing, 269–272
thesaurus, avoidance of, 103–104
thesis, admission essay *versus*, 158
thoughtfulness, within the essay, 11
thoughts, writing about, 239
time management, 89
time order structure, 112–113
timeline
  of application submissions, 222
  early starting within, 308
  gap year and, 188

importance of, 99–100

strategy within, 100–101

theme of, 27

understanding, 14–16

for writing, 291

timing, within writing, 159–160

tone, setting, 154–155

topic, trolling for, 84–85

topic sentence, 162–166

"Total Eclipse" (Dillard), 298–299

touch, sense of, 137, 138–139

Track Changes, 92

transcripts, submission process for, 220, 227

transfer question, 285–288

transition, 167–168, 169, 170

Tufts University, supplemental essay question from, 236, 272–273

tying-up-loose-ends technique, 174–176, 177

U

uncertainty, within structure, 125

University of California

application process within, 14

essay requirements of, 146

supplemental essay question from, 242, 320, 323–324

technology challenges of, 225

as test optional, 9

University of Chicago

supplemental essay question from, 28, 236, 248, 271, 324

as test optional, 9

University of Colorado at Boulder, 18, 236, 246

University of Maryland, short answer question from, 278–279

University of North Carolina, Chapel Hill, supplemental essay question from, 254

University of North Carolina, supplemental essay question from, 248

University of Oregon, 9, 18, 246

University of Pennsylvania, supplemental essay question from, 242, 271

University of Richmond, supplemental essay question from, 271, 272–273

University of Southern California, supplemental essay question from, 263

University of Virginia, supplemental essay question from, 236

University of Washington, 9, 200

University of Washington, Seattle, supplemental essay question from, 257

untruth, avoidance of, 105–106

"Us and Them" (Sedaris), 297–298

V

verbs, use of, 141–142

Villanova University, supplemental essay question from, 236

vision, sense of, 137

visual brainstorming, 61, 62–68, 76

vocabulary, tips regarding, 104

voice, developing, 107–109

voice memo, writing your essay by, 105

vulnerability, 136, 305

W

Wake Forest University, 200, 257, 269

Waltz, Christoph, 159

Washuta, Elissa, 298

websites

ACT, 220

ApplyTexas, 14

Coalition Application, 14

Common Application, 12

My Perfect Resume, 101

SAT, 220

University of California, 14

whining, winning versus, 203–204

"Why us?" concept, 18, 232–236, 279–280, 324

wider-context conclusion, 176–177

winning, whining versus 203–204

Wollstonecraft, Mary, 253

Woodward, Washington, 261

Woolf, Virginia, 299

word count, 221–222

word transitions, 169

word-processing program, 92

writers block, 184, 189–191

writing

actions within, 240

adjective use within, 143–144

adverb use within, 143–144

braindumping within, 61, 72–76

40, 261

...ocks concept within, 60
...ng, 190–191
...antasy, 251, 254, 262–263
...in fiction, 263–264
first impression within, 101
freewriting, 24–25, 33–34, 124, 146
for graduate program, 103
irksome traits within, 103–107
listing for, 61, 68–72, 76
metaphor use within, 66, 144–145
natural, 105
noun usage within, 142–143
pre-writing stage, 50, 52–54, 140
as process, 49–57
recording for, 105
with restraint, 293–294
sifting through ideas within, 61
simile use within, 144–145
sorting the details within, 61
within spare time, 17
specificity within, 130–136
timeline for, 291
timing within, 159–160
tone within, 154–155
verb usage within, 141–142
visual brainstorming within, 61, 62–68, 76
vulnerability within, 136
writing anew, process of, 209
writing questions, answering, 269–272
writing skills, 11
writing supplement
  of Barnard College, 264
  of California Lutheran University, 242
  of Chapman University, 279–281
  of Columbia University, 269
  defined, 12, 37
  directness within, 308

of Emerson College, 242
of Emory University, 269
example questions for, 236
examples of, 320–325
of Gonzaga University, 321–322
honesty within, 246
of Indian University, 243
interest pursuit within, 126–127
mining your life within, 22
of Occidental College, 242, 272–273, 324–325
of Ohio State University Honors College, 263
overlap within, 308
overview of, 16, 232–236
personal experience within, 236–242
purpose of, 265–266
recycling, 18
relevant material within, 237–238
of Santa Clara University, 233–235
of Scripps College, 262
submission process for, 220
themes of, 232
timeline for, 308
tips for, 307–311
of Tufts University, 236, 272–273
of University of California, 242, 320, 323–324
of University of Chicago, 28, 236, 248, 271, 324
of University of North Carolina, 248
of University of North Carolina, Chapel Hill, 254
of University of Pennsylvania, 242, 271
of University of Richmond, 271, 272–273
of University of Southern California, 263
of University of Virginia, 236
of University of Washington, Seattle, 257
of Villanova University, 236
as working together, 196–197
of Yale University, 262

Y

Yale University, supplemental essay question from, 262

About the Authors

Jessica Brenner is an independent counselor and founder of Jessica Brenner Educational Consulting. She has had the privilege of helping students achieve their goals since 2009, and received her Master of Science in Counseling Psychology from San Francisco State University. Previously, she received a B.A. in Comparative Literature from Columbia University and a B.A. in Jewish History from Albert A. List College. When she isn't working with teenagers or writing, she can be found spending time with her husband and their children in Northern California.

Geraldine Woods wrote the first edition of *College Admission Essays For Dummies*. She taught English and directed the independent study program at a high school for gifted students. Throughout her teaching career, she guided a multitude of harried and anxious seniors through the process of writing successful college admission essays. She has written more than 40 books, give or take a few, including *English Grammar For Dummies* and *Research Papers For Dummies* (both by John Wiley & Sons, Inc.).

Dedication

To Robby, Miriam, Judah, and the little one who kept me company while writing this book. You're my reason why my dreams.

Authors' Acknowledgements

Jessica Brenner: Thank you to my literary agent, Margot Hutchison, for believing in and supporting my work. Thank you to the team at Wiley Publishing — Chad Sievers for his expert guidance and feedback, as well as Elizabeth Stilwell, Vicki Adang, Lindsay Lefevere, Pat Orr, and Michelle Hacker — who put their trust in me.

I am indebted to Christy Frantz for giving me my start in the world of college counseling as well as her friendship, and to my counseling colleagues for their continued inspiration.

Lastly, a very special thank you to the students who have allowed me to be a part of their journeys toward college and to the parents who have bestowed me with their trust. Thank you especially to those students who graciously allowed their work to be featured in this book: Tristan Bowen, Grace Casserly, Meredith Cone, Mia Elliott, Amelia Harris, Giorgios Koutantos, Casey Lim, Eliza Van Hamel Platerink, Chris Raboy, Clayton Reid, Aidan Robinson, Claire Robinson, Amelia Solis, Isabella Tole, Katie Uthman, Molly Wachhorst, and Katie Wheeler.

owledgments

or: Kelsey Baird

ger and Editor: Chad R. Sievers

Editor: Pat Orr

Production Editor: Mohammed Zafar Ali

Cover Image: © Antonio Guillem/Shutterstock